Professional Development

Supporting Special Needs

Understanding Inclusion in the Early Years

Penny Tassoni

Heinemann
Inspiring generations

Heinemann Educational Publishers
Halley Court, Jordan Hill, Oxford OX2 8EJ
Part of Harcourt Education

Heinemann is the registered trademark of Harcourt Education Limited

First published 2003

08 07 06 05 04 03
10 9 8 7 6 5 4 3 2 1

British Library Cataloguing in Publication Data is available from the British Library on request.

ISBN 0 435 40162 9

Designed by Artistix, Thame, Oxon
Typeset by Saxon Graphics Ltd, Derby
Cover design by Wooden Ark Studios

Printed and bound in Great Britain by The Bath Press Ltd

Acknowledgements

Every effort has been made to contact copyright holders of material reproduced in this book. Any omissions will be rectified in subsequent printings if notice is given to the publishers.

Crown Copyright material is reproduced under Class Licence Number C01W0000141 with the permission of the Controller of HMSO and the Queen's Printer for Scotland.

Tel: 01865 888058 www.heinemann.co.uk

Contents

Author's acknowledgements

Whilst this book may have my name on the front cover, the words inside have been shaped by the advice, support and wishes of others. I hope that my work will have done justice to their expertise, emotions and experiences. My thanks must therefore go firstly to the families and children who have shared first-hand experiences and emotions with me. Particular thanks go to the Bristow family and Lesley Gilchrist for their powerful words and advice.

Much of the information provided in Part 3 of the book has been shaped by the contacts that I have had with the voluntary organisations who support families and professionals. It is impossible to list every individual from these organisations who has either spent valuable time talking me through the 'getting it right sections' or who has sent me additional materials to aid my work. I know that this section has benefited enormously from their help, time and advice.

Some people have also helped me directly in the writing of this book by allowing me to talk through ideas, material and direction with them. In this respect I would also like to thank Sue Bayliss, Early Years advisory teacher, for allowing me to tap into her wealth of experience in relation to supporting children with special needs and for keeping me on the 'straight and narrow' in terms of interpretation. Thanks also to Debra Cassim at Clive Vale Nursery and Elaine Piper at Gables Day Nursery for their ideas and support.

Thanks must also go to Louise Burnham for helping me out with suggestions, materials and providing me with moral support. I also wish to thank Babette Brown for being ready to share her experience of using persona dolls and also Shirley Eden for giving me her thoughts regarding the tone of the book in relation to anti-discriminatory practice.

In addition to the people who have made this writing possible, I would also like to thank members of the Heinemann production and sales team. Special thanks go to Rachel Gear, Senior Editor, for her interest, efficiency and cheerfulness especially at first proof stage! Special thanks also go to Mary James, Senior Publisher, for her patience and faith in me.

Finally and once again, I would like to thank the Tassoni Team for their continued support, cups of tea and the odd fairy cake.

Penny Tassoni

Photo acknowledgements

The author and publisher would like to thank the children, parents and staff of Elmhurst Infant School in Aylesbury and Coppice Nursery School in High Wycombe for giving us the opportunity to take some excellent photographs for this book. We are also grateful to the following for permission to reproduce photographs and other material:

Haddon Davies, pages 11, 25, 33, 39, 42, 55, 59, 70, 82, 89, 110, 114, 116, 122, 129, 142, 147 and 166

Gerald Sunderland, pages 79 and 168

Babette Brown, page 98

Front cover of *Including Pupils with Down's Syndrome* publication reproduced on page 200 with the kind permission of the Down's Syndrome Association.

Part 1

Special needs – key issues

This book is dedicated to Sophie Bristow who has been an inspiration during the writing of this book.

'Seek first to understand.'

The recent Special Educational Needs Code of Practice, as well as other recent disability legislation, is changing the way that children with special educational needs are educated. It is important that all adults working with children understand the implications of the new Code of Practice as well as other recent legislation aimed at combating discrimination against disabled people. This section is designed to help practitioners understand the concept of inclusion and its history. It also provides a step-by-step practical guide to the process of identifying and making plans for children who may have special educational needs.

Chapter 1

Understanding key issues and perspectives

Introduction

There are some key issues and perspectives that all practitioners need to understand in order to work effectively with children and their parents. They reflect the way in which our society is trying to become more inclusive and valuing of diversity. Isolating children because their learning or physical needs are different to the majority of other children is now seen as being discriminatory and therefore morally wrong. Within education and society steps are now being taken to ensure that children are included rather than excluded, hence the term 'inclusion'.

When working with children, you will need to embrace the move towards inclusion and in your own way look for ways of promoting it. This may mean reflecting on and even challenging your own thoughts as most of us have been brought up in a society that has not been able to value the uniqueness of the individual.

This chapter is designed to give you an understanding of the background of inclusive education and will cover the following areas:

- Definitions of special educational needs.
- Being sensitive to language.
- Attitudes and stereotypes.
- Models of disability.
- Understanding the concept of inclusive education.

Definitions of special educational needs

There are numerous definitions and terms that are used to describe children and people who have previously been discriminated against or excluded in some way because of an impairment. Because definitions can create stereotypes, they are very controversial and many professionals and parents dislike the labelling that they generate. Policy makers, on the other hand, would argue that without definitions, it would be impossible to create any enforceable laws and policies. Funding is often therefore tied to definitions and so it is very difficult for settings to avoid using them. The following definitions are used in current legislation and are referred to in the current Special Educational Needs Code of Practice (2001).

Special educational needs (SEN)

This term is currently widely used in education and care settings. It came into existence as a result of the 1978 Warnock Report. The committee was anxious to avoid labelling children or use words that had negative connotations. The term 'special educational needs' was used as an all encompassing term to describe any child who needed some extra support. It is worth noting that many organisations campaigning for inclusiveness are unhappy with this term.

Children have special educational needs if they have a learning difficulty that calls for special educational provision to be made for them. Children have a learning difficulty if they have any of the following:

- A significantly greater difficulty in learning than the majority of children of the same age.
- A disability that prevents or hinders them from making use of educational facilities of a kind generally provided for children of the same age in schools within the area of the local education authority.
- Are under compulsory school age and fall within the definitions above or would do so if special educational provision was not made for them.

Special needs

This is in some ways an umbrella term and is used in a variety of ways. In some settings it is used to describe children with special educational needs while in others it may be used to describe children with an impairment or medical condition.

Disability

This term has many definitions and can include children who are defined as having special educational needs.

Disability is defined by the Disability Discrimination Act 1995 Section 1 (1) as a person who has a physical or mental impairment that has a substantial and long-term adverse effect on his or her ability to carry out normal day-to-day activities.

Disability is defined by the Children Act 1989 Section 17 (11) as a child who is blind, deaf or dumb or suffers from a mental disorder of any kind or is substantially and permanently handicapped by illness, injury or congenital deformity or such other disability as he or she may be prescribed.

KEY ISSUE: SHOULD WE BE USING THE TERMS 'SPECIAL NEEDS' AND 'SPECIAL EDUCATIONAL NEEDS'?

There is some unease about whether these terms should be used at all. Organisations such as the Alliance for Inclusive Education (ALLFIE) suggest that all children have needs and, as such, they have an automatic right to be met. If society were more inclusive in its structure and nature, there would be no need to have 'special needs' policies or even to label children as having 'special needs'. This book, while endorsing this viewpoint, does however refer to children with 'special educational needs' as this is the term that is used in the Code of Practice 2001.

REFLECT ON YOUR OWN PRACTICE

- Think about diversity and inclusion, not just disability, special educational needs and special needs – all children have particular needs that practitioners must meet.
- Be sensitive to the feelings of children and their parents about the use of labels.

> *I get sick of the way some practitioners talk about the children they work with. It feels that they are collecting trophies when they say things such as 'We've got six SEN children'.*
>
> *Child care practitioner*

Being sensitive to language

As we have seen, definitions can be controversial and damaging. This is because language can be a very powerful tool. Understanding and reflecting on your language is therefore an important part of working effectively with children and their parents. This section is designed to help you feel more confident with your use of language. As attitudes and language evolve, it will be essential for you to continually check that your language is effective and accurate.

A good starting point is to understand that language reflects attitudes and values. Take the term 'invalid' as an example. It actually means something that is not valid! Barriers to communication can appear quickly if someone feels that they are being labelled or negatively viewed. There has been a shift in thinking about disability over the past 20 years and this has been reflected in the language we use; terms such as 'spastic' or 'physically handicapped' are no longer acceptable.

KEY ISSUE: 'DISABLED PEOPLE' OR 'PEOPLE WITH DISABILITIES'?

Currently there is a debate within many voluntary organisations as to which of these terms to use.

Disabled people

The British Council of Disabled People uses the term 'disabled people' in order to clearly signal that people are being disabled because of society's reluctance to be inclusive. It could be argued that if we had an inclusive society, no one would actually be disabled.

People with disabilities

Organisations that use this word order are trying to promote the concept that the person comes first and the impairment is secondary.

Defining disability

- **Impairment** refers to the loss or abnormality of development of growth, for example a hearing impairment means that a person has a loss of hearing.
- **Disability** refers to the restrictions that an impairment causes – for example a person with a hearing impairment has a disability in hearing.
- **Handicap** refers to the disadvantage that the person has in relation to others in certain situations. Note that the person is not themselves 'handicapped' – he or she is being handicapped by situation. For example a person with a hearing impairment is being handicapped when announcements are broadcast in an airport because he or she has a hearing disability. His or her disability does not prevent him or her from reading the signs and getting onto the aircraft, and so he or she is not handicapped all the time.

Terms to avoid	Terms that are preferred
Handicapped person	Disabled person
Invalid	Disabled person
Wheelchair bound	Wheelchair user
Sufferer, victim of, crippled by, afflicted	Person who has ....
Spastic	Cerebral palsy
Categories beginning with 'the' – 'the deaf', 'the blind'	Deaf people, blind people
Mongoloid, mongol	Person with Down's syndrome
Mental handicap	Learning difficulty
Congenital	Genetically impaired
Disabled toilet	Accessible toilet

REFLECT ON YOUR OWN PRACTICE

- Remember that the child is always far more important than any condition or syndrome. Make sure that your language reflects this.
- Avoid drawing attention to a child's disability, difference or condition needlessly.
- Ask the child or their parents about their preferences in terms of language.
- Contact support groups or voluntary organisations if you are unsure about the correct language.

CASE STUDY

Geraldine works in a primary school as a classroom assistant. When asked in the supermarket about her job, she says 'Well, I look after one child who suffers from cystic fibrosis, and in the afternoons I help two dyslexic children'.

1 Why does this type of remark encourage stereotyping of children?

2 Work out what Geraldine might say instead.

Attitudes and stereotypes

The way we think about disability affects the care and education of people with disabilities. This is why it is important to examine the stereotypes and attitudes that are common in society. A good starting point is to understand that discrimination against people with disabilities is not new, but centuries old. In the past, babies with disabilities were left to die, physical differences were mocked and later institutions were built to house the 'defective'. Disability was seen as a 'curse' bringing shame and stigma upon the child and his or her family. Attitudes towards disability were probably founded on ignorance, poverty and religious bigotry. Today, we are faced with the remnants of those attitudes but we no longer have the excuse of ignorance and poverty as we are a relatively well-educated and prosperous society.

> *One of the things I really hate is when people come up to me and say that I must be a wonderful person to have been chosen by God to suffer in this way.*
>
> **Sophie's mum**

Stereotypes

Stereotypes are the images that we hold of groups of people. They tend to reflect society's prejudices and lack of knowledge. They are unhelpful because they lead people to assume that they 'know' about a person who is part of a stereotyped group. These assumptions can prevent us from considering each person as an individual. The controversy surrounding definitions relates to the way that this can reinforce stereotypes.

Stereotypes of disabled people

There are many stereotypes of disabled people, most of which are propagated by the media. It is worth being aware of current stereotypes as there is a danger that they might unwittingly influence our own approach towards children.

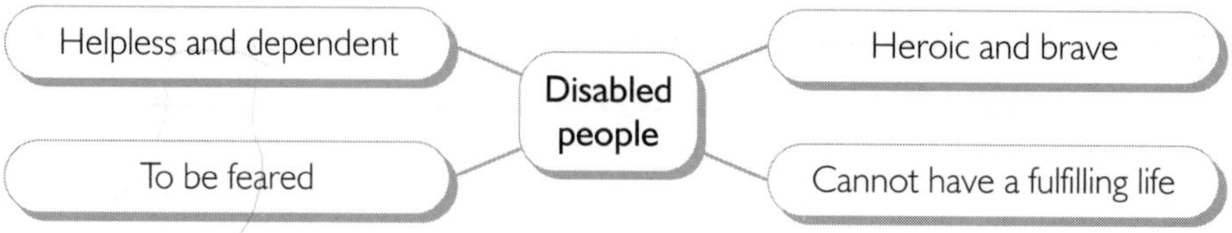

Common stereotypes of disabled people.

Disabled people are helpless and dependent

This stereotype tends to mean that disabled people are to be pitied and are seen as needing others. Traditionally, this stereotype was used by charities in order to raise funds. This stereotype also produces the expectation that disabled people should be grateful.

Disabled people are heroic and brave

This stereotype puts a lot of pressure on disabled people to be cheerful, accepting and ready to 'make the most of their condition'. It is propagated by media stories of disabled people who 'despite the odds' have achieved in some way. This stereotype does not allow for people to have complex emotions and sees disabled people as being different rather than ordinary.

Disabled people are to be feared

Stories about innocent people who have been attacked, and novels and films such as the Hunchback of Notre Dame have produced this outdated stereotype. In the past it largely contributed to the setting up of 'mental hospitals' and the out-casting of disabled people.

Disabled people cannot have a fulfilling life

This stereotype promotes the assumption that disabled people cannot have 'quality of life'. It assumes that disabled people will not be able to have a family, get a job or take on responsibility. The focus remains continually on the person's impairment rather than on the person themselves.

> In a survey conducted by the Leonard Cheshire Foundation, nearly one-third of people questioned thought that wheelchair users were 'less intelligent'; and 44 per cent of opinion leaders thought that using a wheelchair would present a major obstacle to gaining employment.
>
> *Scope: An Introduction to Disability Issues (reproduced with kind permission)*

Models of disability

There are two models or ways of thinking about disability: the medical model of disability and the social model of disability. Understanding both models is important as they reflect underlying attitudes towards disability. As a practitioner, it is important that you understand that the medical model of disability is considered by disabled people to be oppressive.

Medical model of disability

The medical model of disability has its roots in seeing people with disabilities as being imperfect. It reflects society's faith in doctors and came about because of the historic fear of disability combined with scientific advances. The medical model views disability as something that must, whenever possible, be cured. Where this is not possible a feeling of failure results, unless the person can be made to 'look' or 'act' normally. The medical model of disability therefore treats people with impairments as victims and patients; words such as 'handicapped', 'incurable', 'suffering' and 'wheelchair bound' are associated with this attitude. The medical model of disability tends to put the emphasis more on the condition rather than on the person. This results in labelling people according to their impairments, for example 'the one who's wheelchair bound' rather then 'James who uses a wheelchair'.

Social model of disability

The social model of disability reflects a new attitude towards people with impairments. It has been developed by disabled people themselves and aims to challenge the historical view of disabled people as being less worthy. It considers first and foremost that they are people with rights and feelings. The social model of disability looks to empower people as it emphasises their rights to make choices and be independent. It also challenges society to become more inclusive so that disabled people are not seen as being 'problems that need sorting out' or 'victims that need pity'.

The social model of disability has meant that terms such as 'mentally handicapped' and 'wheelchair bound' are now considered unhelpful. The case study below shows clearly how attitudes have changed and the social model of disability is now being increasingly accepted as the way forward.

Jake does not have to hope that someone might open the door. All children's needs are automatically met and he is valued for who he is.

CASE STUDY

Emma was born with one arm foreshortened above the elbow. Her mother was determined that this should not affect Emma's life and she refused to let anyone feel sorry for Emma or consider her a victim. Emma was given a prosthesis (false limb) which although uncomfortable and restricting made her look like all other children. At home Emma never wore her prosthesis as her family completely accepted the way she looked without it. Emma learned to ride a horse, manage everyday tasks and was a very happy and confident child. She left school and started to work in a restaurant. As she became older she gradually started to question society's attitude towards disability and began to feel unhappy that she was in effect disguising her disability. One day she decided that she would no longer wear her false arm. Her employer was unhappy about this decision. He said that seeing a person with only one arm would make customers feel uneasy and it could affect his business. Emma turned the argument around and said that if she had spent her life learning to cope without an arm, perhaps his customers could spend five minutes learning to see her without one, especially as they had already learned to cope with seeing his bald head!

THINK IT OVER

In pairs, consider the following questions:

- Is there pressure on people to look 'perfect'? If so, where do you think this pressure comes from?
- Would you ever consider plastic surgery to improve your appearance?
- Do you use any products to disguise 'imperfections' such as spots or improve your appearance?
- Would you or do you wear contact lenses rather than glasses simply for the sake of your appearance?

Understanding the concept of inclusive education

The medical model of disability has up until now affected the way in which children are educated. Children with any disability were seen as a 'problem' and were segregated. This resulted in many children not fulfilling their potential as expectations of their abilities were often lowered. Segregation also meant that children in mainstream schools grew up without ever meeting a child who had needs that were different to their own. This has served to perpetuate many myths about disabilities.

The concept of inclusive education is the result of parents and disabled people putting pressure on successive governments to change the education system so as to allow all children to have fair and equal access to education. It is important to realise that the campaign for inclusive education is not limited to children who have special needs, but extends also to a wider range of children who have traditionally been discriminated against such as children from travelling families and children who are being 'looked after' by the local authority.

The concept of inclusive education signals a significant mind shift. Instead of expecting children to 'come up to standard' or otherwise be segregated, the emphasis is on schools and settings to adapt and be flexible enough to accommodate each and every child. Organisations seeking inclusive education also point out the importance of significant funding as poor resources, both physical and human, are often barriers to inclusive education.

Inclusive education is about meeting all children's needs

Principles of inclusion

- Inclusive education enables all students to participate fully in any mainstream early years provision, school, college or university.
- Inclusive education provision has training and resources aimed at fostering every student's equality and participation in all aspects of the life of the learning community.
- Inclusive education aims to equip all people with the skills needed to build inclusive communities.

Inclusive education is based on nine principles:

- A person's worth is independent of their abilities or achievements.
- Every human being is able to feel and think.
- Every human being has a right to communicate and be heard.
- All human beings need each other.
- Real education can only happen in the context of real relationships.
- All people need support and friendship from people of their own age.
- Progress for all learners is achieved by building on things people can do rather than what they can't.
- Diversity brings strength to all living systems.
- Collaboration is more important than competition.

Source: Alliance for Inclusive Education
(reproduced with kind permission)

The SEN Code of Practice and inclusion

Recent government initiatives including the 2001 SEN Code Of Practice are designed to ensure a more inclusive education system. The fundamental principles that appear in Chapter 1 of the guidance (see below) have been broadly welcomed by most organisations campaigning for inclusive education.

1:5 Fundamental principles

- A child with special educational needs should have their needs met.
- The special educational needs of children will normally be met in mainstream schools or settings.
- The views of the child should be sought and taken into account.
- Parents have a vital role to play in supporting their child's education.
- Children with special educational needs should be offered full access to a broad, balanced and relevant education, including an appropriate curriculum for the foundation stage and the National Curriculum.

Source: SEN Code of Practice, 2001

THINK IT OVER

Zainab has diabetes. She needs regular snacks. She is told to eat her snack in the corridor by herself so that the other children do not feel hungry.

1 How is Zainab being 'excluded' by the setting?

2 Think of how the setting could change its practice in order to 'include' this child.

Chapter 2

Key legislation

Introduction

The laws of a country often reflect the underlying attitudes and beliefs of the society. Over the past few years, legislation relating to disability in the UK has changed enormously, mainly as a result of powerful campaigning by disabled people and parents of disabled children. The most recent legislation has built upon preceding Acts and it is helpful to understand the chronology and legal background of its formation. This chapter provides a chronological overview of some of the key legislation that has affected disabled children and their families.

The background to current legislation

Mental Deficiency Act (1913)

This Act is significant as it is a powerful reminder of the attitudes that existed and to some extent still exist today towards people with learning difficulties. The Act allowed for the permanent detainment (effectively imprisonment) of children and adults who from an early age appeared to fit into one of four categories: Idiots, Imbeciles, Feeble-Minded or Moral Defectives. There was no appeal system in place. The Act was replaced in 1959 by the Mental Health Act after campaigning by organisations such as the National Council for Civil Liberties.

THINK IT OVER: HAVE WE CHANGED OUR ATTITUDES BUT NOT OUR LANGUAGE?

The words 'idiot' and 'imbecile' are frequently used in everyday language. Most people today no longer understand their dark past. Organisations such as MIND who campaign for people with learning difficulties argue that such language is offensive.

Chronically Sick and Disabled Persons Act (1970)

This Act required local authorities to keep a register of disabled people and to provide services for them. The Act is still current, although it has been strengthened by other pieces of legislation such as the 1986 Disabled Persons Act. Section 2 outlines the range of services that local authorities need to provide if a person is assessed as requiring them. These services include holidays and transport as well as practical assistance in the home. This Act had a significant impact as it suggested that disabled people had the right to a reasonable standard of life.

Education Act (handicapped children) (1970)

This piece of legislation made all children the responsibility of the local education authority. Since 1944 they had been the responsibility of the health service as children with a learning difficulty were considered to be impossible to educate. As a result of this Act many special schools were built in the 1970s in order to give many children an education for the first time.

Warnock Report (1978)

Reports are not pieces of legislation and many findings in reports are often 'forgotten'. This was not the case with the Warnock Report and it is often considered to be a landmark in the education of disabled children. In 1978 a report was published by a committee chaired by Mary Warnock. The committee had undertaken a comprehensive study of the whole area of disabled children, their education and their needs. The committee took evidence from parents, the voluntary sector, educationalists and the medical profession. The report was to prove highly influential and subsequent legislation including the SEN Code of Practice 2001 have evolved from the findings of this report.

For years, people had talked about handicapped children or labelled children according to their disability. The report suggested a title of 'special education need' (SEN) that would include any child who needed some form of extra support. The report suggested that there might be three types of support:

- Special means of access to the curriculum.
- Changes to the curriculum.
- Changes to the environment, including emotional or social support.

KEY ISSUE: SPECIAL EDUCATIONAL NEED

The term 'special educational need' was an all encompassing one and included children who had slight difficulties with their reading and writing as well as children who had major care needs. It also included children who had short-term needs that were causing them to have difficulties in fulfilling their potential alongside children who had long-term needs. In this way it focused professionals on the idea of how to meet the needs that the children might have, rather than on the condition or cause of them. This was a major breakthrough and one that the Warnock Report is noted for.

It is worth remembering here that prior to the report and subsequent legislation, children were categorised and educated according to their disability rather than according to their potential. This meant that a partially sighted child would be educated in a school for the blind and would not have access to the same curriculum and qualifications as other children.

The Warnock Report introduced the following terms in an attempt to remove the previous labelling of children according to their medical condition.

- Speech and language disorders.
- Visual disability and hearing disability.
- Emotional and behaviour disorders.
- Learning difficulties; specific, mild, moderate and severe.

KEY PROPOSALS OF THE WARNOCK REPORT

Assessment The report suggested that early diagnosis and help was essential. It suggested that a team of multi-disciplinary professionals should assess the child's whole needs and these should be reviewed annually.

Supporting pre-school age children The report emphasised that children and parents in the first five years would need support. It suggested that each family should have a 'named person'; a social worker or a health visitor who would support the family.

Integration The report felt that integration of children into mainstream should happen wherever possible.

Parents The report pushed for parents to be more involved in decisions about their child.

Education Act (1981)

This Act was heavily based on the recommendations of the Warnock Report and gave local education authorities (LEAs) legal duties to fulfil. The Act placed a clear responsibility on the LEAs to provide support for children who have special educational needs. It also introduced the process now known as 'statementing'. This is the process by which children are assessed by a team of professionals alongside their parents, and a statement of how the child's needs are to be supported is drawn up. The statement of special educational needs is a legally binding one and commits the LEA to providing for the child.

The Act is also important because it gave parents power for the first time. Parents were to be involved in the process of producing a statement and deciding on the best course of education for their children, but more importantly the parents were given the legal power to challenge LEAs.

The idea behind producing a statement was to ensure that children with special educational needs were given support. The statement was meant to be a legally binding document. By recording their needs and the action required to meet those needs, children were supposed to be more likely to have these needs met. In the early days, LEAs wrote very detailed statements, but the funding to allow the support to be found was often lacking. Some parents took the LEAs to court and this began the trend towards fewer statements.

Disabled Persons Act (1986)

This Act continued the trend towards placing duties on local authorities by requiring them to assess people for services that could be provided under the 1970 Act if asked to do so by the disabled person or their representative or carer. This Act strengthened the Chronically Sick and Disabled Persons Act of 1970.

Education Reform Act (1988)

This Act introduced the National Curriculum into all state schools, including special schools, in England and Wales. This measure was at the time met with some consternation amongst teachers, but the Act allowed schools to modify the curriculum or even not to use it if it was not deemed to be appropriate. It was a significant step as many disabled children were not fulfilling their academic potential.

Children Act (1989)

The Children Act has been in general a well-received piece of legislation. It is still current and many practices such as the compilation of a register of 'children in need' by LEAs are carried out to comply with this Act. It brought together many pieces of legislation that related to children and was based on the idea that children had rights. It sought to protect all children, but also looked at the needs and rights of vulnerable children. The Act is wide ranging and covers issues such as child protection, registration of childcare settings and parental responsibility.

KEY PROPOSALS OF THE CHILDREN ACT

- The welfare of the child must at all times be considered 'paramount'.
- Wherever possible, children should be brought up and cared for within their own families.
- Parents with 'children in need' should be helped to bring up their children themselves (disabled children are considered to be 'in need').
- Children should be consulted and kept informed about decisions that affect their future.

Disabled children are seen as children 'in need' and as such the LEA has legal duties towards them and their families. This means that LEAs are obliged to maintain a register of children and offer them support. Many disabled children therefore have a social worker who visits the family from time to time. The requirement of the Act for LEAs to support children and help them to remain with their families meant that respite care, play schemes and funded places in pre-schools began to be offered. The 1989 Children Act also set the trend for parents and children to be seen as important in the decision making process.

SEEING THEORY IN PRACTICE

A nursery manager explains how she used the Children Act 1989 to get further funding for a child in her nursery.

We were very concerned about one child in particular. The parent was under a lot of stress and the parents were finding the child's behaviour very difficult at home. In nursery, the child was not using any language and seemed withdrawn, while at home he was showing ritualistic types of behaviour. At first, it appeared that no extra funding could be made available because the child did not have a statement. Everyone involved with the child recognised that the child needed additional help, but because there was no 'actual' diagnosis, there seemed to be no funding available. In the meantime, his parents were finding it increasingly difficult to manage the child and were desperate for us to take him in for more sessions, but could not afford the fees. Eventually, by researching the 1989 Children Act, I argued that this was clearly a 'child in need' and that the family also needed supporting. The parents were delighted and the child has since made fantastic progress.

1. Why did the LEA have to make funding available for this child?
2. Why can it be helpful for settings to have an understanding of legislation?

NHS and Community Care Act (1990)

Under part three of this Act (which is still current), the government sought to help people who previously would have been in residential care to have their needs met at home and thus remain in the community. Services such as domestic help, equipment and modifications to accommodation are examples of the help that can be provided.

Education Act (1993)

The 1993 Education Act was based on the 1981 Education Act. Its key points are summarised below and are important because they still form the basis of the Education Act of 2001.

KEY PROPOSALS OF THE EDUCATION ACT (1993)

Code of Practice The Act required that the Secretary of State for Education publish a code of practice which was to give LEAs and others practical guidance in following the legislation. The Code of Practice came into effect between September 1994 and December 2001.

Parents The 1993 Act made it clear that local education authorities needed to work alongside parents. It also established SEN tribunals that would hear cases where parents and local authorities were unable to agree. Parents' rights of appeal were extended and information was published to help parents understand their rights.

Definition of special educational needs The Act also defined what was meant by special educational needs. It stated that to be defined as having special educational needs, children had to have a learning difficulty that required special educational provision because the learning difficulty was greater than that for the majority of children of the same age, or because of a disability that prevents them from using the same provision as other children. It also made it clear that children who had a different home language to the one used in the setting were not to be classified as SEN.

Co-operation between agencies The Act stated that where health services identified that a child under five years old might have special educational needs, they had a duty to both the LEA and the parents to inform them. It also stated that they should pass on information about voluntary organisations that might be able to assist parents. This was significant because it encouraged voluntary, education and health services to work together in the interests of the child.

Assessment of children under two years The Act gave parents the right to ask for their child to be assessed and if appropriate to be given a statement of special educational needs

As a result of the 1993 Education Act, a Code of Practice was produced. This legally binding document was available for everyone involved in the care and education of children with special needs, including parents. The availability of this information meant that parents were able to challenge schools and LEAs if they were not fulfilling their obligations. The Code of Practice introduced a new role into settings; that of the Special Educational Needs Co-ordinator or SENCO (a named person responsible for co-ordinating support for children with SEN). The Code also required all maintained schools (schools receiving public funds) to have a policy on special needs. These two measures gave SEN a higher profile in schools that has since been built upon by the current Code of Practice.

Disability Discrimination Act (1995) and Disability Rights Commission Act (1999)

The Disability Discrimination Act 1995 (DDA) came into force on 2 December 1996. It is considered to be a landmark in terms of addressing discrimination against disabled people. For the first time, it was against the law for shops, employers and landlords to discriminate against disabled people.

The Act gave disabled people new rights in the following areas:

- Employment.
- Education.
- Goods and services including transport.
- Buying / renting of property.

The Act also created a Disability Rights Council, but this did not have statutory powers. After campaigning from many groups, a Disability Rights Commission was created in April 2000, following the Disability Rights Commission Act 2000. This Commission has statutory enforcement powers, which means that it can conduct investigations into discrimination and also support an individual in bringing court proceedings where unlawful discrimination is alleged to have taken place. The Commission also has a key role in educating employers, service providers and the general public in order to prevent discrimination occurring.

The DDA Act is divided into seven parts. It defines disability as a physical or mental impairment that has a substantial and long-term adverse effect on a person's ability to carry out day-to-day activities. To allow shops, restaurants and other service providers time to make 'reasonable' adjustments, different parts of the Act have been phased in gradually. For example from 2004, service providers will have to make 'reasonable adjustments' to the physical features of their building to overcome physical barriers to access.

The Act ensures recognition of the needs of disabled people wishing to study and the provision of better information for parents, pupils and students. The aim is that students will not be discriminated against because of their impairments. This Act has been strengthened further by the SEN and Disability Act 2001.

Schools have to explain their arrangements for the admission of disabled pupils, how they will help these pupils gain access and what they will do to ensure they are treated fairly.

- Further and higher education institutions funded by the Further and Higher Education Funding Councils have to publish disability statements containing information about facilities for disabled people.
- LEAs have to provide information on their further education facilities for disabled people.

Education Act (1996)

This Act incorporated all previous Education Acts since 1944. Part four of this Act included the main elements of the 1993 Education Act in relation to SEN. It gave parents more rights to appeal and also set a limit of 26 weeks to complete the legal process for identifying and assessing special needs. This Act is still current, but has been amended by the Special Educational Needs and Disability Act 2001 to give parents and children stronger rights to be included in mainstream education.

Human Rights Act (1998)

This Act came into effect in October 2000 and incorporates provisions from the European Convention on Human Rights. It has wide ranging implications for many areas of people's lives as all government initiatives and decisions must be interpreted in line with the agreed articles and the protocols of the convention. These include the Right to Education (Article 2 of Protocol 1) and the Prohibition of Discrimination (Article 14).

Carers and Disabled Children Act (2000)

This Act came into force on 1 April 2001. The aim is to recognise the role of carers and to provide for their needs as well as the needs of children. Parents of disabled children are therefore asked about the family's needs as well as the needs of the disabled child. The Act also allows councils to make direct payments to families so that they can purchase services. As well as direct payments to the family, short-break vouchers are also provided which are intended for families to use to gain respite care.

Special Education Needs and Disability Act (SENDA) 2001

This Act is divided into two sections. The SEN Code Of Practice 2001 is the product of this Act as it gives practical guidance to LEAs, schools and parents about the implementation of the Act. Part One of the Act reforms the framework of SEN to strengthen the rights of parents and children to access mainstream education. Part Two extends the Disability Discrimination Act (1995) to education, extending the civil rights of disabled children and adults in schools, colleges and universities.

KEY PROPOSALS OF THE SPECIAL EDUCATION NEEDS AND DISABILITY ACT (SENDA) 2001

- The right of children with special educational needs to be educated in mainstream schools (where this is what parents want and where it is appropriate for the child).
- The requirement of LEAs to arrange to provide parents of children with special educational needs with advice and information, and a means of resolving disputes with schools and LEAs.
- The requirement for LEAs to comply with orders of the Special Educational Needs Tribunal.
- The requirement of education settings to tell parents where they are making special educational provision for their child and to request a statutory assessment of a pupil's special educational needs
- The introduction of disability discrimination rights in the provision of education in schools, further education, higher education, adult education and the youth service.
- The requirement not to treat disabled students less favourably than non-disabled students.

THINK IT OVER

Zara is five years old. She is about to start school. Her parents want her to attend the local school where her two brothers already go. The school has told her that because she needs a wheelchair and help with toileting and other day-to-day tasks that it cannot accommodate her.

1. What legislation might her parents use to challenge this decision?
2. Why is it likely that going to the local school will be best for Zara and her family?

Chapter 3

Working with the SEN Code of Practice 2001

Introduction

The Special Educational Needs Code of Practice 2001 is the latest Code which practitioners, LEAs and other professionals should use to interpret the legislation relating to children with special educational needs. The Code of Practice applies to any setting that takes government funding. These include pre-schools and nurseries that receive the Nursery Education Grant as well as schools. It is important for your setting to have at least one copy of the guide, although many settings find that it is useful to have several copies so that if necessary they can be taken home or lent out.

This chapter looks at the principles behind the Code of Practice as well as how the Code might affect your setting and day-to-day practice.

Fundamental principles of the Code of Practice

It is helpful to understand that the Code of Practice reflects a changing philosophy in terms of our perception of children who have special educational needs. Chapter 1 of the Code of Practice lists the fundamental principles that were used to draw up the Code.

Critical Success Factors

The Code of Practice also lists factors that will be important for the successful implementation of the Code. These are entitled 'Critical Success Factors'. The first factor stresses the importance of the willingness of settings to meet all children's needs and to find ways of meeting them. Emphasis is given to the needs of children being identified early on in their education and also that professionals from different sectors should work together.

The Code assumes that practitioners will always show good practice by differentiating the curriculum to meet the needs of children. For example, instead of sorting plastic objects in order of size, a child might begin by sorting objects that are the same colour. Children whose needs can be met in this way are not considered to have special educational needs. In the same way, it is assumed that the setting will automatically adjust the layout or use other resources so that children's needs can be met without any further action being required.

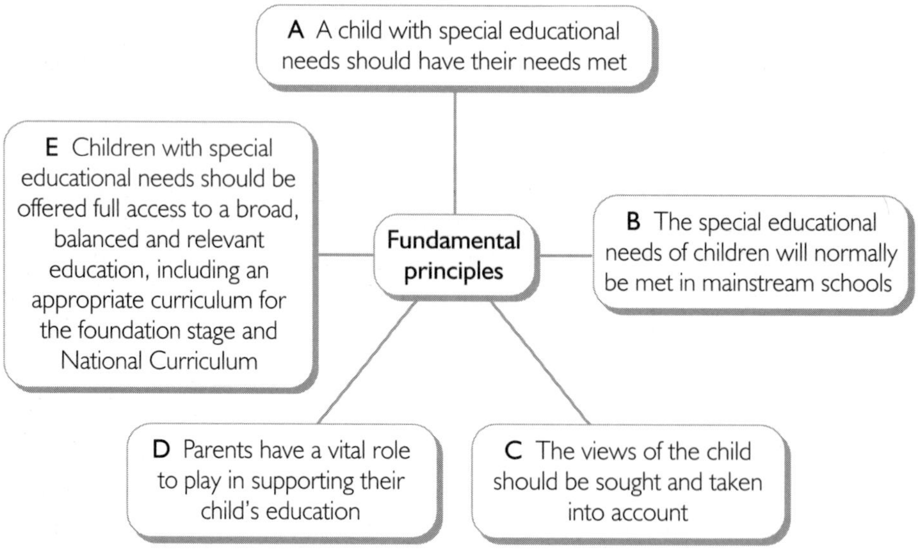

Source: SEN Code of Practice 2001

A *The Code of Practice reflects the principle of the social model of disability, i.e. that it is society that must change to meet the needs of disabled people rather than disabled people being expected to 'put up' with second class treatment unless they can manage otherwise. In terms of education this means that the emphasis is now on us to change the way we work, the environment and the curriculum in order to meet the child's needs rather than see the child as being the 'problem'.*

B *This is an essential principle to understand as it suggests that nearly all children will be playing and learning alongside each other, regardless of whether or not they have 'special needs'.*

C *This is a key change to the way that most children have been treated. The Code encourages children to take responsibility and some control over their care and education. Chapter 3 in the Code is entitled 'Pupil Participation' and gives guidance as to the ways in which children are expected to be involved.*

D *The Code of Practice strengthens parents' involvement and rights in relation to their child's education. Settings must work effectively with parents and involve rather than just inform them.*

E *The idea behind this principle is that all children should be able to learn in a way that suits them and not be discriminated against because of any disability. In practical terms, this means that you may have to change your way of working or the layout of a room to make sure that all children can take part.*

Fundamental principles of the Code of Practice.

Early years settings should adapt to meet the needs of all children

Meeting children's needs: a 'graduated response'

The Code of Practice suggests a 'graduated response' to meeting children's needs. This replaces the five 'stage' approach in the previous Code of Practice. The graduated response can be thought of as layers of a cake as each layer builds upon the previous one.

Early Years Action

This is the first 'layer' and is used once the normal differentiation of the curriculum has been tried out, but staff remain concerned about meeting the child's needs. The aim of Early Years Action is to provide 'in house' support. This means that the SENCO and practitioner will talk to the parents and the child. Individual Education Plans (IEPs) will then be drawn up showing strategies and resources that will provide more support for the child. The plans will then be monitored and reviewed to see if this level of support is effective.

Early Years Action Plus

This is the second 'layer' and means that other professionals outside of the setting will be contacted, with the agreement of the parents. IEPs will still be used, but other professionals are likely to contribute ideas and strategies to make them more effective. The setting will continue to review and monitor the child's progress and will still be expected to differentiate activities or resources to suit the child. Note that in order to trigger Early Years Action Plus, settings will need to show what action they have been taking 'in house'. This will mean keeping a record of the IEPs and other strategies that have been used.

Statutory Assessments (Statementing)

Statements are legally binding documents that set out the support that is required to meet a child's needs. They were first introduced in the 1980 Education Act, as a way of ensuring that children's needs were met following an assessment of their needs. Statements are reviewed each year in consultation with parents, the child and every professional that has some input.

The Code of Practice suggests that very few children will require a statement as the aim is that children's needs should be automatically met through Early Years Action and Early Years Action Plus. This means that the number of statutory assessments will be reduced considerably and are only likely to be carried out where a child has 'demonstrated significant cause for concern'.

The statementing process

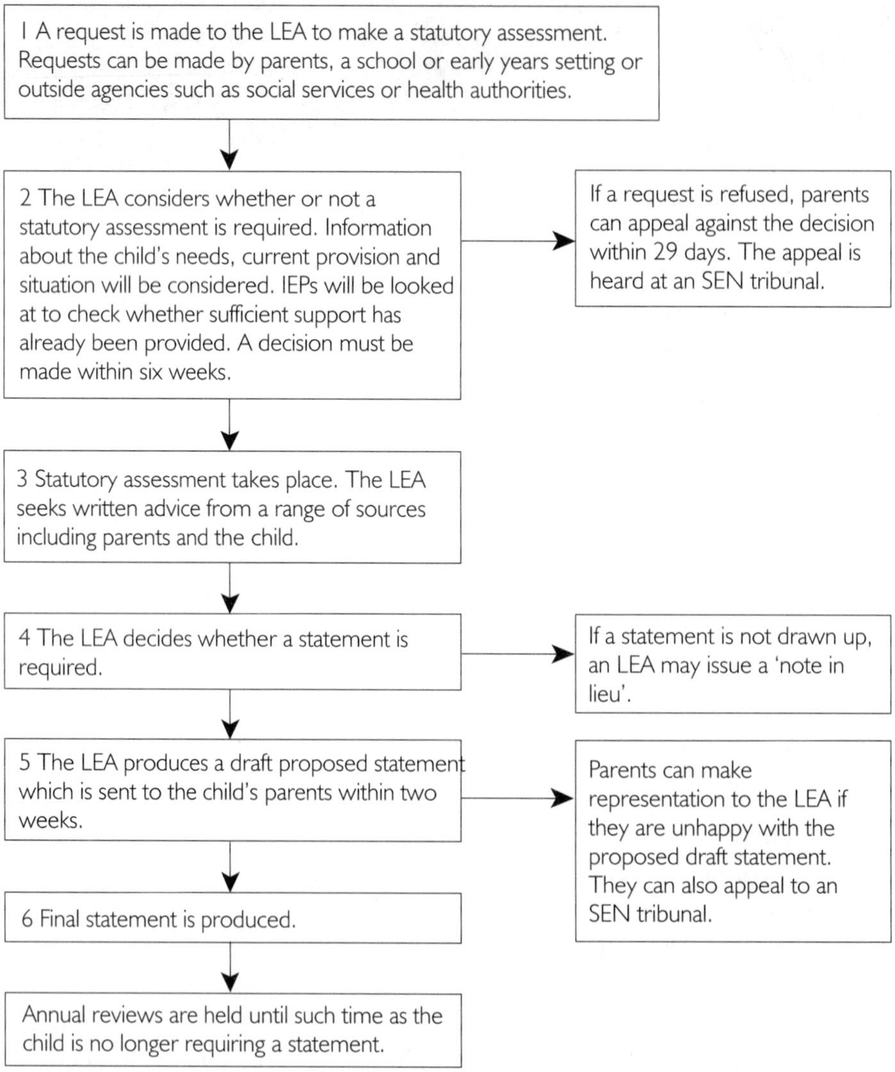

The statementing process.

1 The statementing process begins with a request to the LEA for a statutory assessment of the child's needs. A statutory assessment can be requested by the following:

- The child's school or early education setting (for children aged four and over, although as from 2004 an early education setting can make a request for three year olds).
- The child's parent(s).
- An external agency, e.g. health authority or social services.

Parents have to be informed that a statutory assessment has been requested.

2 Within six weeks of receipt for a request for statutory assessment, the LEA must make a decision. The decision will be based on the checks that the LEA takes to ensure that a statement is necessary. It will, for example, ask to see the child's records and IEPs to check that best uses of resources, teaching strategies and available support have already been explored. An LEA can refuse a statutory assessment, although it has to provide a reason for doing so. Parents can appeal against the decision to refuse the request at an SEN tribunal.

3 Once a statutory assessment is deemed necessary, the LEA must seek the following in writing:

- Parental advice.
- Educational advice.
- Medical advice.
- Psychological advice.
- Social services advice.
- Other advice that might be relevant, including the child's wishes.

The LEA has to find out what the current and future educational and medical needs of the child are. Comments about the best provision for meeting these needs are also invited, although the Code of Practice states that these should not include the naming of particular schools.

4 On receipt of the advice, the LEA will consider whether a statement is necessary. It is recommended that where a statement is not drawn up, a 'note in lieu' is sent to the parents. The Code of Practice suggests that the note in lieu should be similar in layout to a statement but should give the reasons why a statement has not been proposed. The idea of a note in lieu is to reflect the advice that has been given and make some suggestions as to how best to meet the child's needs.

5 If the LEA has concluded that a statement is necessary, a draft proposed statement is issued. The statement is divided into six parts.

Part 1 Introduction: the name, address and date of birth of the child and his or her parents. The child's home language and religion.

Part 2 Special educational needs: details of each of the child's special educational needs as identified by the LEAs during the statutory assessment.

Part 3 Special educational provision: details of the provision that the LEA considers necessary to meet the child's needs.

Part 4 Placement: the name and type of school where the special educational provision is to be made

Part 5 Non-educational needs: details of non-educational needs as agreed between the health services, social services and other agencies and the LEA.

Part 6 Non-educational provision: details of how the non-educational needs are to be met.

Once the proposed statement is drafted it is sent to the parents. They are able to make representations to the LEA within 15 days if they are unhappy with the proposals. If the parents and the LEA are unable to agree a statement, the parents can appeal to the SEN tribunal. In practice, most parents are in agreement as they have been involved in the assessment process.

6 A final statement is produced and statements are reviewed annually until such time as they are no longer needed.

Understanding how the Code of Practice might affect your setting

In many ways, the Code of Practice reflects good practice that should largely be in place in your setting. It is important for all staff to understand that following the Code of Practice is compulsory if the setting receives government funding and so it is in everyone's interests that some time and attention is spent on understanding it.

> "*Provision for children with special educational needs is a matter for everyone in the setting.*"
>
> 1:29 SEN Code of Practice 2001

SEN Policy

Your setting needs an SEN policy that reflects the Code of Practice and the conditions of the Nursery Education Grant.

A member of staff needs to take on responsibility for co-ordination of Special Educational Needs. This position is referred to in the Code as a SENCO.

Planning

Planning should reflect how you differentiate the curriculum to meet all children's needs. Plans should be evaluated so that you can consider if they are meeting children's needs. Some children will need IEPs where their needs are additional or different to what is being provided. These will need to be reviewed regularly.

Layout and resources

The layout of the setting should allow all children to be able to play and learn. Resources may need to be provided to enable learning or to remove barriers to learning.

REFLECT ON YOUR OWN PRACTICE

- Observations and records of children's progress and needs should be kept, as early identification of children's needs is stressed in the Code.
- More detailed observations and assessments should be made for those children who are the focus of Early Years Action and Early Years Action Plus.
- Good working relationships with parents should be in place.
- Ways of seeking children's ideas and listening to their views should be used.

Reports as part of statutory assessment or review of a statement

Reports and IEPs may be requested as part of the statutory assessment or review of a statement. Note that the majority of early years settings will not have children who have (or who are in the process of gaining) statements.

Developing an SEN policy

Policies outline the attitudes as well as the actions that settings should take about various areas that are important to their everyday practice. Your setting should have a behaviour policy, a child protection policy and a health and safety policy. Good policies are there to be used and understood by everyone including parents and others who may come into the setting, e.g. volunteers, visitors and advisers.

Who should write the policy?

The policy is best written and thought about as a team effort, although in many settings the manager, owner or SENCO will co-ordinate the actual writing of the policy. Settings that plan and write policies together tend to find that they work more effectively because everyone understands the purpose of the policy. It is worth reminding any reluctant members of staff that the Code of Practice expects a shared involvement in relation to SEN and that they will have a day-to-day responsibility to make sure that the SEN policy of the setting is effective.

KEY ISSUE: WRITING A POLICY

- Involve staff and others throughout the process.
- Use clear and simple language.
- Use headings to help the reader find information quickly.
- Avoid long sentences; use bullet points where possible.
- Number paragraphs so that they are easy to find.

1. Begin by considering what information is needed

The key starting point is to jot down the type of information that will be helpful and is needed in the policy. It is useful to meet with all the staff and write down their suggestions as to what they feel should be included.

Your policy is likely to need paragraphs on the following:

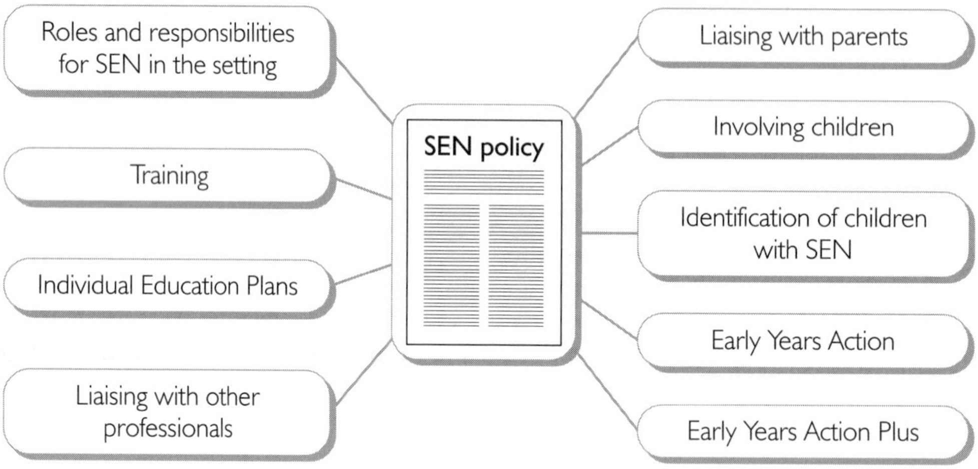

The content of an SEN policy.

2. Review what your setting is currently doing

For many settings, the SEN policy should simply put into words what they are doing in practice. Look at what is currently happening; consider what is working well, what needs to be changed in line with the Code of Practice and how this might happen. If changes are needed, you will need to consider these with the other staff and also seek advice from your local Early Years Development and Childcare Partnership (EYDCP).

REFLECT ON YOUR OWN PRACTICE

- What is the setting's overall belief in terms of anti-discriminatory practice and meeting children's needs?
- What is your admissions policy regarding children with SEN and how does this reflect the Code of Practice?
- Who has the overall responsibility for the SEN policy?
- Who is acting as the SENCO?
- What is the responsibility of the SENCO in your setting?
- Who will be responsible for identifying children with SEN and how will this occur?
- How will parents be informed of any concern that staff have about children?
- How can parents raise concerns that they may have about their child?
- How will parents be made aware of the Parent Partnership service in the local area?
- How are IEPs drawn up and reviewed?
- How will records relating to children be stored and who will be responsible for updating them?
- How will the setting make sure that staff are given on-going training so that they can meet the needs of children?
- Who will monitor the effectiveness of the SEN policy and when will it be reviewed?

> *"Once we began to write the policy, we realised that the SENCO should be given some time each week to meet with parents and staff and also to carry out observations on children."*
>
> **Nursery manager**

3. Order your headings and produce the first draft

Use clear headings and stick to these. Check through your draft with the staff involved to ensure that the text is clear and that everyone is in agreement. This can be a good time to gain feedback from an early years adviser or local SEN team. It is also useful to ask sympathetic (but objective) parents to make some comments, as the policy will be needed when working with parents.

SEEING THEORY IN PRACTICE

The Gables Day Nursery is a private day nursery that takes children from 0–4 years. Elaine Piper, the owner, explains how she and her staff wrote their SEN Policy.

We were keen to develop our own policy rather than just adopt or adapt one. I felt that if we did it ourselves, the staff would find it easier to use and understand. I also wanted the policy to be written in everyday language so that any parent, student or new member of staff could understand it.

Our starting point was the Code of Practice. First the management team sat down and drew up a list of points that we felt our policy needed to address. These included how to identify that a child had special needs, how to speak to parents as well as how we would help to include and support a child with special needs. We also reflected on our own 'mission' as a nursery. As a nursery we believe in taking a holistic view towards children's development that centres around play.

We then used staff meetings to work our way through the headings that we had drawn up. This took two meetings and at the third meeting, a draft policy was presented to the staff. The time spent was an investment as staff are now very confident about the policy and it is not seen as just another document sitting on the shelf.

Elaine gives the following advice to others who are about to write their own policies:

- Make sure that everyone in the setting works on the document.
- Write in a straightforward way so that everyone can understand it.
- Look at other settings' policies, but be confident enough to use your own headings and language.
- Consider asking for feedback about your policy from the early years advisory team while it is in draft.

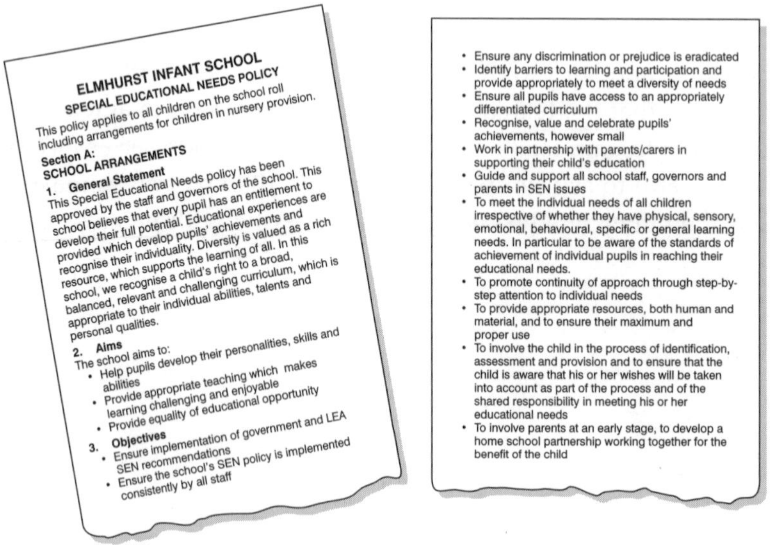

ELMHURST INFANT SCHOOL
SPECIAL EDUCATIONAL NEEDS POLICY

This policy applies to all children on the school roll including arrangements for children in nursery provision.

Section A:
SCHOOL ARRANGEMENTS

1. General Statement
This Special Educational Needs policy has been approved by the staff and governors of the school. This school believes that every pupil has an entitlement to develop their full potential. Educational experiences are provided which develop pupils' achievements and recognise their individuality. Diversity is valued as a rich resource, which supports the learning of all. In this school, we recognise a child's right to a broad, balanced, relevant and challenging curriculum, which is appropriate to their individual abilities, talents and personal qualities.

2. Aims
The school aims to:
- Help pupils develop their personalities, skills and abilities
- Provide appropriate teaching which makes learning challenging and enjoyable
- Provide equality of educational opportunity

3. Objectives
- Ensure implementation of government and LEA SEN recommendations
- Ensure the school's SEN policy is implemented consistently by all staff
- Ensure any discrimination or prejudice is eradicated
- Identify barriers to learning and participation and provide appropriately to meet a diversity of needs
- Ensure all pupils have access to an appropriately differentiated curriculum
- Recognise, value and celebrate pupils' achievements, however small
- Work in partnership with parents/carers in supporting their child's education
- Guide and support all school staff, governors and parents in SEN issues
- To meet the individual needs of all children irrespective of whether they have physical, sensory, emotional, behavioural, specific or general learning needs. In particular to be aware of the standards of achievement of individual pupils in reaching their educational needs.
- To promote continuity of approach through step-by-step attention to individual needs
- To provide appropriate resources, both human and material, and to ensure their maximum and proper use
- To involve the child in the process of identification, assessment and provision and to ensure that the child is aware that his or her wishes will be taken into account as part of the process and of the shared responsibility in meeting his or her educational needs
- To involve parents at an early stage, to develop a home school partnership working together for the benefit of the child

Sample SEN policy (reproduced with kind permission of Elmhurst Infant School).

THINK IT OVER

Jennie is a member of staff in a day care nursery. She is fed up because she has been told that everyone is to talk about the new SEN policy that is about to be written. She moans that it has nothing to do with her and in any case there are no children in wheelchairs in the setting.

1 Why is it important that everyone in the setting understands and contributes to the SEN policy?
2 What would you say to Jennie?

The role of the SENCO

Every early years setting and school in receipt of government funding has to have a named person who is responsible for co-ordinating support for children with SEN – this is the Special Educational Needs Co-ordinator or SENCO. SENCOs have several responsibilities which include meeting with parents, observing children and supporting their colleagues.

The position of the SENCO is regarded by the Code of Practice as an essential role. For many settings, the role of the SENCO is a promoted post as it requires an experienced practitioner, although not necessarily someone who has had any specific training in SEN. Enthusiasm, the ability to work with colleagues and parents and a good level of administration and organisational skills are the key

SENCOs need to be able to work with parents and staff in ensuring the best support for children with special educational needs

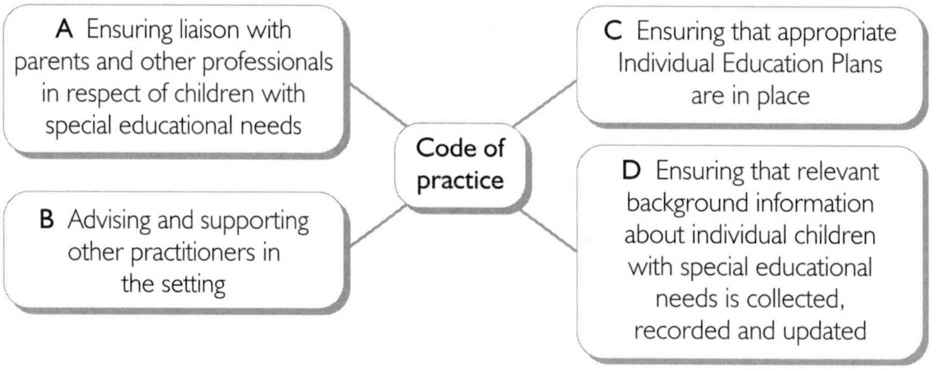

Source: 4:15 SEN Code of Practice 2001

A The liaison role is essential. SENCOs need to be able to work with parents, children and other professionals such as SEN advisers, social workers, health visitors and specialists such as teachers from the Speech and Language team. As well as meetings, SENCOs may also have to write reports to assist other professionals. The liaison role means that SENCOs need to have good communication skills.

B SENCOs need to be able to lead, motivate and inform other members of staff in matters relating to SEN. This may mean working alongside colleagues to devise strategies to support a child, organising training or finding out further information and cascading it back. Most SENCOs find that they become more skilled at suggesting strategies as they gain experience and build up contacts with other professionals.

C The production of IEPs is key to implementing the Code of Practice. The SENCO must make sure that IEPs are being used where children need additional or different support from that which is normally provided in a setting. In some settings the SENCO jointly draws up the IEP with the colleague who works with the child, while in other settings the SENCO offers a 'checking service' where colleagues feel they need reassurance. Note that it is not the intention of the Code of Practice to make SENCOs responsible for the actual writing of children's IEPs unless they are the child's key worker.

D The SENCO also has responsibility for the maintenance of records in the setting relating to children with SEN. The records have to be accurate and up to date which may mean checking the information that is being stored. It is important for SENCOs to be aware of the Data Protection Act and have good systems in place to review the records.

The responsibilities of the SENCO.

qualities in effective SENCOs. It is also essential that the SENCO is given sufficient time during workplace hours in order to meet with parents and staff and to carry out observations on children.

It is important to note that the SENCO does not necessarily work with individual children or draw up the IEPs. The Code of Practice expects that practitioners will be responsible for the day-to-day work with children.

STARTING POINTS FOR SENCOs

- Form or join a network of other SENCOs in your area.
- Subscribe to organisations offering support for SENCOs such as the National Association for Special Educational Needs (NASEN) as well as campaigning for organisations such as the Alliance for Inclusive Education.
- Look out for training opportunities for you and staff members.
- Look for ways of making contact with the parents when their child first joins the setting so that a link has already been established.
- Make sure that parents are aware of the role of the SENCO as part of the services that your setting offers children.
- Devise a brief information sheet for new members of staff to help them understand your role in the setting.
- Ask for a regular 'slot' for SEN at staff meetings to update colleagues.
- Consider setting up a resource shelf for colleagues, e.g. books, articles, blank IEPs.
- Develop a file of resources relating to areas of need, e.g. ideas for activities to support communication, etc.
- Make sure that other members of staff understand how and where records are stored so that they can be easily accessed in your absence.
- Look for ways of recognising and valuing colleagues' work in supporting children – a word of reassurance goes a long way.
- Keep a diary that highlights when reviews or updates are needed – remind staff if necessary.

SEEING THEORY IN PRACTICE

Debra Cassim has been the SENCO at the Clive Vale Nursery for six months. She explains her feelings about taking on the role.

To be honest, at first I felt quite daunted. I feel a bit guilty to say it now, but I also felt that I had been 'landed' with a huge task. I thought that I needed to be trained in order to do the role, but actually looking back, I had already acquired a lot of the knowledge about working with parents and children. In some ways I was three quarters of the way there. The support from within the nursery and the Early Years team helped me get the extra quarter. Now, I feel quite privileged to have been asked to take on the role. I like knowing that I am helping to make a difference.

Debra's advice to new SENCOs is:

- Don't worry about not being trained; you will already have many of the skills as an early years practitioner.
- Go to as much training as possible. This will help to improve your confidence and you will meet other SENCOs.
- Make sure you use the support in your area from early years advisers and SENCOs.

THINK IT OVER

Gavin has been asked to become a SENCO in a nursery. He is worried because he does not have any training and although he has worked with a range of children, he has never had to fill in or use an IEP.

1. What advice would you give Gavin?
2. What support would be available in your local area to support new SENCOs?

Resources

Copies of the SEN Code of Practice 2001 are available from:

DfES Publications
PO Box 5050
Sherwood Park
Annesley
Nottingham
NG15 0DJ
0845 6022260
www.dfes.gov.uk

Chapter 4

Identifying and assessing children who need extra support

Introduction

The early identification of children who may need some kind of extra support is very important, as children whose needs are not being met are essentially in danger of losing out. They may not be able to play alongside others or experience the learning benefits of play and feel part of the setting. This chapter looks at how you might observe and identify children who may need additional support or resources.

Early identification is not about 'sorting' children

It is important to understand that early identification is not about sorting children into groups of 'less able' and 'more able', nor about labelling children. Early identification should be about considering how we can best meet children's needs. A child whose needs have not been noticed may not be able to access the curriculum fully and so is effectively being discriminated against.

In some cases it is the parents who may bring their concerns to us hoping that we will listen to them and look out for their child. In other instances, it is an early years practitioner who notices or has a 'hunch' about a child. The observation of children is therefore important as it is not uncommon for a child's impairment to be thought of as part of their 'personality' by their immediate family or as 'something that they have always done' as the example below shows.

> *I wasn't picking up that he wasn't fully hearing. I just thought that his speech was quite sweet and because I was at home I knew what he needed as I was very much tuned into his speech. I was amazed when I realised that he really couldn't hear properly.*
>
> ***Gail, mother of Hugh, who had conductive hearing loss***

Understanding the limits

While it is important to observe children and consider the needs of particular children, it is essential that practitioners understand that their role is not to 'diagnose'. This is the role of other professionals such as educational psychologists, paediatricians and language therapists. Inaccurate diagnosis or speculation can mean that children become 'labelled' and potentially cause considerable anxiety for parents. The early years practitioner's role is to notice, observe and then, if necessary, act to inform parents and to refer.

Building a picture of the child

Most practitioners are quick to notice children who do not appear to show the same behaviour, progress or development as other children. When this happens, it is important to begin to look more closely, not only at the child, but also at the provision in your setting. Remember that the Code of Practice assumes that before any IEPs are drawn up, settings will have already tried a range of strategies including differentiating the curriculum.

Focusing on the provision in your setting

The key to good identification of children's needs is to be as objective as possible. Your starting point should be to consider whether or not the environment, activities or system of deploying adults in the setting is 'disabling' a child. This is particularly important where a child is perceived as having behavioural difficulties or is reticent to communicate. At the same time, you should also have a clear idea of the 'normal' ranges of children's development. In some cases, by standing back and considering what is being provided, and also by referring to normative development charts, you may find that a child does not have any particular needs, but that the setting needs to consider its approach.

REFLECT ON YOUR OWN PRACTICE

The following questions can be used to help you think about the effectiveness of your setting:

- Are there any periods of time when children are 'waiting', e.g. registration, snack time, lining up?
- Are group sizes during adult-led activities small enough to encourage children to talk and participate?
- Do children have a key worker who spends some time with them each day?
- Does the key worker greet the child at the start of the day?
- What opportunities are there for children to get individual attention in each session?
- Is a range of sensory activities available during each session, e.g. sand, water, dough?
- How attractive are the equipment and activities?
- Are there sufficient activities and equipment available to prevent squabbles?
- Are children encouraged to choose their own resources and play activities?

Think about the equipment and activities you provide in your setting – are there plenty of opportunities for children to participate in group activities?

SEEING THEORY IN PRACTICE

The Busy Bees pre-school had concerns over one child who appeared to lack concentration. After attending a training session, the supervisor decided to focus on the layout of the setting and the activities that were being offered. She noticed that when sand and water were put out, the child in question was able to concentrate for as long as 20 minutes at a time. She also noticed from carrying out the observation that several children were looking bored during snack time, including the child who she was focusing on. She concluded that the child could concentrate, but that the setting needed to be more pro-active in looking at the activities and also the routine of the session.

1. What may have been the consequences for this child had the setting not reflected upon its practice?
2. Suggest two ways in which this setting might change its practice in order to allow the child to concentrate.

Focusing on the child

Once the routine, layout, etc. of your setting has been considered, it will then be important to carry out some observations and to gain a fuller picture of the child in question. In some situations it can be better to ask another member of staff who is not closely involved with the child (or the SENCO) to observe the child as the key is to be objective as possible. It is well known in research that preconceptions about children can influence what we perceive and see.

Types of observation methods

There is a range of methods that can be used in order to collect more information about children. The type of observation method that is used will depend very much on personal preference but also on what area needs to be considered. Confidence is often the key to observation, so be prepared to adapt a method to suit your observing needs.

KEY ISSUE: OBSERVATION METHODS

Method	Aspect of development	Useful for
Event sample	Behaviour Interaction Social skills	Good for identifying how often a child shows a particular behaviour or is interacting
Checklist	Physical skills Language Cognition	Useful in identifying the skills a child has acquired and can be re-visited to check for progress
Target child	Behaviour Concentration Interaction Social skills	Good for providing a range of information about what a child does over part of a session
Time sample	Concentration Interaction	Good for providing a range of information about what a child does over a session
Free description	Behaviour Interaction Physical skills Concentration	Good for providing a detailed but snapshot record of a child's activity

Event sample

Event samples are very useful as they can be used to gain a more accurate picture of how frequently any kind of behaviour is being shown. This means that they can be used to look at how often a child interacts with other children, how often they play in groups as well as how often a child shows aggressive behaviour. Event samples can be used to monitor the effectiveness of IEPs; for example a target may be to increase the number of times a child interacts with other children and an event sample could be used to see if the number has increased.

Method

A sheet is prepared and each time the child shows the behaviour or action that is being monitored, the sheet is filled in. The number of columns is dictated by the type of information that is sought.

- Prepare a sheet beforehand.
- Add a column for each piece of information that you want to collect, e.g. the time, what happened, who the child was with.
- Make sure that everyone in the setting knows what behaviour is being monitored and where the sheet is being kept. This is important as you may be out of the room or not available when the action or behaviour occurs.
- Repeat the event sample on other sessions to build up a picture of what is happening.

CASE STUDY

Dora is four years old and the staff feel that she hardly plays with the other children. Dora's key worker, Chris, has decided to use an event sample to log down the number of times she plays with other children during a session. He is also interested to see whether Dora actually talks to the other children as she seems very quiet. Chris drew up an event sample to collect the following information:

- How many times Dora played with other children during a session.
- How long Dora played for.
- Who Dora played with.
- Where the play took place.
- Whether there was any interaction.

No.	Time (start and finish)	Who	Where	Interaction	Comments
1	9.45–9.46am	Niamh, George, Ali, Mark	Sand tray	No	Dora made eye contact and smiled at Niamh
2	11.13–11.15am	Sandie, Elliot	Toilets (washing hands)	Yes	Sandie and Elliot were singing. Dora joined in and giggled
3	11.35–11.53	Zainab	Dressing up corner	Yes	Dora took on the part of the baby and both girls played co-operatively

1. How many times was Dora seen interacting?
2. Which activity appeared to stimulate the most interaction?
3. Do you feel that the staff should be concerned at the level of her interactions?
4. What further information might be useful?
5. Suggest one way in which staff might help Dora to interact more?

Checklists

Checklists are quick to complete and many settings use them to assess children's development. A checklist is literally a list of skills and/or behaviours that can be ticked off when the observer has seen them. Checklists are useful because they focus the observer on particular things, for example, whether or not a child uses plurals, or can stand on one foot.

Checklists are an effective method for assessing children's stage of development

Method

Checklists are extremely simple to use, but a decision needs to be made as to whether or not to intervene in a session and actually ask the child to show certain skills so that they can be ticked off. Intervening (known as structuring) can put the child under pressure, but has the advantage that the observer can fill in the checklist more rapidly.

Child's name .... Date ....

Date of birth .... Observer ....

Developmental checklist

By 12 months	Yes	No	Sometimes
Walk with some help?			
Pick objects with finger and thumb?			
Transfer items from one hand to the other?			
Look for an object hidden under a beaker?			
Look at a person who is speaking to him or her?			
Make tuneful babbling sounds such as Da-da			
Respond to different sounds, e.g. drum, bell			
Imitate gestures such as pat cake and bye bye			
Hold beaker using two hands?			
Use fingers to eat finger foods such as squares of bread?			
Pick up dropped toys?			
React to the word 'No'?			
Reacts to own name?			

An example of a checklist.

CASE STUDY

Rebecca is very quiet and sometimes withdrawn. Her key worker has decided to use a checklist to consider whether Rebecca may have a hearing impairment. The key worker looks carefully at all of the statements and then observes Rebecca during the session.

Target child

Target child observations are used to track individual children during a session or part of a session. They are useful because they can give a fuller picture of how a child spends his or her time and can be designed to look at several aspects of a child's development.

Target child

Child's name: Annie   Sex: Female

Age: 3 yrs 4 months   Date: 22/3/02

Time	Activity	Language	Task	Social group
1 minute	T.C scooping sand with hands	T.C directing himself	Sand	Sol
2 minute	T.C scooping with beaker		Sand	Sol
3 minute	T.C patting down sand in beaker	A–T.CV 'Are you going to make a sandcastle?'	Sand	A
4 minute	T.C turning beaker over	T.C–A 'It won't come out'	Sand	A + 1 C
5 minute	T.C protects sandcastle	T.C–C 'Don't, it's mine'	Sand	A + 1 C

Code

T.C = Target child   A = Adult

Sol = solitary   C = Child

An example of target child observation.

Method

A sheet needs preparing in advance of the observation. A column is needed for each piece of information that is required. The observer needs to be aware of the time as this is a minute-by-minute recording system. Codes are often useful as more information can be jotted down and it is useful if you develop your own 'shorthand' or code.

Time sample

The time sample method allows an observer to record comfortably for longer periods of time. Instead of continuously observing the child, the recording takes place at regular intervals such as every 5 or 10 minutes. Some observers prefer to use a time sample in a general way and simply record down what a child is doing, others use columns to focus on particular skills and areas of development that a child is showing during each 'time slot'. Time samples can be used to observe more than one child as the example below shows.

Method

- Prepare a sheet with the timings running vertically.
- Add in a column for each type of information required, e.g. speech, social grouping.
- Use a watch during the recording to help record time accurately.
- At the appointed times, note down what the child is doing. Remember that this is not a continuous observation.

Sanjeet

Time	Location	Social grouping	Activity
10.00	Sand	Solitary	Scooping, pouring with bucket (LH)
10.10	Sand	Pair	Digging – imitating Sophie
10.20	Puzzle table	Solitary	Sits down, puts in one piece, moves off
10.30	Dough	Group	Rolling dough into sausages (LH)
10.40	Dough	Group	Showing how to make 'cakes'

Harriet

Time	Location	Social grouping	Activity
10.05	Home corner	Pair	Knocking on door, going in and out
10.15	Home corner	Pair	Lying down, pretending to be a baby, eye contact and interaction with Ciara
10.25	Home corner	Pair	Pushing pram with both hands, steers around objects, talks to Ciara
10.35	Book area	Solitary	Sitting on mat, looking at the Rainbow Fish, turning pages one by one
10.45	Book area	Pair	Showing book to Ciara, pointing to pictures and explaining

Free description

This method is used to provide detailed information about a skill or situation that a child is involved in. This type of observation does not have to be planned ahead as only a paper and pen are required. Note however that this method only provides 'snapshots' of the child and sometimes other methods need to be used alongside it.

Method

This method can be compared to taking 'written photographs' of children. Spend 2 or 3 minutes observing a child and write down as much as possible. The present tense is normally used. Immediately afterward, write up the observation as it can be difficult to decipher what has been written at a later date.

> Robbie is standing up in front of Sofina, who is sitting on a chair. Robbie seems to be looking down at Sofina. She is saying 'Shall we dress up?' Sofina nods and smiles. Robbie smiles too and they both walk over to the dressing-up corner. Robbie takes a green dress, grasping it in her right hand, and places it on the floor. She pulls the back of the dress open with both hands. She steps into the dress using her right foot first and pulls up the dress gradually to a standing position, placing her right arm into the dress and then her left. Robbie walks over to the nursery and looks up. She asks 'Can you do my buttons up?' and turns around.

An example of a free description.

THINK IT OVER

Sanjeet is sitting next to an adult sharing a story. He points to a picture and says 'Look'. He pulls the book towards him and brings the book closer to his face . 'Look, dog.' He passes the book back to the adult. He smiles.. Another child approaches. Sanjeet looks up abruptly. Sanjeet takes the book and holds it closely to his face. He points to a picture. He shows the page to the other child. He pushes the book close to the other child's face. the other child takes the book. Sanjeet reaches out with his left hand. He does not make contact with the book. The adult asks the other child to pass her the book. Book children sit down with the adult and look at the book. Sanjeet leans closely towards the book.

What to observe

There are some signs that can indicate that a child has an impairment or condition. While conditions and impairments that are likely to seriously affect a child's development are noticed during routine health visits, slight impairments can go undetected. It is therefore useful to hone in on the following as you observe a child. Remember, however, that the role of the early years practitioner is not to diagnose and that some skills are linked to stages of development such as being able to use scissors or play with another child.

Physical development

- How controlled and co-ordinated are a child's movements?
- Does the child bump into objects or fall over frequently?
- Does the child have difficulty in holding and manipulating objects?
- Does the child have a dislike of messy play, e.g. dough, sand?
- Has the child begun to show a hand preference?
- How confident is the child at using tricycles, climbing and balancing?
- Is the child aware of his or her body in relation to the space around them?

Vision

- Does the child need to be very close to books, pictures and posters?
- Does the child ever peer or frown?
- Does the child appear to be 'accident prone'?
- Is the child sometimes frustrated when using small toys and equipment such as puzzles or farm animals?
- Is the child uninterested in watching videos and television?
- Does the child look at objects in an unusual way, e.g. holding things very closely to the eyes.

Hearing

- Is speech muffled or unclear?
- Do adults who are unfamiliar with the child have difficulty in understanding what is being said?
- Does the child mispronounce words that other children of his or her age manage easily?
- Does the child appear to stare intently at adults and other children's faces when they are talking?
- Does the child at times appear to be unsure as to what is happening, e.g. after some instructions have been given?

- Does the child look and copy what other children are doing?
- Does the child appear to be in a world of his or her own especially at story time?
- Does the child respond immediately to his or her name or to a loud sound?
- Is the child prone to runny colds?
- Does the child often 'shout' rather than talk at a normal volume without realising it?
- Does the child show aggressive or frustrated behaviour?

Speech and communication

- Does the child make eye contact with adults and other children?
- How often does the child interact with adults or children?
- Does the child have difficulty in understanding what is being said?
- Does the intonation sound monotone and flat?
- Does the child often keep repeating nonsense words or phrases?
- Are the child's responses not in keeping with what would normally be expected?
- Does the child stutter or stammer or have difficulty in pronouncing words?
- Does the child repeat words or phrases spoken by the adult in inappropriate contexts?
- Can the child follow simple instructions, e.g. put your apron on the peg?

Social and emotional development

- Is the child aware of other children, e.g. watches others, copies their play?
- To what extent does the child interact and play with other children?
- Is the child able to take turns and show some awareness of other's needs (over three years)?
- Is the child aggressive towards others for no apparent reason?
- Is the child constantly restless and finds it hard to concentrate even on self-chosen activities with adult support?
- Is the child aware of the routine of the setting?
- Does the child have great difficulties adapting to changes in routines or new members of staff?
- Is the child clingy towards adults and seeks their attention?
- Does the child play in a ritualistic way, e.g. always using the same pieces of equipment in a repetitious way?
- Does the child avoid imaginative play, e.g. dressing up, home corner?
- Does the child become distressed for no apparent reason?

Using the information gained from observations

There is little point in carrying out observations if the information gained is not effectively used. It is therefore important to spend some time analysing your information. A good starting point is to consider whether or not it is the setting that is 'disabling' the child. The child may be responding in a certain way because equipment is not accessible or the activities are not interesting.

The next step is to consider whether a developmental need has been identified. If this is the case, it is worth checking the charts of normative development to gain some kind of benchmark. If at this point, you still have concerns, it will be worth talking to the child's parents as they may wish to refer the child via their G.P. or health visitor for more specialist advice. In the early stages of identification, it is essential to avoid 'labelling' or 'diagnosing' as a child who at three years may appear to have some delay may be making adequate progress in a few months time.

Early Years Action

It is useful to look at the Code of Practice's suggestions for when a setting needs to implement Early Years Action. It is important to note that in the initial stages of identification of a child's needs, the setting must look at ways to differentiate the curriculum and remove any barriers to learning by providing equipment, resources, etc. before Early Years Action is appropriate.

The triggers for intervention through Early Years Action could be the practitioner's or parent's concern about a child who, despite receiving appropriate early education, experiences the following:

- Makes little or no progress even when teaching approaches are particularly targeted to improve the child's identified area of weakness.
- Continues working at levels significantly below those expected for children of a similar age in certain areas.
- Persistent emotional and/or behaviour difficulties, that are not ameliorated by the behaviour management techniques usually employed in the setting.
- Has sensory or physical problems, and continues to make little or no progress despite the provision of personal aids and equipment.
- Has communication and/or interaction difficulties, and requires specific individual interventions in order to access learning.

Source: 4:21 SEN Code of Practice 2001

Using charts of normative development

Normative development charts show what 'most' children are able to do at various ages, although it is essential to remember that there is no such thing as a 'normal' child, as all children develop at their own pace. This means that charts can only be used a guide. They are, however, helpful as they show the sequences

Normative development charts

Stage	Age	Development
Pre-linguistic	0–3 months	Cries to show hunger, tiredness and distress Recognises different tones of voices Coos and gurgles when content By three months can recognise carer's voice and is soothed Smiles in response to other's faces
	3–6 months	Still cries to show distress, but is more easily soothed Babbles and coos Babbles consist of short sounds 'ma, ma, da, da' Laughs, chuckles and even squeals
	6–12 months	Babbling makes up half of baby's non-crying sounds Strings vowels and consonants together to make repetitive sounds – 'mememememe, dadadadada' Babbling becomes more tuneful and inventive and by nine months most of the sounds used are the ones needed for the language being learnt At ten months understands about 17 words such as 'bye bye' Uses gestures to ask for things – points hand and whines to show adult what he or she wants Enjoys games such as pat-a-cake
Linguistic	12–18 months	First words appear at around 12 months, although will only be recognisable as a word to carer, e.g., ;dede', to mean drink Words are used to mean more than one thing depending on the intonation the baby uses, e.g. 'dede' used to mean I want a drink, my drink is finished or I want more drink Linguists call these one-word expressions holophrases By 15 months will have about ten words that carers can understand
	18–24 months	Puts two words together, e.g. 'bye-bye dog' Telegraphic speech appears – uses key words in a grammatical way, e.g. 'dada come' Vocabulary increases – 10–30 words in a month! By two years, most children have 200 words
	2–3 years	New words are quickly learnt Uses plurals, e.g. dogs Makes errors such as 'sheeps', 'drawed' Starts to use negatives such as 'There no cats' Begins to use questions 'Where cats?'
	3–4 years	Imitates adult speech patterns accurately, e.g. 'We liked that, didnt we?' Speech is understood by strangers Sentences contain four or more words and are grammatical Vocabulary is large – knows parts of the body, names of househol objects, animals Errors are still made, especially when using past tenses, e.g. 'I taked it' Knows and understands nursery rhymes Enjoys asking questions
	4–8 years	From four years, language is developed and refined Mistakes beciome fewer – starts to enjoy using language as a means of socialising with others, expressing needs and recounting what he or she has done. By five years vocabulary is about 5000 words Uses complex sentences correctly Enjoys telling and hearing jokes Understands that language can be written with symbols By eight years most children are fluent speakers, readers and developing writers of their language

Language development.

Age	Fine manipulative skills	Gross manipulative skills
12 months	Picks up objects with thumb and forefinger Picks up toys such as rattles Points to objects Holds cup with help Puts small objects in a container	Mobile – either crawling, rolling or shuffling (Some children may be walking) Sits up insupported for long periods Walks with assistance Tries to crawl up stairs
15 months	Holds and drinks from cup using two hands Builds tower of two blocks Makes marks with crayons Tries to turn pages in books	Crawls down stairs feet first Walks independently Seats self in small chair
18 months	Strings four large beads Turns door knobs and handles Pulls off shoes	Bends down from the waist to pick up toys Squats down to look at toys Rolls and throws a ball Walks down stairs with adult help Pushes and pulls toys whilst walking
2 years	Uses a spoon to feed him or herself Zips and unzips large zippers Places five rings on a stick Puts on shoes Draws circles and dots Builds a tower of five to six bricks Begins to use a preferred hand	Kicks a ball that is not moving Climbs on furniture Puts together and pulls apart snap-together toys Walks up and down stairs confidently
3 years	Turns pages in a book one by one Holds crayon and can draw a face Uses a spoon without spilling Washes and dries hands with help Puts on and takes off coat	Walks and runs forwards Walks on tiptoes Throws large ball Kicks ball forward Jumps from low steps Pedals and steers a tricycle
4 years	Buttons and unbuttons own clothing Cuts out simple shapes Draws a person with head, trunk and legs Puts together 12-piece puzzle	Walks on a line Aims and throws ball Bounces and catchces large ball Runs, changing direction Hops on one foot Pedals and steers a tricyle confidently
5 years	Forms letters, writes own name Draws recognisable picture of trees, houses, people and animals Colours in pictures neatly Dresses and undresses easily Completes 20-piece jigsaw puzzles Cuts out shapes using scissors quite accurately Draws around a template	Skips with a rope Runs quickly and able to avoid obstacles Is able to use a variety of large equipment, e.g. swings, slides Throws large ball to partner and catches it Hits ball with bat or stick
6–7 years	Is able to sew simple stitches Cuts out shapes accurately and neatly Handwriting is evenly spaced and may be joined Drawings are detailed and representative Makes a simple sandwich Ties and unties laces	Rides a bicycle without stabilisers Runs Chases and dodges others Hops, skips and jumps confidently Kicks a ball with direction Balances on a beam or wall

Physical development.

Age	Development
Birth to 1 year	
1 month	Watches primary carer's face
3 months	Smiles and coos
	Enjoys being handled and cuddled
6 months	Laughs and enjoys being played with
8 months	Fears strangers
9 months	Plays peek-a-boo
	Discriminates between strangers and familiar adults
12 months	Is affectionate towards family and primary carers
	Plays simple games such as pat-a-cake
1–2 years	
15 months	Begins to explore environment if familiar adult is close by
	Begins to use words to communicate with
	Has a stronger feeling of being an individual
18 months	Language is increasing
	Points to objects to show familiar adults
	Explores environment and shows some independence but still needs familiar adults
	Strong emotions, e.g. anger, fear and joy, are shown
2 years	Plays near other children – parallel play
	Begins to talk when playing – pretend play
	Imitates adults' actions
	Strong emotions, e.g. anger, fear and joy, are shown
2–3 years	During this year most children will: • move out of nappies • have a strong sense of their identity, including their gender and age • be happy to leave their primary carer for short periods • start taking an interest in other children and playing with them • show concern for other children, e.g. telling primary carer if baby is crying • start to wait for their needs to be met
3–4 years	• Affectionate towards family, friends and carers • Wants to help and please primary carers and other familiar adults • Imitates – in play – actions seen, e.g. putting teddy to bed, feeding dolls • Shares playthings • Plays with other children – mostly pretend play • Shows concern for other people, e.g. rubs back of crying baby

Emotional and social development.

involved in gaining skills and so can be used to track a child's progress. They can also be useful in cases where children are in danger of being labelled 'difficult' or 'slow' as reference to such charts can sometimes show that it is the adult's expectation of children that is too high. Referring to charts can be a useful starting point if concerns are expressed about a child.

THINK IT OVER

Rajeet is four years old. The pre-school finds that he is very boisterous and does not concentrate. During story time he fidgets and often tries to wander off. The pre-school have a rule that all the children must sit down and listen to the story time. English is not his home language and although he understands some English, he is not yet fluent. His parents are surprised that the pre-school finds his behaviour difficult as he plays well with his cousins and other friends at home.

1 What additional information do you feel would be helpful in this case?

2 What observation methods would you choose to gain this information?

Chapter 5
Working with parents

Introduction

The need to work effectively with parents is not just restricted to children who have 'special needs' but should be one of the driving forces within your setting. All children have needs, and all parents therefore should feel included in their child's education and care. Settings that work well with parents and see them as equal partners are more likely to provide the necessary care and attention that will help children to fulfil their potential. Good working relationships should be based on mutual respect allowing everyone to be able to comfortably exchange information and points of view.

In reality, many parents feel that practitioners do not listen to them or treat them as equal partners. It is not uncommon for parents who have children with special needs to report feelings of anxiety, frustration and anger in relation to their meetings with practitioners as a result of feeling that they were not being listened to.

> "*They listened, and somehow you felt their empathy and you felt that you weren't on your own. You felt that they were committed, and they cared and were trying to bring out the best in Sophie. They made a big contribution not only to Sophie but also to us.*"
>
> *Sophie's mother*

Parents and the Code of Practice

The Code of Practice 2001 places a strong emphasis on the need to work in partnership with parents. Section 2 of the Code of Practice outlines the importance of working in partnership with parents and outlines clear principles that practitioners should bear in mind.

> Parents hold key information and have a critical role to play in their children's education. They have unique strengths, knowledge and experience to contribute to the shared view of a child's needs and the best ways of supporting them. It is therefore essential that all professionals (schools, LEAs and other agencies) actively seek to work with parents and value the contribution they make.
>
> *Source: Paragraph 2.2, SEN Code of Practice, 2001*

Settings have a duty to tell parents when they first identify that a child has special education needs. The Code of Practice also asks LEAs to make arrangements for parent partnership services so that parents can be supported.

KEY ISSUE: DEFINITION OF 'PARENTS'

The definition of 'parent' is quite wide as the term parent includes anyone with parental responsibility. In general, all mothers have parental responsibility as well as fathers married to the mothers at the time of birth. Parental responsibility can be sought by fathers, but can also be granted to others in some circumstances by a court. This may mean that a guardian, grandparent or social services department may have parental responsibility if a child lives with them and a court order has been granted.

Principles of effective communication with parents

The Code of Practice outlines seven key principles that you should adopt when working with parents. They emphasise the vested interest that parents have in their children's lives and also the knowledge and contribution that parents are able to give to practitioners.

1 Acknowledge and draw on parental knowledge and expertise in relation to their child

Parents usually have a great deal of background knowledge about the child and may have tried out a range of strategies, equipment or have contacts with different professionals and support groups.

Sharing information with parents about their child is vital

2 Focus on the children's strengths as well as areas of additional need

Parents can become frustrated by practitioners who focus on the 'problem' or the 'condition' as in their role as parents they are seeing the 'whole' child. Sharing and talking about a child's interests, pleasures and personality is not only a more positive way of working, but can help you to plan more effectively to meet the child's needs.

3 Recognise the personal and emotional investment of parents and be aware of their feelings

The emotional tie between parent and child is a powerful one. Parents do not see their children in terms of 'key learning intentions' and 'normative development'! The only 'target' that most parents have for their child is that they should be happy and fulfilled. It is therefore essential that you are thoughtful and consider the effect of your words in the light of this when you are talking about their child.

> *The only thing I want for my child from her education is that she will be able to have another child home for tea.*
>
> **Parent**

> *The word normal should be taken out of the dictionary. I became sick of hearing how Robert wasn't normal.*
>
> **Parent**

4 Ensure that parents understand procedures, are aware of how to access support in preparing their contributions, and are given documents to be discussed well before the meetings

To involve parents in their child's education, they will need to understand any paperwork and procedures that are being used. While they may be an expert on their child, they may need some help in familiarising themselves with how you draw up IEPs, review the child's progress, etc. It will be essential that you have the local contact details of the Parent Partnership Service.

5 Respect the validity of differing perspectives and seek constructive ways of reconciling different viewpoints

Many practitioners view any disagreement with parents as a challenge to their authority or expertise. This can create very negative meetings and eventually block out any hope of effective communication. Accepting that parents may have a very different view of their child and how to best provide for him or her is an essential starting point in any open communication.

6 Respect the differing needs that parents themselves may have, such as a disability or communication and linguistic barriers

Some parents may have particular needs which, if we are not sensitive to them, may create a barrier to effective communication and information sharing. To overcome potential barriers, we may need to be flexible in our approach. A parent may wish to bring along an interpreter or advocate or we may need to translate or tape documents. The key is to find out sensitively from the parents how best we can meet their needs in order that they can participate fully in the process.

7 Recognise the need for flexibility in the timing and structure of meetings

To achieve true involvement with parents, you will need to make sure that you are 'user friendly'! Are meetings formal and stiff, thus creating an unnecessarily charged atmosphere? Will parents have to take time off work or make complicated child care arrangements? The key to getting meetings right with parents is to imagine that you are in their position.

REFLECT ON YOUR OWN PRACTICE

- Recognise that parents may have a different perspective on their child's development and may have different priorities from you.
- Acknowledge that while you may be an expert on your setting, parents are experts on their children.
- Do not make comparisons between children in the setting.
- Remember that trust can be shattered by breaches of confidentiality and thoughtless words.

Confidentiality

If you have developed a good relationship with parents, it is likely that they may provide you with personal information, both about the child and themselves. It is essential to regard all information that is passed to you as confidential, unless you are told otherwise.

CASE STUDY

Hannah has been working as a classroom assistant for two terms. She knows some of the parents of the children in the class. One Saturday outside a supermarket, one of the parents asked Hannah why one of the children in the class received individual support. Hannah told the parent that it was because the child had behavioural difficulties as well as poor speech. She went on to tell the parent that the child was now having speech and language therapy and that the whole family was having some type of counselling.

1 Why is this a serious breach of confidentiality?
2 Give a suggestion as to how Hannah might have replied without breaking confidentiality.

Data Protection Act

While it is good practice for all records to be 'open' so that parents feel part of the process, you should also be aware that any written personal information that you hold will be subject to the Data Protection Act whether or not it has been processed on computer or by hand. The Act is designed to protect everyone's right to know what has been written about them and to safeguard information being given out without consent.

SEEING THEORY IN PRACTICE

- Check that your setting has registered with the Data Protection Commission.
- Make sure that your records are secure as well as being accurate, relevant and relevant.
- Invite parents to check written information as part of 'open communication'.

Communicating with parents

There are no magic 'tricks' that are needed to work with parents. You will however need to be a good listener, be supportive and create environments and situations that help parents to feel at ease. You will also need to show empathy for parents. Note that empathy is not sympathy, but reflects concern, care and warmth towards another person.

> *There were times when I couldn't help but cry because the emotions inside me were building up, but they made me feel that I was no longer alone.*
>
> Parent

Listening to parents

Many parents comment that some practitioners do not listen to them. This perception is more likely to occur when parents feel that they are being hurried or that the environment in which conversations are taking place is hectic or noisy. In these conditions, a practitioner's attention might be divided or time may be so short that instead of listening to a parent's perspective, the practitioner concentrates only on what he or she wishes to say. It is therefore essential to find quiet areas and times in which to talk to parents.

It is also important to show parents that you are actively trying to understand their viewpoint and are listening to their messages. There are many ways in which we can do this. First, show through your body language that you are keen to listen. Take the time to sit down with the parent, nod and make eye contact. Remember to avoid interrupting what a parent is saying. Good listeners also check that they are receiving the message by clarifying points, for example, 'So if I have understood you correctly, you are finding that Jo points rather than uses

Early years practitioners should show good listening skills when talking to parents

words at home.' As well as checking that you are receiving the message well, you can show parents that you really are listening to them by reflecting back their words, for example, 'So Jo was very frustrated yesterday'. This can help parents to keep talking as they feel that they are being listened to.

> *He just needed stimulating in a different way; it felt like the whole education system didn't listen to me.*
>
> **Parent**

Talking to parents

It is easy to forget that our words can be very powerful. They can destroy the trust and confidence that a parent has in a setting or a person. Words can also make parents feel guilty and defensive or make them feel that their child is 'not good enough'. This means that while you are talking to parents, you will need to be aware of the effect of your words and notice their body language and responses. It also means that you should prepare for meetings carefully. Look again at the child. Notice the strengths of the child. Consider what this child can bring to the setting. It can also be a good idea to think about what the child now needs from the adults in the setting. In this way, you are more likely to show that you care and have the child's best interests at heart.

REFLECT ON YOUR OWN PRACTICE

- Do not focus on what the child can or cannot do. Focus on what adults need to do to help the child.
- Monitor parents' body language as you talk; consider the effects of your words.
- Make sure that you talk about the child in positive ways.

Understanding that parents may have strong emotions

Many parents will have strong emotions when they talk about their children. This is perfectly natural as the emotional bond between parent and child is after all what makes parents parents! Understanding this is essential, and allowing parents to express their emotions without feeling embarrassed will be a cornerstone in a good relationship.

> "*I have to work quite hard to come across as strong and sensible, almost as if I have to deny who I am. I dare not cry or show any emotion, otherwise they will think that I am just some silly neurotic mother.*"
>
> **Parent**

KEY ISSUE: COMMUNICATING WITH PARENTS

- Find a quiet and private space for conversations so that parents can really get an opportunity to talk. Consider using a 'do not disturb' sign on the door.
- Always remember that you are talking about a child, not a 'problem' or a 'syndrome'. Make sure that this is reflected in your tone of voice and language.
- Make sure that you are really listening to parents. Check that you have understood what they are saying by asking them if you can summarise it and invite them to correct you.
- Do not show embarrassment or surprise if a parent openly cries; have tissues to hand and make sure that the parent does not feel rushed.
- Some parents may need to be reassured that their emotions and feelings are normal and that this does not make them 'silly' or 'neurotic'.
- Consider whether a parent's anger is based on frustration; have you really been listening and acknowledging his or her viewpoint?
- Consider whether you would benefit from some basic counselling training as this should teach you how to listen effectively.

Parents as an invaluable source of information

Parents can usually provide information not just about the child, but also about strategies, equipment and resources that they use to 'enable' the child to live happily in the home environment. This is worth remembering because often a child who appears to be 'disabled' in some way in a setting may well be 'abled' in their own home. It can therefore be a good idea to visit a child at home, especially if you are worried about managing a medical condition or making sure that your setting is accessible.

Some parents also become 'experts' on their child's impairment and can provide up-to-date information and also contacts with other professionals. Tapping into this information can therefore be helpful in finding effective ways of supporting and enabling the child.

CASE STUDY

We had a partially sighted girl coming to join us. At first I was really worried because I have never worked with a partially sighted child. I was scared that we would not know what to do or how to help. In the end I visited the child at home. It was amazing and I learnt so much simply by watching and talking to the mum. It also meant that we had all got to know each other.

What should I do if I notice that a child's behaviour or development is giving me cause for concern?

Early identification of children with additional needs is essential in order for children to gain any support that they might need. It is also important that children are not 'labelled' and so you should always start by carefully observing the child. Once you have carefully assessed a child and are sure that the child has some additional needs that will require further action, you will need to talk to the parents. Hopefully, you will already have developed a good working relationship with the parents as this forms the basis of good practice within all early years settings. Parents who feel the most dissatisfied with settings are often those whose first contact with staff is when they are called in to talk about a 'problem'. It is essential that early meetings work well for everyone involved as it is likely that further meetings will be required. The tone of the first meeting needs to be reassuring and supportive rather than accusatory. It is also worth pointing out to parents that children under five years old often show a wide range of development and that some apparent delay at this age does not necessarily signal difficulties in later schooling.

> *I was made to feel from day one, that Stephen's difficulties were in some way my fault and that I was expected to sort them out.*
>
> **Parent**

REFLECT ON YOUR OWN PRACTICE

- Find out when parents are able to come in to talk; make sure that your tone is reassuring rather than accusing.
- Begin any meeting by explaining that you are hoping to help the child and that it would be helpful to exchange as much information as possible about the child.
- Talk through the child's overall progress in the setting, emphasising the strengths of the child in order for parents to understand your perspective on the child.
- Ask the parents for their perspective emphasising that they will have a more global view of their child.
- Make sure that any meeting ends with everyone involved having a clear idea of what the next steps might be. These may be further assessment in the setting, drawing up an IEP or the parents drawing on outside assistance.

What should I do if I am concerned about a child's progress and the parent does not seem to accept that there is a developmental delay?

If, when talking to parents, you sense that they do not share your view of the child's progress, it will be important to acknowledge this. The child they see at home may be very different to the one you see in your setting, especially in terms of behaviour and language. The starting point is therefore to find out more about the child and to keep in contact with the parents. You may consider jointly carrying out some observations so that the areas of concern can be more accurately assessed. It is also important to go back to charts of 'normative development' on pages 50–52 so that you can be sure that these assessments are accurate.

It is essential to remember that a parent's concerns may be different to your own. A parent may focus on the happiness of their child rather than have an educational perspective. You must take care to consider the 'whole' child and not just focus on the child's weaknesses. Parents will also need to feel that you are on the child's side and that any concern you may have does not reflect badly on either the child or the parent. Some practitioners who are concerned that parents are not taking on board the message that they are trying to give can make the situation worse by almost building a case against the child. This makes parents defensive as it can feel as if the child is being blamed and victimised. You should be clearly reflecting the idea that, by considering the child's needs, your aim is to 'enable' the child by changing your approach, resources or strategies.

It is also worth recognising that some parents may be at the start of a potentially emotional journey. Some parents are afraid that their child will be labelled or treated less favourably than others and may distrust any attempt to record the child's needs. This is a natural reaction in view of how children with disabilities have been treated in the past. It is therefore essential to reassure parents that your records will be open to them and that they will be able to contribute towards the planning of the child's education. They may also be interested in finding out about the Parent Partnership Service as well as the Code of Practice's principles of inclusion.

In other cases, parents may need some time to consider your perspective and to allow them to adjust to this other view of their child. This may mean arranging further meetings so that parents can come back and ask further questions and learn more about their child.

> *I was presented one day with a list of everything that was 'wrong'. I was so angry that in the end I tore the paper up and asked them who they thought they were.*
>
> *Parent*

REFLECT ON YOUR OWN PRACTICE

- Make sure that your assessments are accurate.
- Remember to focus on children's strengths as well as areas causing concern.
- Listen to and acknowledge any differing perspectives that parents may have.
- Avoid making meetings 'adversarial'; parents should feel that you are on the child's side.
- Remember that parents want the best for their child and want to protect him or her.
- Consider whether it is your setting that is 'disabling' the child.
- Talk to parents about any fears that they may have.
- Give parents information about the Parent Partnership Service in your area.

Parent Partnership Services

The Code of Practice requires LEAs to arrange Parent Partnership Services. The aim of these services is to ensure that parents get access to support and information. Parent Partnership Services will vary considerably from area to area, as the Code of Practice allows LEAs to choose how to provide the service. In some areas LEAs are building upon and funding existing services provided by the voluntary sector, while in others LEAs are setting up their own service. Parent Partnership Services also have a variety of names and so it will be important for you to find out the name and the way in which the service is provided in your area.

In some cases, parents may ask a member of the Parent Partnership Service to a meeting, especially if they find it hard to put their own views across. It is important that you do not see the service as a threat or challenge, as its role is to help everyone involved with the child to be able to communicate effectively.

Tameside Parent Partnership Service

Newsletter 3 — July 2002

INSIDE THIS ISSUE:

1. PPS roles and responsibilities
   Feedback on PPS events
2. Special Educational Needs Code of Practice
   North West Disagreement Resolution Service
   Local SEN news
3. Events
4. Council web addresses
   Local Support Groups
   Comments Sheet

ROLES & RESPONSIBILITIES

Hello, my name is Jackie Woolstencroft.

I am Tameside Parent Partnership Service Support Worker and have been with the service since November 2001.

Prior to joining the service I was employed by Social Services for 12 years. I worked with young children and their families in Early Years Centres.

Since joining the service I have dealt with various enquiries - I am gradually forming links with schools in the borough and have received valuable input from experienced colleagues within Education and Cultural Services.

Jackie

Since Jackie commenced with the service, it has allowed me (Debbie Wood, Service Co-ordinator) time to refocus my role. I am responsible for planning and reviewing the service. Although I am still involved in supporting parents this is now mainly Jackie's role. I have several large projects to work on in the future, all of which aim to support parents and aid communication with agencies involved. I look forward to keeping you updated in the next newsletter.

Debbie

FEEDBACK ON EVENTS

CODE OF PRACTICE DAY

On 27th February 2002 the Parent Partnership Service in association with Afasic hosted "An Awareness of the Code of Practice" day for parents/carers of children with special educational needs.

During the day we covered the changes to the new Code of Practice, the Parent Partnership Service and meeting SEN. We also outlined the Disagreement Resolution Service, Individual Education Plans, Statements and Annual/Transitional Reviews.

The day was well attended with 53 parents/carers participating.

At the close of day parents/carers were asked to complete an evaluation form. Feedback from them was very positive, almost all who completed the form said they felt the day had been very informative and was well organised and presented.

All parents/carers who attended were given a pack of information, which contained information on PPS, SEN, IEPs, Annual Reviews, Transition Plans, a Glossary of terms used in the Code of Practice and contact numbers.

A very successful day

SEN INFORMATION DAY

Our information day was held on Monday 11th March 2002 at Ashton Town Hall. Along with the Parent Partnership Service stall were numerous other stalls, giving information to members of the public about special educational needs. Other stalls included services from Health, Education, Social Services and the Voluntary Sector.

Again the day was a great success with over 70 people calling in and collecting information.

Tameside Parent Partnership Service

What is the Parent Partnership Service?

The Parent Partnership Service works to promote partnership between parents and carers of children with special educational needs or disabilities and those who provide services that can support them-voluntary and community groups, schools and professional groups. We are funded by Nottinghamshire County Council and Nottingham City Council Education Departments and so we only operate in those local areas. If you live in another part of the country you can find out about parent partnership services in your area from your own local education authority. In the meantime you are welcome to browse our site to see what's there.

Parent Partnership Services provide information through websites, telephone helplines and newsletters

(reproduced with kind permission of Tameside Parent Partnership Service and the Parent Partnership Service for Nottingham and Nottinghamshire)

REFLECT ON YOUR OWN PRACTICE

- Make sure that you have the contact details of your local Parent Partnership Service.
- Make contact and build a relationship with the service, as it can provide support and information to help you work more effectively with parents.
- Provide parents with information about the service so that they can independently contact them.
- Remember that you must ask for parents' permission if you wish to refer them to the Parent Partnership Service.

THINK IT OVER

The Drayton pre-school has some concerns about a child who is now three and a half years old. He finds it hard to play alongside or co-operatively with other children. He often plays repetitive games by himself, and at times it seems as if he is in his own world. Staff also find his speech and thoughts difficult to understand and he often repeats words and phrases in odd contexts. Staff have also noticed that he rarely plays in an imaginative way. To help get a better picture of what is happening, the SENCO has decided to talk to the parent.

Look at the following snippets of conversation:

Conversation A

SENCO: Hello, would you like to sit down? I have brought Joshua's file along with me as I want to make some notes as we speak. We have many concerns about Joshua which is why we wanted to talk to you.

Parent: Oh, I didn't know that anything was wrong.

SENCO: Well, actually we find Joshua very difficult at times and we think that he is not normal.

Parent: In what way?

SENCO: I think you know that he bites, as we have told you that already, but his language is very poor for a child of his age. We think that he is autistic.

Conversation B

SENCO: Hello, thank you so much for coming in, I was looking forward to meeting you. Shall we find somewhere quiet to sit for a moment? If I can start by just letting you know why we wanted you to come in. We are concerned that we are not quite meeting Joshua's needs at the moment and we wanted to find out more about him from you.

Parent: I see. What do you want to know?

SENCO: Well to start with, we have noticed that Joshua isn't always playing with the other children and we were wondering if he plays with friends or your other son at home.

Parent: He does play a bit, but not like his brother did.

1 Which style of conversation is likely to produce information about Joshua?
2 Analyse the differences between the two conversations and consider the likely effects on the parent.
3 Why is it important that practitioners should approach parents with the idea of 'sharing' rather than telling information?

Chapter 6

Individual Education Plans

Introduction

Individual Education Plans, often referred to as IEPs, are essentially action plans. They are useful because they help to provide a focus for future work with individual children. IEPs are not 'statements' and can be drawn up by the practitioner and/or the SENCO if it is realised that a child needs additional or different support in the setting. IEPs are used to support children on Early Years Action as well as Early Years Action Plus. This chapter looks at the process of writing, using and reviewing IEPs.

The purpose of IEPs

IEPs are designed to focus on small steps of a child's development, needs or behaviour. They act principally as an action plan, focusing on areas that will benefit the child. Breaking down and focusing on particular targets has been shown as an effective way of helping children. Practitioners and parents also benefit because they are able to see and measure the success of the strategies that have been put into place. As well as acting as an action plan, IEPs also have other purposes, as shown in the diagram below.

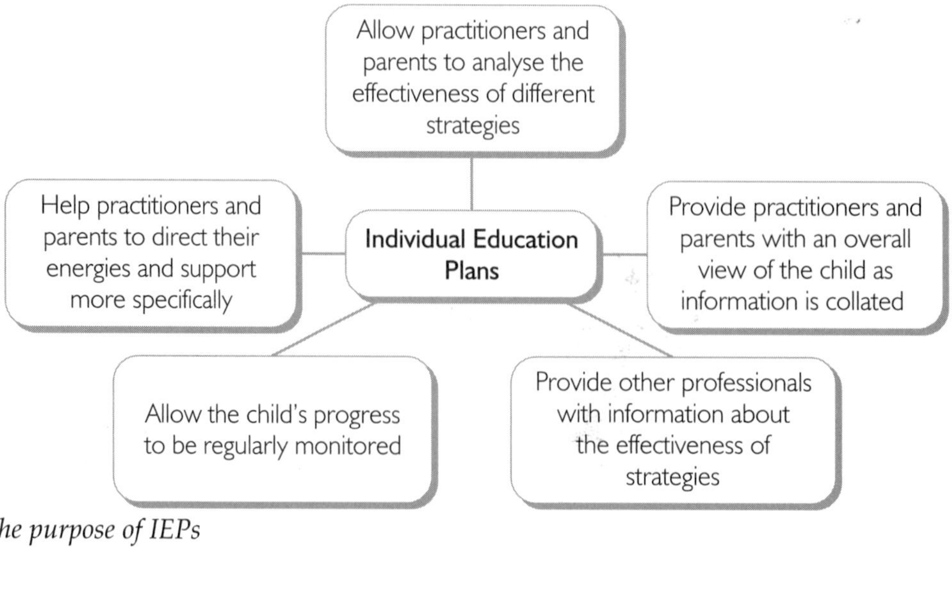

The purpose of IEPs

Understanding when children need an IEP

The key test of whether a child needs an IEP is whether or not you will need to provide very different or extra support to help the child. A child with a medical condition such as diabetes or asthma is unlikely to need an IEP because these types of conditions do not usually affect children's learning and overall development. In the same way, a child who uses a wheelchair may not need an IEP as once adjustments are made to the environment to 'enable' the child, he or she will be able to enjoy the same play, activities and learning experiences as other children.

KEY ISSUE: WHEN AN IEP IS NECESSARY

Children are likely to need an IEP if any of the following apply:

- The child makes little or no progress even when teaching approaches are particularly targeted to improve the child's identified area of weakness.
- The child continues working at levels significantly below those expected for children of similar age.
- The child experiences persistent emotional and/or behavioural difficulties that are not ameliorated by the behaviour managements and techniques usually employed in the setting.
- The child has sensory or physical problems and continues to make little or no progress despite the provision of personal aids and equipment.
- The child has communication and/or interaction difficulties, and requires specific individual interventions in order to access learning.

Source: 4:21 SEN Code of Practice 2001

People involved in writing the IEP

Effective IEPS will draw upon expertise and information from a range of people. At the level of Early Years Action, it is likely that IEPs will be drawn up by SENCOs, the key worker or practitioner with responsibility for the child, the parents and also the child themselves. See also page 76 on the involvement of Early Years Action Plus.

The role of the SENCO

While it is the responsibility of the SENCO in the setting to ensure that IEPs are in place, the SENCO's role is not necessarily to produce them. The idea is that practitioners who work on a day-to-day basis with a child will have a greater understanding about the child and therefore will be in a better position to draw up an IEP. In many settings SENCOs support their colleagues and help them to check that the IEPs are likely to be effective and will also suggest strategies and teaching methods.

Involving parents

When it is recognised that a child will need additional and/or different support and will need an IEP, additional and/or different parents need to be involved. Parents will need information about how IEPs are used and should be encouraged to make comments or suggestions about the targets that are going to be set. It is essential to gain as much information about the child as possible as the parents may be able to suggest strategies that they find helpful at home.

Involving children

The Code of Practice has as one of its key features the involvement of children in their own education. While very young children will not necessarily understand the process of IEPs, they can still be involved, as working from children's interests is likely to make more impact. This means that before an IEP is drawn up, the child's parents or key workers can ask the child about what they enjoy doing most in the setting and who they like being with. It is also possible to use observations and videos of children to help build an IEP that reflects their interests.

CASE STUDY

Yannick does not interact with the other children. His keyworker and parents have decided as part of the IEP to encourage him to take part in one game involving another child each day. Yannick is very interested in playing with cars. The keyworker talks to Yannick about his favourite cars. She uses this information to devise simple games that involve the cars. Yannick and one other child are given boxes into whcih the put their favourite cars. They take in turns to choose a car.

What information should an IEP contain?

There is no standard form on which IEPs are recorded. Settings are free therefore to design their own, although it can be useful to look at others. It is essential that the following information is recorded:

- ✓ Child's name and date of birth.
- ✓ Date of the IEP.
- ✓ Number of IEP (where there has been more than one).
- ✓ Date and level of support, e.g. Early Years Action/Early Years Action Plus.
- ✓ A brief summary of the child's difficulties and needs.
- ✓ Child's strengths, interests and views.
- ✓ Targets that the plan is to cover.
- ✓ Criteria for success.
- ✓ Teaching methods and strategies.
- ✓ Staff to be involved.
- ✓ Date to be reviewed.
- ✓ Signatures of parent and staff.

Writing IEPs

The actual IEP should not be a lengthy document. Most settings use brief bullet points and simple sentences as lengthy documents tend to go unread and create unwieldy demands on staff.

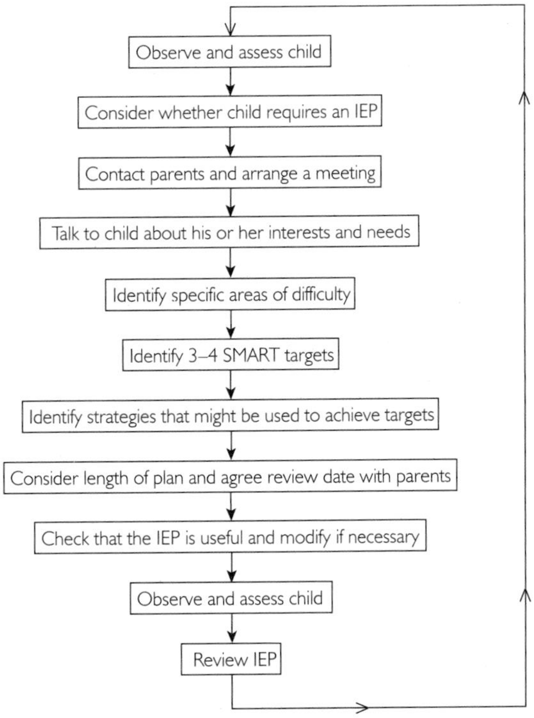

The stages of writing an IEP.

Areas of difficulty

This section should be quite short and simply record the reasons why the child needs additional or different support. Try and be specific as the targets should reflect the area of difficulty. For example 'Dora does not interact with other children' or 'Damien has difficulties with fine motor skills'.

Using SMART targets

Setting targets allows us to focus on developing or improving children's particular skills. The acronym SMART is often used when target setting to help practitioners think carefully about the targets that they are setting:

S specific

M measurable

A achievable

R relevant

T time bound

The SEN Code of Practice suggests that an IEP should have three or four targets. However, for children attending a setting for only two sessions, the number of targets should reflect the shorter time available to work on targets and use strategies. Once these targets are met, new ones can be developed. In this way, you can build a step-by-step approach to your support.

KEY ISSUE: TARGET SETTING

The key to setting targets is that they are focused and small enough to make them achievable. By continually meeting targets, children learn about success. It also helps parents and others in the setting to feel positive and to notice children's strengths rather than weaknesses.

Setting unrealistic goals can cause enormous difficulties as staff, parents and children may feel that no progress is being made. This can quickly erode the 'can do' feeling in a setting and actually create further problems. It is important to remember that although targets are being set, we should see them mainly as targets for us and our work. There is otherwise a danger of creating a system where the child is seen as failing if he or she is not meeting targets.

Specific

Every area of development and every skill needs to be seen as a journey. The key to setting targets is to break down the journey into tiny steps. It is these steps that can be used as targets. To work out the 'steps' of the journey, you need to think about what is involved in the task or skill, for example in order to use a pair of scissors, a child has to develop strength in the hand as well as being able to hold them correctly.

Using SMART targets can help when monitoring the development of children's skills

Steps can be worked out by referring to charts showing normative development and looking at the sequence that most children follow in the different areas of development. For example in terms of language development children often learn to point to draw an adult's attention to an object before using a word. Ideas for targets can also be gained from referring to the Nuffield Portage programme, the P scales and also from talking to others such as the SEN advisory team in your area.

In some cases, it might be hard to decide which area of need to concentrate on. In such cases, it is often a good idea to begin by choosing the area that will have the greatest impact on the child, but also one that will be easy for the child to achieve.

Measurable

As part of the thinking process, it will be important to decide how targets can be measured. How will you be able to check that the child has made progress and is ready for a new target? For each target, you will need to record how you intend to check or monitor that the child can achieve it. The advantage of recording the 'criteria for success' or 'outcomes' is that everyone will have a clear idea of exactly what they are aiming for. It is at this point in writing the IEP that practitioners often realise that their targets are too big and too 'wide'. A target such as 'to concentrate more' is very hard to measure. How long for? On what type of activity? By thinking about the measurability of an outcome, the target often becomes smaller and more focused.

To help you think about how to measure the outcomes consider these type of questions:

- How many times will I need to see the child demonstrating that they can achieve the target?
- How confidently/easily must the child be able to achieve the target?
- In what type of situations, does the child need to achieve the target, e.g. during adult-directed activities, with support of another adult, at home as well as in the setting?

Achievable and relevant

By thinking about how your targets are going to be measured, it is more likely that you will choose achievable targets for the child. Choosing targets that are relevant is also important. Ideally, the targets should concentrate on helping the child rather than just helping the setting. What targets will best help the child to access the curriculum and meet his or her needs? It is also worth checking that efforts are being focused appropriately, for example, choosing a target of sitting for a group story may not be appropriate for a child who finds it hard to sit on an adult's knee and share a picture book.

Time bound

The idea behind 'time bound' is that it creates a sense of priority and urgency. Having time limits helps everyone to focus on helping the child and so progress is likely to be made. Most settings draw up their IEPs with a time frame of six to ten weeks although this depends on the amount of time the child spends in the setting. This should provide enough time for the programme to take effect but not so long that inertia sets in.

Teaching methods and strategies

After deciding on the targets and ways of checking the targets, the next step is to consider the role of the adult and the strategies that need to be provided. This is in some ways the most important part of the IEP as targets alone will not help the child. This section of the IEP is the 'how' part. You will need to consider how best to support the child. In some cases, you may decide that the child needs more one-to-one adult support, but it may also be worth considering if a child can be given this support as part of a small group.

Again, it can be helpful to talk to parents and gain their input. In some cases, parents will be able to suggest strategies that have worked in other settings or at home. Some parents are also very knowledgeable about their child's impairment and are often in contact with support organisations. Part 2 of this book provides examples of strategies and activities that are often used in relation to four areas of need.

SEEING THEORY IN PRACTICE

Daniel was born ten weeks early. He is small for his age and he has poor motor skills, both fine and gross. He has poor concentration. He changes activity frequently even when supported with an adult. He is a sociable child and enjoys watching and being with other children. He particularly enjoys painting and playing games. Staff have noticed that he responds well to sensory activities such as sand and water. His parents report that at home he enjoys having friends round and playing in the tent in the garden. They have noticed that he finds it hard to follow instructions.

Louise, his key worker, has decided, in consultation with Daniel's parents, to focus on his fine motor skill development and concentration. It was also felt that his overall poor co-ordination might be affecting his concentration. It was felt that as Daniel was just four years old and that he was unaware of his difficulties, it would not be appropriate to address them directly with him. He was however asked by both his parents and his key worker about the things that he enjoyed most at nursery. He mentioned the sandpit, playing with water and being with one child in particular. To get a feel of what Daniel wanted to achieve, his key worker asked him what he would most like to be able to do. Daniel said that he wanted to be able to build a sand castle.

This information was used to help the key worker link the teaching strategies to Daniel's interests. As it is was the first IEP that Daniel had had, the review date was set quite early on as both the setting and Daniel's parents wanted to look at his progress.

Individual Education Plan

Name: Daniel	Early Years Action
Area/s of concern: Fine motor skills/concentration	
Review Date: 14 March 2003	
Early years practitioner: Miss Fletcher	Start date: Jan 2003
DOB 4-12-99	IEP No.1
Proposed Support:	
Support began: Jan 2003	

Targets to be achieved	Achievement Criteria	Possible resources/techniques	Possible class strategies	Ideas for support/assistant	Outcome
1. To grasp a small object between finger(s) and thumb	1. Pick up 5 beads and transfer to a pot in under 3 minutes.	1. Sorting activies e.g. beads, using spoons in sand tray Play-doh.	1. Provide a variety of small objects within Daniel's reach. Encourage him to pick them up with fingers.	1. Demonstrate how to pick up objects with a pincer grip. Praise success.	
2. To maintain attention in a small group activity and participate appropriately.	2. To participate fully in a sensory activity for 10 minutes.	2. Building sand castles. Sorting objects that float and sink	2. Provide opportunity for Daniel to participate and take turns at an appropriate level with 1:1 support.	2. Encourage Daniel to participate and take turns. Praise him.	

Parents/practitioner contribution Work with Daniel on related activities at home. Practise taking turns at home. Playing games.

Parent's signature ____________________

Practitioner's signature ____________________

Daniel's IEP.

Storage of IEPs

The complete IEP should be stored in a safe place whe confidentiality can be maintained. It is not appropriate for them to be displayed where adults who are not connected to the setting might see them. All adults who work with the child should be given access to the IEP and should be aware of the strategies that are being used. Note that access to the child's complete file may be more limited so that personal details about the family can be protected.

IEPs can be modified

IEPs are meant to be a tool. They should not be consigned to a filing cabinet and forgotten about until the review date is about to dawn! This means that if you realise that an unrealistic target has been set or the targets are no longer appropriate, it is good practice to amend them. This should be done in conjunction with parents as they are a vital part of the process. Most practitioners find that as they become more experienced, they also become more skilled at working out achievable targets and strategies.

Reviewing IEPs

To prevent IEPs from becoming just another piece of paper in your setting, you will need to review the plans. This will help you decide whether the strategies and targets that you have chosen have been effective. In some cases, children will need no further plans drawing up because their needs can be met through the programme that you are offering for the other children. In other cases, further plans will need to be drawn to build on the progress that the child has made. Reviews should be carried out in consultation with parents as it is important to gain their perspective. With very young children, it can be hard to see how to include them in the process, but we can ask them questions about what they have enjoyed doing so that we can build further on their interests.

How to review an IEP

Begin by closely observing the child and thinking about his or her progress and/or continuing needs. Think carefully about the environment that is provided and the effectiveness of the strategies that have been used. It is also important to gain information from other colleagues as they too will have their own perspective. Once you have begun to pool information, you will then need to hold a review meeting with the parents. It will be important to make sure that meetings are held at convenient times; in some settings, reviews are held during parents' evenings, while in others separate times are chosen. For the review process to work well, it will be essential that sufficient time and privacy are made available in order for everyone involved to be relaxed.

As with all meetings, remember to consider the 'whole' child. What are the child's strengths? What are the child's interests? What has been the impact of the strategies so far? You should also consider whether the targets have been achieved and if so, can the child maintain this skill or is further reinforcement or practice still needed?

The analysis and exchange of information should then help you to decide on the next step for the child. In some cases, no further IEPs will be required, in other cases further support will be required and so a new IEP will need to be drawn up.

Deciding on whether further IEPs are required

The key question to consider is whether or not the child is making progress and can the progress be sustained by simply differentiating the curriculum? The Code of Practice clearly states that 'IEPs should only record that which is additional to or different from the differentiated curriculum plan that is in place as part of normal provision' (4:27 Code of Practice). It is worth remembering that the concept of inclusion accepts that all children have needs and that we should be meeting these automatically without the need to 'label' children. This guidance should also prevent situations where practitioners are spending large amounts of time on paperwork rather than actually using their time to be with children.

This may mean that no IEPs will be drawn up for children who are showing signs of slower development than their peers, but whose needs can be met by adjusting the type of activities and the routine of the day. Where no further IEPs are required, it will be essential to explain to parents how you will make sure that the child's ongoing needs are to be met. Some parents may feel that without an IEP, their child will no longer be able to make progress and that he or she will just be left to 'fend' for him or herself. It is also useful to explain to parents that you will be making ongoing observations on the child's progress and that if necessary in the future, further IEPs can be drawn up.

Frequency of IEPs

There is no 'magic' number of IEPs that children should have, although the Code of Practice suggests that IEPs should be reviewed at least three times a year. In practice this is not likely to be sufficient, as young children's needs can change, and progress at times can be quite rapid. It is therefore probable that you will need to consider writing and reviewing plans on an eight weekly basis.

THINK IT OVER

It is important to remember that not all children will need an IEP as often adjusting an activity or making changes to the setting will be sufficient. Look at the following children's needs:

- Anya is five years old. She has diabetes which means that she must have regular snacks and meals.
- Paul is four years old. He has a visual and hearing impairment. He requires speech therapy and also needs help in socialising with other children.
- Marcos is five years old. He has difficulty in controlling his fine manipulative movements. He needs specific activities and one-to-one support to build his co-ordination.
- Krishna is four years old and has epilepsy. Her epilepsy is controlled by medication.

1. Decide which children are likely to require an IEP.
2. Give reasons for your decision.

Chapter 7

Gaining additional support for children: Early Years Action Plus

Introduction

While many children's needs can be met within the setting and through working closely with parents, some children will need additional support from other professionals. The 1989 Children Act sent a clear message that health, social services and education teams should work together to meet children's needs. This approach has been followed up in subsequent legislation. There are therefore a range of services that are provided for children with special needs. Understanding the roles of other professionals and the types of support that are available is therefore very useful. This chapter provides a general overview of the support that is found in most areas. However, services tend to vary from area to area and it is advisable that you develop your own local directory.

Early Years Action Plus

Early Years Action Plus is the title used in the Code of Practice to indicate a level of support for the child in which other professionals will work alongside your setting to meet a child's needs. Responsibility for drawing up IEPs and differentiating the curriculum will still remain with the setting, but other professionals might provide guidance, resources and training to help you meet the child's needs. In some cases, other professionals may also work directly with the child, although the current trend is to encourage practitioners to be taught the skills and the strategies that should be used. This is considered to be a more effective approach as a practitioner may be seeing the child every day, whereas a speech therapist may only see a child once a week.

Referring children

In order to gain the support of external agencies at Early Years Action Plus, you will need to show how the setting has already tried to provide additional and/or different support for the child. Likely exceptions to this are children who come into your setting with a statement or children whose needs are so great that you feel that immediate support is required. IEPs will be looked at to see whether sufficient strategies have already been tried, as well as notes and information gained from parents. This means that you will need to keep good records of the work that you have carried out with the child and as well as observations and records of meetings with parents.

KEY ISSUE: PARENTS' RIGHTS

One of the major changes to the Code of Practice is the strengthening of parents' rights of information. This means that you should not refer a child to any service unless you have informed and preferably gained parental consent.

Sources of support and information

Systems for gaining additional support and advice can vary enormously from area to area. While one service will accept direct referrals in one area, another may have a different process. It is therefore useful to develop your own directory and network of contacts so that you can easily find help or advise parents of who to contact. It is worth noting that many of the services outlined in this chapter offer training courses and workshops.

As well as gaining support from specialist professionals, remember too that in your local area, there will be other SENCOs working in early years settings. By exchanging phone numbers, you can potentially pool ideas and suggestions.

Early Years Development and Childcare Partnerships (EYDCP)

Your local EYDCP is likely to be your first port of call when seeking advice and additional support, even if the child is not requiring Early Years Action Plus. EYDCPs were formed to support the government's National Childcare Strategy.

EYDCPs often provide information on the internet (reproduced with kind permission)

Partnerships consist of representatives from a range of sectors including health, social services, private, voluntary and statutory childcare providers as well as training providers. As part of their role, EYDCPs provide training and support to early years settings. Each EYDCP is structured differently. In some areas, the role of the EYDCP has been combined with the education department, while in others it is quite separate. The advantage of contacting your local EYDCP is that although they may not actually be responsible for a particular service, they should be able to provide you with the correct contact details.

Early Years advisory teams

Most EYDCPs or education services have some system of providing advice for early years settings. Early years advisers often put on training, organise link groups and visit individual settings. Early years advisers can be an invaluable source of support, particularly if you require help with planning the curriculum or evaluating the effectiveness of the routine of your setting. Some advisory teams provide a resource bank so that settings can borrow books, posters and even equipment.

> “*I often begin by observing what is happening and also by talking to the staff and children. I like everyone to know that my role is not that of an inspector but in some ways that of an 'objective friend'. I can point out positive things and this is an important part of my role because many people need reassurance about what they are doing. I am also able to talk to staff about ways of meeting individual children's needs and developing curriculum areas. Sometimes I am like a fresh pair of eyes as it can be hard when you work in a setting to find the time to stand back.*”
>
> *Sue Bayliss, advisory support teacher*

SEN advisory teams

These are sometimes referred to as inclusion support teams or SENCO area teams. Most LEAs have a service to support teachers and early years professionals who are working with children who have special educational needs in mainstream settings. The exact title of the teams can vary and so it will be important to find out the name of the service in your area, as well as how it operates. Following the Code of Practice's emphasis on mainstream education, many teams are now offering advice and training. In some areas advisory SEN teachers who specialise in early years visit settings to support SENCOs and to help draw up IEPs. During a visit an SEN advisory teacher is likely to look at the setting's planning, layout and also at the child.

Speech and language teams

Every area will have a speech and language service or team. Technically, this service is provided by the health service, although some units may be housed

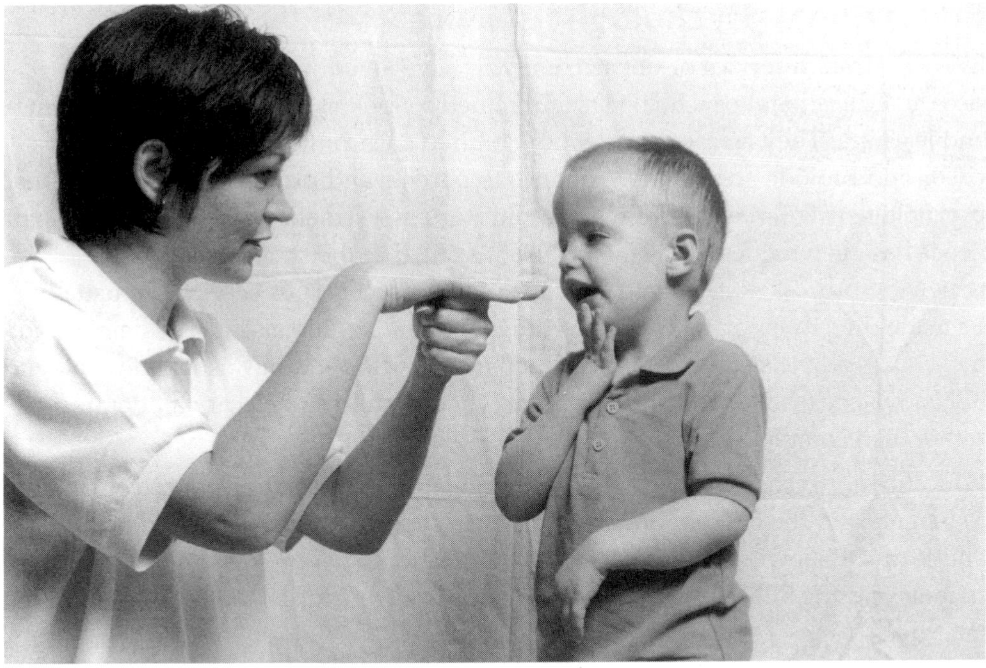

Using sign language to help with communication difficulties

within the education department because of the collaborative nature of their work. Speech and language therapists assess, diagnose and work out a programme of exercises to help children's communication and speech. This may include children who have hearing impairments, stammers, language delay and communication difficulties.

They work closely with parents, early years professionals and teachers. The type of support that a child receives will depend on his or her need, but usually exercises and strategies are shared with everyone involved in the child's care and education, especially parents. Children can be referred directly by parents to the speech and language team or by the setting with parental consent.

CASE STUDY

Joachim was nearly four years old and staff at the pre-school were a little concerned that his speech was still hard to understand. The supervisor began by sharing her concerns with the parents and it was agreed that they would listen carefully to his speech at home over the weekend. On Monday, the parents came into the setting as agreed and it was decided that it might be beneficial for Joachim to be referred to the speech and language team. The parents decided that they would seek a referral themselves via the health visitor. A few months later, Joachim was seen by a speech and language therapist.

1. Why was it important for the setting to voice its concerns to the parents rather than directly to the speech and language team?
2. Why should parents be involved in deciding how to refer the child?

Educational psychologist service

Every education service or department will have an educational psychologist service. Educational psychologists are trained to look at children's development and learning. They assess and identify children's learning and developmental needs and provide advice and guidance to parents and professionals. Educational psychologists will have input when a statutory assessment of special educational needs has been requested. They are also involved in the statementing and reviewing process. Referrals to the educational psychologist service can usually be made directly by parents or by settings with parental consent. The demand in most areas on the service is high, so many early years settings usually involve the SEN advisory teacher as a starting point where a child's needs are moderate rather than complex.

Educational psychologists usually observe a child in the setting as well as talking to parents and the child in order to build up a picture of how the child behaves and learns. Following an assessment, an educational psychologist may provide parents and the SENCO with advice and may arrange to see the child again at a later date.

Sensory impairment team

Many education services have a team dedicated to helping children who have visual and/or hearing impairment. While the title of this service can vary from area to area, the role of the team is similar. Most teams employ specialist teachers who visit families to work directly with the child and their parents. They also visit settings to advise them on the effects of the child's impairment and to give them practical suggestions as to how best to meet the child's needs. This service can also become involved in the drawing up of IEPs as the teacher will be assessing and monitoring a child's progress. Most sensory impairment teams also have strong links with the speech and language service. If you are aware that a child is coming to you with a sensory impairment, it may be possible to contact this service for some advice before the child starts.

Parent Partnership Service

Following the Code of Practice, every LEA has to ensure that a Parent Partnership Service was available for parents of children with special educational needs. The aim of the service is to support parents and to give independent advice. Some Parent Partnership Services offer training so that settings can update or gain skills in communicating and working with parents. Parents should be told about the service when you first discuss that a child may have special educational needs as many parents find the service invaluable.

Health visiting service

Health visitors are trained nurses who have undertaken specialist training in health promotion. Their role is to promote health across all age groups in the local community, although many health visiting teams divide their work to focus on particular groups. The health visiting service can be organised in a variety of ways. In some areas, health visitors are attached to clinics, while in others they are attached to GPs' surgeries. Health visitors who are involved with parents and their children carry out routine health checks and are also able to provide support by giving advice about child care and development. It can be very useful to talk to a child's health visitor, but it is essential that the parent gives permission for you to do so. Health visitors can refer children to further services and are usually good at giving advice. It is important to remember that they are not education specialists.

Paediatric occupational therapy service

Paediatric occupational therapists work with children to maximise their physical movements and development so that they can become as independent as possible. They work with a range of children including those who may have a physical impairment, perceptual disorder or difficulties with hand-eye function. As well as working directly with children, they also tend to work closely with the child's family. In early years settings they will advise how best to make a setting accessible and some services are able to lend equipment and resources. Paediatric occupational therapists may also ask settings to become involved with the programme that they have devised for the child.

Physiotherapists

Physiotherapy is usually provided by the health service. Children who may need physiotherapy include those with medical conditions such as cystic fibrosis, children who have injured themselves and children who have a physical impairment. As well as directly treating children, physiotherapists will provide advice and guidance to parents and settings about exercises and movements that will help the child. Referral to physiotherapy is likely to occur via a GP or paediatrician.

Social services

By law, local authorities have a duty to provide services for 'children in need'. This means that most children who have complex and severe needs are likely to have a social worker involved with their families. Assessments will be regularly carried out to see how the LEA can support the child and the family. A social worker will be involved in the annual review of a child's statement.

THINK IT OVER

1 Why is it important for everyone in the setting to understand the type of support that is available?
2 Why might parents also be a valuable source of information?

Support groups and voluntary organisations

Local and national support groups and voluntary organisations can provide settings with advice, fact sheets and in some cases resources. Many organisations hold awareness training or workshops for professionals and so it is useful to develop contacts.

Portage

Portage is a home-based teaching service for children under five years and is provided for children whose needs have already been identified. The portage system relies heavily upon parents, as it is recognised that by involving parents in the teaching of skills the child is likely to make more progress. The portage teacher, or volunteer in some cases, visits the home regularly and works with the parent to devise a structured programme to build on a child's skills.

If you have a child in your setting who is receiving portage, it will be helpful for you to talk to the parent about he or she is doing at home as you may be able to incorporate and reinforce the skills in your planning. Developing a contact with the portage service can be extremely helpful as it may be able to give informal advice on how to 'break' down skills into small steps.

Toy libraries

Toy libraries lend a wide range of toys and equipment to parents, but also in most areas to early years settings. They pride themselves on providing a good

Toy libraries are a good source of toys and equipment for children

range of resources aimed specifically at children who have special needs. The way the service is run can vary, with some being staffed completely by volunteers while others form part of the LEA. To find out details of your nearest library, contact the National Toy Library and Leisure Association (Tel. 020 8387 9592).

Internet

The Internet is not a perfect tool, but can be an extremely useful source of information, particularly if you are trying to track down contact details of organisations or are looking out for ideas and up-to-date information. It is important to be aware that anyone can set up a website and this means that there is always a danger of gaining inaccurate information. The Department for Education and Skills' website has a section designed to give advice and information about SEN (*www.dfes.gov.uk/sen*).

SEEING THEORY IN PRACTICE

Complete the contact details for the organisations in your area on this reference sheet:

Early Years Development and Childcare Partnership (EYDCP)

____

Early Years advisory team

____

SEN advisory team

____

Speech and language team

____

Toy library

____

Sensory impairment team

____

Paediatric occupational therapy service

____

Parent Partnership Service

____

Health visiting service

____

Physiotherapist

____

Social services

____

Educational Psychologist service

____

Part 2
Working with children

It is sometimes thought that to work with children who have been identified as having special needs requires new skills. This is not really the case. All children require adults to be patient, thoughtful and be flexible in their approach. They also need adults to give them time and respect. Armed with these requirements, adults should be able to help all children regardless of their 'label'.

Having said that, most practitioners find it helpful to have an understanding of child development and examples of strategies that they can use in order to help specific children.

This section is divided into five chapters. The first chapter looks at the importance of building good relationships with children, while the remaining four chapters consider each of the 'areas of need' that are referred to the Code of Practice. Each chapter ends with examples of activities that might be used to address particular children's needs.

Chapter 8

Valuing and empowering children

Introduction

The starting point for working effectively with any child is to respect and value the child for being him or herself. A common criticism of practitioners is the tendency to focus so much on the area of development, the impairment or condition, that the child becomes a problem that has to be solved. This chapter looks at the importance of building strong relationships with children, but also finding ways of empowering them through building strong self-esteem.

> *School had in some ways haunted me. I left feeling that in many ways I was not good enough and that I didn't measure up. The best thing that I ever did was going back to school when I was in my late twenties for a reunion. I showed them and myself that I was worth more.*
>
> *Chris, a former 'remedial' pupil*

The Code of Practice and children

One of the key changes to note about the Code Of Practice is the emphasis on the rights and involvement of children. Chapter 3 of the Code is entitled 'Pupil Participation'. It clearly instructs all practitioners, including those in early years settings, to look for ways to involve children in their own care and education. This includes looking for ways of involving children while drawing up IEPs. The acknowledgement that children should be consulted and listened to is a reflection of the growing understanding that children have rights.

> 3:6 All children should be involved in making decisions where possible right from the start of their education. The ways in which children are encouraged to participate should reflect the child's evolving maturity. Participation in education is a process that will necessitate all children being given the opportunity to make choices and to understand that their views matter. Very young children can be encouraged to choose and to share their wishes and feelings with families and staff. The Early Learning Goals recognise the importance of children's ability to develop competency and confidence progressively and to have opportunities to develop a range of social as well as educational skills.
>
> *Source: SEN Code of Practice, 2001*

KEY ISSUE: INVOLVING CHILDREN

To be able to involve children meaningfully it is important to develop good relationships with them, and also to look for ways of boosting their self-esteem so that they can be assertive.

Developing a key worker system

Relationships are the starting point for working effectively with children. Many children will need one person in particular in whom they can trust and rely. This is particularly true of children who are very young, emotionally insecure or who have had many changes in their care and education. It is good practice for all early years settings to have a key worker system, regardless of whether a child is seen as having additional needs. A key worker is an adult who will take an especial interest in the child and provide a secure emotional bond. The key worker needs to spend time with the child and be there for the child especially when he or she first joins a setting.

CASE STUDY

Sarah was very unsure about coming into the nursery. She was quite clingy and needed to be with her mother for support. The nursery found out that Sarah was very keen on 'Bob the Builder' and so Sarah's key worker looked out for some puzzles and books about him. The key worker also found a set of tools and showed these to Sarah. With her mother standing nearby, Sarah watched as the key worker showed her the tools and how they worked. The key worker also chatted to Sarah's mother and gradually Sarah began to relax. It took several sessions before Sarah was confident enough to leave her mother and for two weeks, Sarah only wanted to be with the key worker.

1 Why is it important to find out about a child's interests?
2 Why it is essential to allow the settling-in process to move at the child's pace?
3 Why should parents be involved in the settling-in process?

Building relationships

Children learn best when they are happy and secure. A child who enjoys being with you is more likely to respond and consequently to learn. This creates a positive cycle, with children achieving their potential because they are enjoying what they are doing.

Building a relationship with a child is a very individual process as each child brings his or her own special qualities and attributes. Focusing on these rather than any 'impairment' or 'condition' should be your primary concern. You will also need to find out about the child's interests and what he or she enjoys doing. Parents can be extremely helpful here. They may share some anecdotes about their child and give you information about interests and toys that their child enjoys outside of the setting.

Developing a trusting relationship with children can boost their self-esteem

Thinking about the child's interests, likes and dislikes should help you to find points of contact with the child. It is also worth remembering that children enjoy being with adults who are attentive to them and also have a sense of fun.

STRATEGIES FOR BUILDING RELATIONSHIPS

- Avoid focusing only on the child's impairment or IEP targets.
- Look and value things that are of interest to the child.
- Be attentive to the child; this may mean listening to the child, using eye contact and playing with him or her.
- Make sure that time spent with you is seen as being fun and interesting.
- Involve parents; young children will find it easier to trust and be with you if they can see that their parents 'like' you.
- Find out and remember events that are special for the child, e.g. birthday, outings, clubs.
- Understand that children form relationships at different speeds.

Empowerment

The word 'empowerment' is frequently used in the context of working with groups of people who are discriminated against. Empowerment in the context of disability is about understanding and ensuring that children (and their parents) are not seen as helpless victims. To empower children means to consider their feelings and rights and to look for ways of making them independent and assertive. A major obstacle to empowerment is often self-esteem. A child who comes to believe that he or she is helpless or 'lacking' in some way will find it harder to be assertive.

Self-esteem

Self-esteem is sometimes referred to as having 'confidence'. Children who have additional needs are vulnerable to developing a low self-esteem. This is important because low self-esteem can limit children's expectations of themselves and others towards them. This means that a child may not feel confident enough to try out a new activity, take the initiative or see him or herself as worthy of respect. In short, low self-esteem will limit children's ability to fulfil their potential. Low self-esteem is also linked to behaviour. Some children quickly learn that to avoid being in a situation that they are unsure about they should 'misbehave'. By doing this they may be taken away from the activity or be given extra adult attention.

We are not born with a low or high self-esteem. Our levels of inner confidence are the result of an ongoing process. This begins in the early years of children's lives when they develop a self image or a view of themselves. As children get older, they begin to consider whether their view of themselves matches up with what they want to be like; their ideal self. If a child views him or herself as being very different to the child he or she wants to be like, the result will be a low self-esteem.

Understanding how the self image is built

We come into the world knowing nothing about ourselves, not even our names. The first step for children is to find out about themselves. This they do mainly by listening and noticing other's responses to them, especially key adults in their lives.

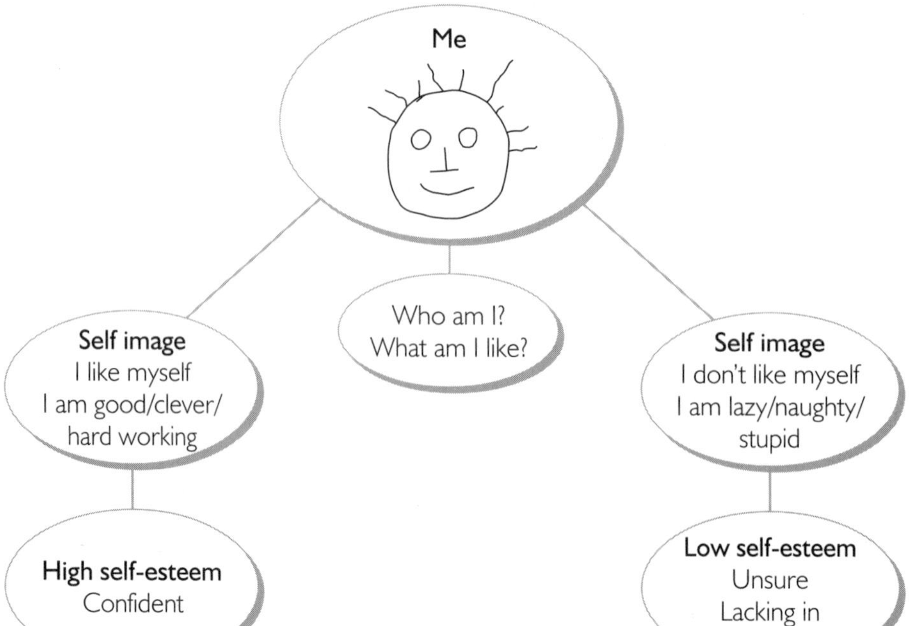

Self-esteem.

What children learn from listening

Children will listen to the comments that adults make about them and to them. Children try to use the words that are used to find out about themselves. A phrase such as 'Good girl, Sam, you were very kind' may give this young child four messages:

- I am good, the adult is pleased with me.
- I am a girl.
- My name is Sam.
- I am kind.

If we look at another comment such as 'I really wish you would try harder, Samantha, this isn't really that difficult', we can see that the child may gain some other information:

- The adult is not happy with me.
- I am not trying hard enough.
- When this adult is not pleased with me, my full name is used.
- The adult thinks this is easy, but I am not doing it well.

As well as the actual words, children are also good at tuning into the intonation of the voice used. Research has shown that most babies are able to distinguish an angry sounding voice from a relaxed voice, even when the language is unfamiliar to them.

What children learn from non-verbal responses

As well as learning through words and signs, children also notice our non-verbal behaviour towards them. Children can sense whether someone is happy to see them and genuinely enjoys being with them. They are also able to notice when adults are irritated, disappointed or frustrated with them. Children notice our eye movements, facial expression and overall body language.

THINK IT OVER

Joseph has been away with a cold. Today he comes back to the pre-school. Staff were hoping that he would be away for longer as they find his behaviour challenging. The supervisor says hello, but doesn't bend down to make eye contact or to smile.

1. What messages will Joseph be learning from this welcome?
2. Why is it important for staff to concentrate on relationships rather than behaviour?
3. Give two suggestions as to how the setting could 'include' rather than 'exclude' this child.

Why children need a positive self image

Children need to be gaining positive responses from us if they are to develop a strong self image. If a child constantly hears that he or she is 'naughty', 'lazy' or 'difficult', he or she will begin to believe that this is the way he or she has been 'made'. This in turn creates situations where the child acts in line with the adults' expectations. By contrast, children who hear and sense positive things about themselves, develop a strong and healthy view of themselves. A strong positive self-image needs to be developed when children are young as once children become older, the pressure on their self image can increase.

Becoming aware of others

The pressure on children increases as they become more aware of others. For many children this will happen in their primary school years, although for some children this may happen earlier and for others not at all. Children who become aware of others are likely to compare themselves, and in some cases this may make them feel that they are 'lacking' in some way. This can have serious implications. A child who becomes aware that he or she is not fast at running may decide not to bother any more, even though the child previously enjoyed this. In school and some early years settings, comparisons are actually inherent in the structure of the day. Children may see that they are on the 'lowest' reading shelf or that they are put on a table with 'slower' children.

The development of an ideal self

As well as comparing themselves to others, some children will go on from this to develop an 'ideal self'. This is an imaginary picture of what they would like to be. Children gain this ideal self by working out what others around them value, i.e. what seems to impress teachers, their parents and their friends. Children can also be influenced by what the media portray as being important. Low self-esteem is often seen as resulting from the difference between the child's ideal self and his or her own self-image or picture of themselves. While confident children may wish that they were a little different to how they see themselves, children who have low self-esteem will see themselves as being nowhere like the 'perfect' child.

CASE STUDY

Rashida wears a foot brace. She was a happy girl and had settled well into her pre-school and then into her first year of school. In her second year, her parents started to notice a change in her. She no longer seemed to be enthusiastic about school and her teacher began to notice that she appeared to be less and less motivated. After one story time about dreams and wishes, Rashida commented that she wished that she could be pretty. The classroom assistant said 'but you are pretty'. Rashida replied that pretty girls did not wear callipers.

1 Explain why Rashida's feelings about herself have changed?
2 Why is it important that children see positive images that reflect society's diversity?

Helping children to develop a positive self image

There are many ways in which we can help children to develop and maintain a positive self image. It is important to remember that as practitioners, we should be doing this to help all children that we are working with, regardless of any additional or special needs.

What messages are children receiving from adults' interactions and body language?

We have seen that children learn about themselves by noticing the reactions and interactions of adults towards them. This has strong implications as it means that we should consider carefully what messages we are sending out to children. When we are working with children whose behaviour is challenging, we need to make sure that a child is not receiving so many negative signals that he or she comes to believe he or she has been born 'naughty'. It is important to remember that children will need more positive signals to counteract any negative ones they have received.

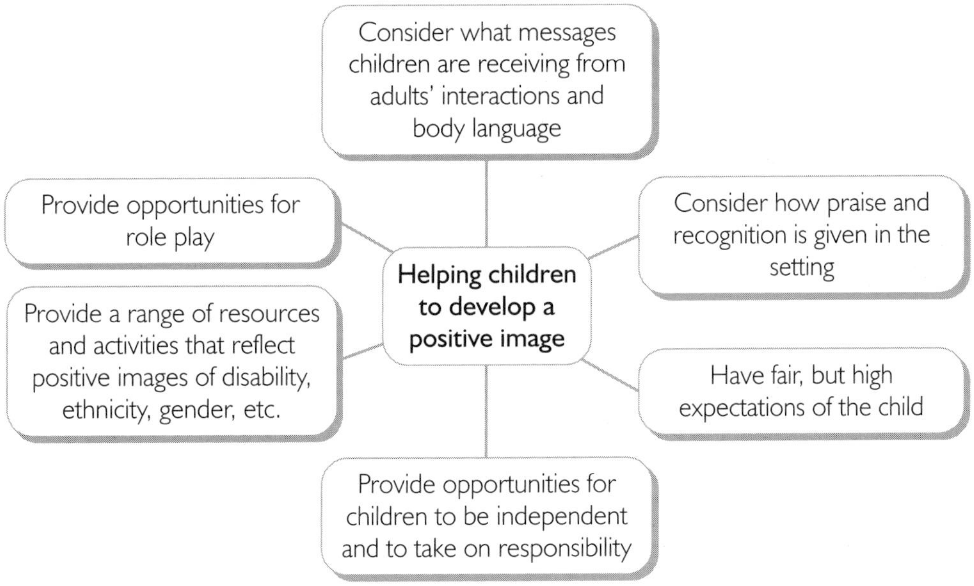

Helping children to develop a positive image.

THINK IT OVER

Most practitioners do not realise that they are sending out more negative messages than they think. Be careful of signals that focus on what the child cannot or is not doing. Always try to turn negative messages into positive messages. Look at the following example:

Negative	Positive
'No, you have got the wrong piece there.'	'I don't think that piece wants to go there.'

Now try and make the following statements more positive:

- 'You can stop that right now.'
- 'Stop running.'
- 'Don't touch that.'

Changing the balance

Try monitoring the number of positive interactions that a child in your setting receives in a session. Keep a simple tally sheet. Does the child gain more positives or negatives by the end of the session?

REFLECT ON YOUR OWN PRACTICE

- Consider the ways in which children are greeted and made to feel welcome.
- Look for opportunities to positively recognise children's special attributes and skills.
- Make sure that you signal to children when you are working with them that you enjoy being with them, e.g. eye contact, smiles, touch.
- Remember that children respond to adults' who have a sense of humour and are fun.
- Be very clear when managing behaviour that you are not unhappy with the child, but with the behaviour that he or she is showing.
- Consider carrying out a simple observation to check that interactions are positive.

Consider how praise and recognition is given in the setting

It is very important that children learn that adults care and cherish them for themselves, not only for what they can do. This means that while it is important to praise children when they achieve, you also need to strike a balance so that children do not feel that praise is conditional only on performance. You should also be careful that love is not associated with pleasing the adult. Phrases such as 'Be a good boy and do that for me?' will give children the message that in order to be a 'good boy' you have to please the adult. This is a dangerous message as a child might worry about not being liked if they are not 'good enough'.

Where children are at the stage of comparing themselves to others, it will be important to consider if the environment is structured to negatively reinforce 'differences' between children, i.e. competitions, prizes for some children, but not for others. You may therefore consider encouraging everyone to share an individual's achievement, for example, 'Today, everyone is getting a sticker so that we can all celebrate Marty's success. Let's all have a clap'. This type of approach helps children to be recognised, but also makes everyone in the setting feel good.

REFLECT ON YOUR OWN PRACTICE

- Remember that qualities such as kindness should be positively recognised as well as achievements.
- Do not withhold affection from children on the basis of poor performance or behaviour.
- Avoid using phrases that encourage children to believe that affection is linked to pleasing adults.

Have fair, but high expectations of the child

Children are quickly able to sense whether adults believe in them. Having too low expectations of children can mean that they too do not believe that they are capable of certain things. Phrases such as 'Never mind, you have done your best' can actually give children a signal that the adult does not believe that they are capable of any more. The path between encouraging children and putting them into situations where they might fail is therefore a sensitive one. Too many apparent 'failures' can result in children losing confidence, while not being challenged can deny children the opportunity to develop their skills further. In the past, there was a tendency to underestimate what children were capable of. This resulted in many children missing out on opportunities to learn new skills and have a wide range of experiences. This effectively discriminated against children.

The key here is always to observe children carefully so as to get a feeling of what will be challenging but within their reach. By considering what children really can do, and working out what they may be capable of will help children in the longer term achieve their potential. It is also important to vocalise your expectations so that children know that you believe in their potential, for example, 'Why don't you have another go at pouring the drinks out. It is tricky and it takes a little practice, but you can do it' will be far better than saying to a child 'Never mind you have done your best' and taking over for them.

STRATEGIES TO HELP DECIDE WHAT A CHILD IS CAPABLE OF

- Find out from parents what type of things the child can do at home.
- Observe children carefully so that you can gain a picture of their capabilities.
- Avoid 'taking over' if a child is struggling; this teaches children that they cannot do it.
- If children are struggling, consider breaking down the task or restructuring or adapting it.
- Praise children when they are persevering and concentrating.
- Take the attitude wherever possible that children 'can' rather than 'can't'.

Provide opportunities for children to be independent and to take on responsibility

The more children can do for themselves, the stronger their confidence can grow. It is often easy for adults working with children to 'take over' rather than to give children the time and encouragement to master a skill or finish a task. Children in this way can be disempowered because they learn to rely on an adult rather than themselves.

There are many ways in which we can help children to take on some responsibility and have some control over their care and education. Children can be involved in their own self care, choice of clothes, food and activities. The key is to adapt the routine or the way we work to allow for choices and for children to take control. A child may not be able to manage to pour a drink from a large jug, but may be able to do so if he or she is provided with a much smaller jug. It is always worth asking yourself why a child cannot do something for themselves. The answer may be to break down the task, provide different resources or to find an alternative system of communication.

Sometimes, you may find that a child resists being independent. Children may become so used to someone else tidying up that they refuse to do so. Many adults find it helpful in these situations to look for ways of turning the activity into a game or by asking the child to do just part of it at first. A child who does not want to tidy up may be given the box to hold while the adult puts the objects in it. In this way, children learn to be involved and can see for themselves that they are capable.

REFLECT ON YOUR OWN PRACTICE

- Look carefully at the routines within the setting. Do they encourage choice and independence?
- Build choices within activities, e.g. different sizes of paper, a choice of several puzzles, a choice between what to do first.
- Praise and encourage children's attempts to take the initiative.
- Make sure that children have opportunities to play freely and so can experience situations where they are thinking for themselves.

Provide a range of resources and activities that reflect positive images of disability, ethnicity, gender, etc.

It is important for children to see positive images of disability as well as gender, ethnicity and culture, in order to learn that everyone has differences and that these should be valued. Being different does not mean that you are less important or worthy must be the message that all children learn. It is important that this message is embedded into the books, resources and images that you present to children. A child who wears spectacles or is in a wheelchair will need to feel that he or she is not alone and 'different'. This is especially important when children become aware of others and compare themselves. You should also look for some activities that encourage children to talk about differences and see differences in a positive way, for example, we may all have different food preferences or enjoy wearing different clothes. It is also a good idea to encourage all children to talk and ask questions about differences. This allows misconceptions to be put straight and prevents children from acquiring stereotypes and potential prejudices.

STRATEGIES TO DEMONSTRATE POSITIVE IMAGES OF CHILDREN

- Choose books and resources carefully; do they portray a range of positive images of children?
- Provide activities that encourage children to realise that everyone is different, yet special.
- Allow children to talk to express their feelings about themselves.

Provide opportunities for role play

Role play is often seen as important for all young children. Pretending to be someone else allows children to act out different roles; they may pretend to be a figure of authority. Role play also allows children to act out scenes that they have experienced. By watching children's role play, we may come to understand more about how individual children are feeling and perceive themselves. There are different types of role play; sometimes a child will use small toys such as play people, dolls and cuddly toys and 'direct' their movements and actions. At other times children may use dressing up clothes, masks and props to put themselves into a role. Some practitioners use role play as a way of strengthening children's views of themselves. They may put a child into a position of responsibility so that the child learns through play to feel more in control.

STRATEGIES TO ENCOURAGE ROLE PLAY

- Provide a good range of resources including small toys and dressing up clothes.
- Intervene if other children are making discriminatory comments or are playing in a way that will lower the self image of another child.
- Be ready to join in with play as a way of helping children to feel more in control.
- Observe role play carefully to gain more information about a child.

Provide puppets and persona dolls

Working with all children to develop positive attitudes towards disability is crucial as a child's self-esteem will be influenced by the attitudes of the children around them. Using resources that help children to develop positive attitudes towards others is therefore essential. Such resources include puppets and persona dolls. Persona dolls are dolls that have been specifically designed to help children develop positive attitudes towards disability, ethnicity and gender. Each doll is an individual with a life story and character rather than a plaything. They are used to tell stories. The children can talk to them and ask them questions in a comfortable and non-threatening way. This allows children to find out more about abilities and disability as well as helping individual children to feel positive about themselves.

Self-conscious children will often forget themselves as they become captivated by their characters. Their ability to encourage children to respond easily makes them good tools. They can be introduced with a story line that echoes how a child might be feeling, for example, a puppet who is fed up because it cannot run as fast as its friend.

Persona dolls can help children develop positive attitudes towards disability, ethnicity and gender

Suggested activities

ACTIVITY 1: FAVOURITES

Children need to learn that everyone has differences and specific preferences. This activity encourages children to learn on a basic level that it is fine to have your own tastes and differences.

Aim: To help children gain a sense of pride in their own choices and differences.

Resources: Any group of objects that have some dissimilarity, e.g. buttons, shells, small boxes, labels with children's names.

Activity: Put the collection of objects on to a tray. Encourage children to handle and touch them. Talk about which ones they prefer. Do they have favourites? Give each of the children their own small box and ask them to put their favourite item inside. This box can then be labelled with the child's name. Display the children's favourites on a table. As the children are sorting out their favourite objects, notice carefully any children who seem particularly keen to change their favourites to fit in.

Possible adaptations:

Encourage children to talk about what makes the object their favourite. Repeat this activity with a variety of different objects

ACTIVITY 2: MY BOOK ABOUT ME

Children need to develop a strong sense of self-worth and identity. Using photographs and books can help children to value themselves.

Aims: To help children value themselves. To encourage children to talk about their identity. This book can also be helpful for new adults in the child's life to see.

Resources: Photographs of the child, paper, glue, pens, etc. to make a book.

Activity: Show the child the photographs. Ask the child about the photographs. Does the child have a favourite? Talk to the child about the photographs and why you particularly like them. Together make a book about the child. Anything can be put into the book that will help the child learn and think about themselves. What does the child enjoy doing? Who are the special people in the child's life? What does the child enjoy eating?

Possible adaptations:

Use the books as a starting point for children to talk about themselves. Make a book about the child's day. Make a book about particular aspects of the child's life, e.g. their friends, their home, etc.

ACTIVITY 3: I LIKE THE WAY YOU ... GAME

Positive recognition is important for all children, especially children who are in danger of being excluded. It is also important that children learn to positively recognise others

Aims: To help children to learn to recognise others and to be able to accept positive recognition.

Resources: Two bean bags of different colours or other objects that can be passed around.

Activity: This activity will work best with a small group of children (no more than six). Begin by teaching children the line 'I like the way you ...' (this could be sung). Go around the group and say to each children 'I like the way you ...' and then add in something special about each child, for example 'I like the way you smile when you are happy'. Ask the children to turn to the person next to them and to think about something that they like about that child using the line 'I like the way you ...'. Once children are able to do this, you can then play a game with two bean bags. The bean bags are passed or thrown around the circle. When you clap your hands the children with the bean bags must say to each other 'I like the way you ...' adding on the positive recognition.

Possible adaptations:

Devise a song to accompany this game. Singing is a powerful tool for learning. If children find it difficult to think of things to say about each other, increase the amount of positive recognition that children are getting in the setting and focus on the words 'I like the way you ...'.

Resources

The *Persona Dolls in Action* video and support book are available from:

Persona Doll Training
51 Granville Road
London
N12 0JH
020 8446 7056

Chapter 9

Supporting children's communication and interaction

Introduction

A large proportion of children with special educational needs have difficulties with communication and interaction. For some children their difficulties in communicating their needs, or in not being able to understand what is happening, can create feelings of frustration and isolation. The ability to understand how to support children's communication and interaction is therefore important when working with them.

Why communication is an important skill

Communication is an essential part of most people's daily lives. It is used in a variety of ways, for example, to help people express their needs and to build and maintain relationships. It is a skill that is often taken for granted, but actually plays an important part in children's overall development.

KEY ISSUE: COMMUNICATION

Most children rely on spoken language and non-verbal communication as a key way of interacting, although as children's language becomes more developed, they are introduced to reading and writing as further methods of communicating.

THINK IT OVER

For most people, communication is taken for granted.

1. Write a list of the number of times you have communicated today.
2. Think about the ways in which you communicated, e.g. speech, signs, reading and writing.
3. What purpose did the communication serve?
4. What would have been the effects on you, had you been unable to communicate effectively today?

Links between challenging behaviour and communication skills

There is a significant correlation between children who have difficulty in communicating and those showing inappropriate behaviour. Some children show behaviours that are linked to their frustration while others may withdraw and opt out of activities. This means that while strategies that work on behaviour may have some success, the key for staff is to identify the nature of the child's communication difficulty and work to support the child.

Links between language and thought

Language is also important because it is linked to thought. Language allows us to organise our thoughts as it is used as a way of classifying and storing information in our memories. Children who have difficulties in communicating and using language may therefore sometimes find it harder to retain information and may not be able to process and organise their thoughts easily. This can place children at a significant disadvantage and so finding ways of helping children's language to develop is essential.

Specialist support

The importance of speech and language in children's overall development is so important that it is essential for children whose language development is atypical to be referred for professional assessment. Specialist intervention in children's early years can be extremely helpful as there appears to be a 'critical period' in children's lives when it is easier for them to acquire speech. Speech and language therapists often produce a tailored programme with specific activities for the child. It is likely that your setting will then have some responsibility to implement the programme and to monitor the child's progress.

THINK IT OVER

Anjah's speech therapist has produced a programme which focuses on developing the muscles in the mouth as sometimes her speech is unclear and she has a tendency to dribble. The nursery has therefore planned activities that will encourage her to blow and suck. At snacktime, the nursery now puts straws in all the children's drink and games such as blowing feathers have been planned into the programme.

1 Why is it important that the nursery looks for activities that will support the speech and language programme?

2 Why is it good practice to look for ways of planning speech and language activities in ways that all children can participate?

3 Think of two more activities that involve blowing movements which all children might enjoy doing.

Understanding the components of interaction

It is useful to have an understanding of what is involved in interaction. Children may have difficulties that link to one or more components.

Non-verbal communication

It is thought that around 60 per cent of communication is expressed through non-verbal communication. Children need to learn to interpret and respond to others' gestures, facial expressions and body movements. They also need to become aware of their own expressions and use them appropriately. Some children with autistic spectrum disorders may have difficulties in understanding the non-verbal signs that people send out, while some children with a visual impairment may have limited experience of using and seeing non-verbal communication.

Language

Using and understanding language is complex as it is divided into several components.

Syntax

Language is rule based, although once the rules are learnt, the communicator can be quite creative. The rules of language are important because language is a two-way process and other people have to be able to understand what is being said. Some children find it difficult to acquire and understand the rules. This can affect their understanding and also their ability to use language.

Semantics

As well as being based on rules, language is also based on meaning and thoughts. Children have to know what the words mean in order to be able to understand what is being said. It is also important to understand that written and spoken language are abstract. The collection of sounds or symbols are used to

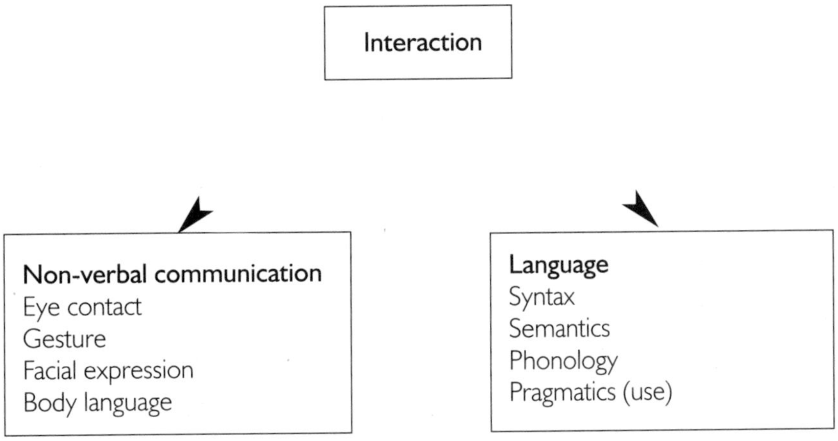

Interaction.

represent something and children have to learn the link between the sound / symbol and the object or idea. Some children with cognition difficulties may find it difficult to process their thoughts into words and thus require visual cues alongside spoken ones.

Phonology

For spoken language, children need to be able to recognise and produce the sounds that are required in the language they are using. Some children have particular physical difficulties in producing sounds, while others may not be able to hear them properly, thus making it difficult to understand what is being said and difficult to reproduce the sounds accurately.

Pragmatics (use)

Children also have to learn about the purpose of language and what type of language is appropriate in different situations. Being able to alter the way in which we use language allows us to communicate more effectively. Some children with communication difficulties may need guidance to use language appropriately, for example not constantly changing subjects as this confuses the listener.

Understanding interaction as a process

As well as understanding the individual components that make up language, it is important to understand that interaction is a two-way process and so can be represented as a cycle. When thinking about children who have difficulties in communicating, it can be worth considering where this happens within the cycle.

Common difficulties for children

There are some common difficulties that can affect children's speech and communication.

Hearing problems

When looking at children's communication skills, it is always worth considering whether or not the child is hearing properly. It has been estimated that as many as one in four children in a reception class at any time may have mild or slight hearing loss caused by otitis media, a conductive type of hearing loss. Otitis media occurs when fluid collects in the eustachian tube and results in the child receiving distorted sounds. This type of hearing loss can be fluctuating, as the fluid in the ear may drain away but may build up again if the child has a cold. The fluctuating and sometimes slight nature of this type of hearing loss can make it harder for adults to identify. It does however have an enormous impact on a child's ability to communicate, learn and socialise.

If you suspect that a child is not fully hearing, it is essential to encourage the parents to visit their doctor or their health visitor. It is worth explaining to parents that the nature of otitis media means that on one day a child could be

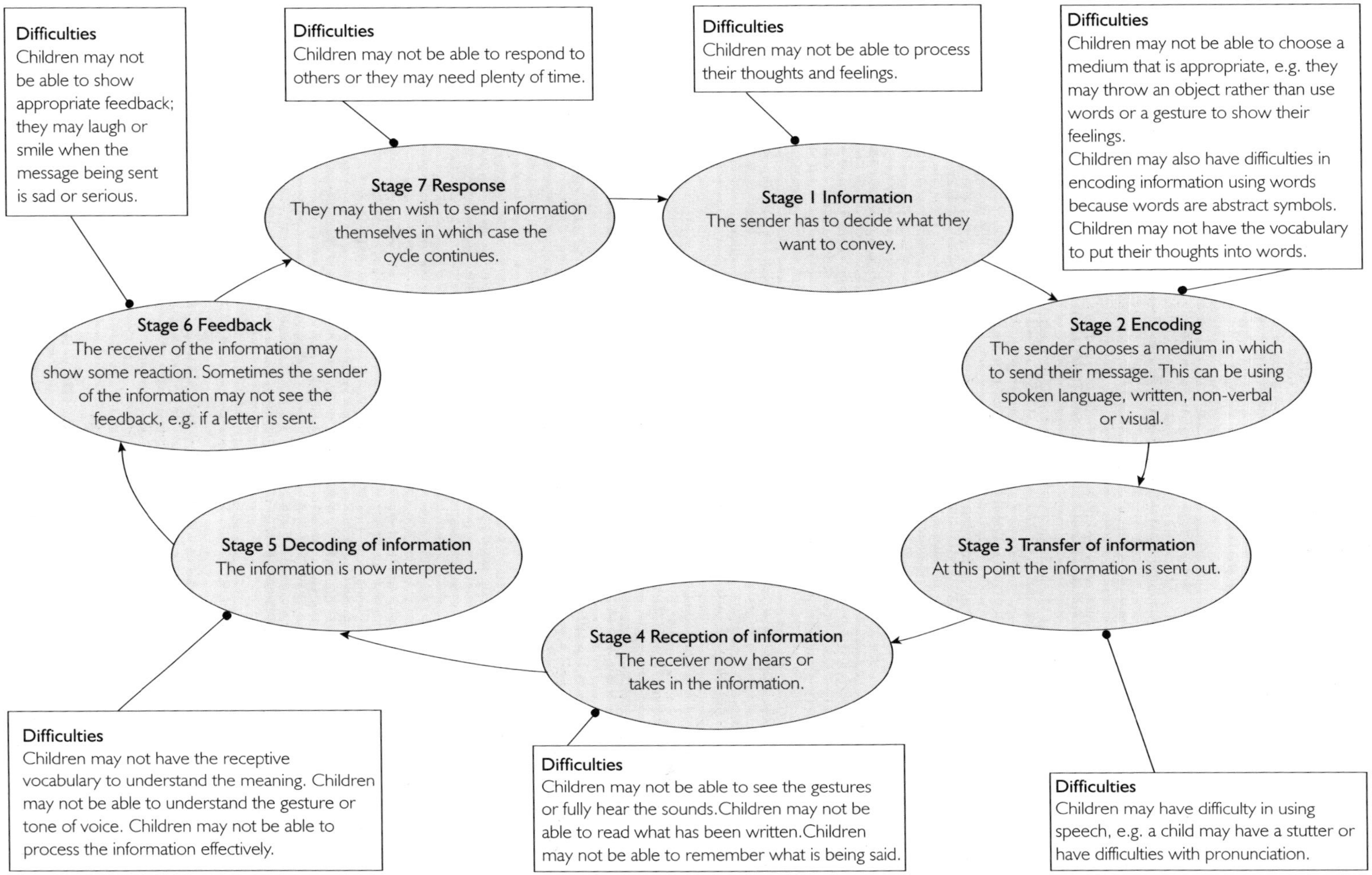

The interaction cycle.

hearing well, but on another day the child's hearing may be restricted. Therefore, just because their child has 'passed' a hearing test in the past, it does not necessarily mean that the child is hearing at that level all the time.

Checklist for hearing impairment

✓ Does the child have frequent coughs and colds?

✓ Does the child often fail to respond to his or her name or instructions when engaged in an activity?

✓ Does the child find it hard to follow simple instructions?

✓ Does the child watch other children when instructions are given?

✓ Does the child appear to study a speaker's face intently?

✓ Is the child withdrawn or does he or she appear to be in his or her own world?

✓ Is the child's speech muffled or very unclear?

✓ Does the child appear to lack concentration during group activities such as story time?

✓ Do parents report a lack of interest in watching television or listening to story tapes?

Supporting children who are not hearing fully

If you are aware that a child is not fully hearing because he or she has a cold or ear infection, you will need to take extra steps to help the child understand what is happening.

STRATEGIES FOR SUPPORTING CHILDREN WHO ARE NOT HEARING FULLY

- Always turn to the child so that he or she can clearly see your face.
- Make sure the lighting allows your face to be seen.
- Do not cover your mouth with your hands, hair, etc.
- Make sure that children understand the subject of conversation early on.
- Emphasise key words in a sentence.
- Use props, gestures and facial expression to help the child follow what is happening.

Visual impairment

As well as considering whether children are fully hearing, it is also worth considering whether a child is seeing well. A child who cannot see the expression on other children's faces or pick up clues from their body language may find it hard to act appropriately, especially as children rely heavily on non-verbal communication. Look out for children whose own facial expressions and gestures are limited or who appear not to understand what is happening. (See page 47 for a checklist for visual impairment.)

Stammering

Stammering affects children's fluency in speech and is therefore also known as dysfluency. Stammering is not unusual in young children's speech, and for most children is simply a phase which, if handled sensitively, they will move on from. Stammering in young children often reflects their thoughts not always being as fluent as their language. They may therefore stumble over initial sounds of words, particularly if they are feeling under pressure to speak quickly. Stammering is likely to increase when children are tired, excited or nervous. If you hear that a child is stammering, it is essential that all members of staff look for ways of reducing the pressure on the child.

STRATEGIES TO HELP REDUCE STAMMERING

- Avoid situations where the child has to compete to say anything, e.g. first child to put up a hand or shout out an answer.
- Avoid asking many direct questions. Answering questions can increase children's stress levels.
- Avoid finishing off the sentence or letting other children interrupt the child.
- Reduce the speed at which you talk. This can help the child to relax and to speak more slowly to you.
- Make sure that you are on the same level and are making eye contact with the child.
- Nursery rhymes, songs and poems can help children to speak fluently if the child becomes familiar with them.
- If a child is stressed and stammering because of feeling emotional, talk to the child about the emotion that he or she is feeling, e.g. 'You are upset because you cannot find your picture'.

Seeking help for dysfluency

It can be difficult to assess at what point 'natural' dysfluency has become a habit, but a good indication is to consider the effects of the stammer on the child. Once children become aware of and frustrated by their stammer, they are more likely to put themselves under pressure. This leads to the child being less relaxed and a further increase in stammering. If you are concerned about a child's stammer, it will be wise to talk to parents about the frequency with which the child stammers at home. If they too feel that the child is frequently stammering, seek advice from the speech and language unit or SEN advisory teacher.

THINK IT OVER

Harry is the youngest of four children in the family. At pre-school he appears happy in himself, but often stammers. At snack time, which the children have altogether, the children are asked to put their hands up if they have something that they wish to say. Some of the children shout out while others seem almost ready to explode with their hands up in the air. Today, the key worker says that it is Harry's turn because he has brought in a model aeroplane from home. Harry holds up the model and begins to speak. He stammers slightly and then another child shouts out that he has an aeroplane like that.

1 Explain why large group situations may not be helpful in developing young children's speech.
2 Why is it important that Harry has opportunities to talk in a relaxed atmosphere?
3 Make two suggestions as to how the setting might include rather than exclude Harry.

Principles of supporting children's communication and interaction

We have seen that there are many skills that children need to master in order to be able to communicate and interact effectively. While many children appear to be able to 'pick up' language effortlessly, children who have difficulties in communicating and interacting need optimum conditions for language learning and interaction.

Be a language partner rather than a teacher

Children can learn about communication and language from responsive adults. If children enjoy being with an adult, they are likely to want to interact with the adult and will learn about the process of shared communication. This means

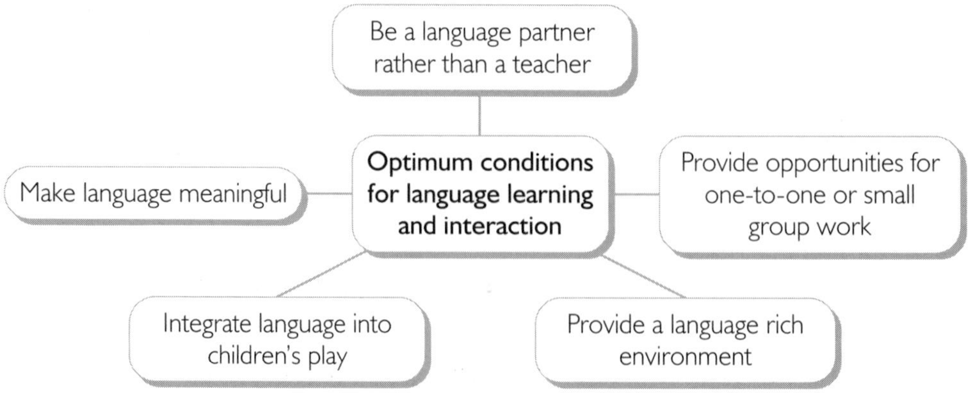

Optimum conditions for language learning and interaction.

thinking about your role as that of a partner rather than as an instructor, and thus concentrating on building a good relationship with the child.

STRATEGIES FOR BEING A LANGUAGE PARTNER RATHER THAN A TEACHER

- Make good eye contact with the child.
- Smile and express genuine pleasure when the child tries to involve you.
- Avoid 'interrogation' of the child and learn a 'chatty style'.
- Acknowledge by reflecting back what the child has said rather than giving praise.
- Give the child time to reflect.
- Value children's non-verbal communication.
- Avoid rushed conversations.

THINK IT OVER

Look at the following examples of how an adult interacts with a child. The child is sitting on the floor playing with some building bricks.

Interaction 1

Adult: That looks nice. Well done. What colour is this? (Adult holds a brick.)

Child: Red.

Adult: Well done. What about this one, do you know what colour it is? (Holds up another brick.)

Child: Blue.

Adult: Nearly, but it is green like your jumper. Good, I'll come back when you have done some more.

Interaction 2

Adult: Hello Daniel. Can I come and play with you because I love bricks too. I think my favourite ones are those with the wheels on. What about you?

Child: (Passes a sheep across to the adult.) This.

Adult: Oh yes, he's a lovely sheep. I wonder if he likes going on wheels?

Child: (Puts sheep onto the brick with wheels.) There. He goes brmm, brmm, brmm. (Child laughs.)

Adult: Wow, he's going fast. He's the fastest sheep that I have ever seen!

1 Which approach is likely to help the child learn about the purpose of interaction?
2 What is the danger of children associating language with being praised?
3 Why is it important that children enjoy using language?

Provide opportunities for one-to-one or small group work

Children who have difficulties in communicating will require one-to-one or small group work. It is important that they are not just 'left to get on with it'. This does not necessarily mean 'teaching' language, but actually making sure that children have adequate contact with language. A child playing alone and silently, however happily, is not gaining any new language or communication skills. Playing alongside children or involving them in small group activities where their language 'output' can be monitored is therefore essential. Targeting children in this way for extra language support can also be beneficial in terms of reducing unwanted behaviour and encouraging the acquisition of social skills.

Provide a language-rich environment

A language-rich environment is one where children are encouraged to talk freely and where adults are consciously using every opportunity to develop children's language. This includes using songs, rhymes and action games with children so that they can explore sounds, patterns and intonation.

Using gestures and varying your intonation during story time can make learning more exciting for children

Integrate language into children's play

Play is pleasurable and thus provides a perfect backdrop to learning language. Children who are more relaxed are more likely to acquire and use language and so using games and providing for imaginative play can be very effective. Adults can play alongside children and thus introduce new language, but can take a back seat at times if children are communicating with their peers.

Make language meaningful

We communicate for a purpose and the same is true for children. Children will learn language more effectively when it has some meaning for them. This means that we need to check that we make the most of everyday situations and link language to play and activities. Taking children away from an activity that they are enjoying to 'do' some language may therefore not always be the best approach. It may be better to incorporate the language within the activity.

Adjust language to suit the child

To help children gain the most from play activities, story times and conversations, it is essential that the language being used matches the child's level of comprehension. It is worth remembering that children who cannot understand what is being said often show disruptive and unwanted behaviour. Grouping children according to language development for story time can therefore be very effective as the complexity of stories can be matched to children's needs. It is also important when we talk to children to monitor their responses and to check that our language and gestures are being understood.

Strategies to develop children's language

There is a range of strategies that can be used to build and develop children's language. When selecting particular strategies, it is important to bear in mind a child's stage of language and cognitive development. Speech and language therapists may also give you direction as to strategies that you should be adopting with children.

Using 'parentese'

Parentese or motherese is the style of speech that most adults naturally use with babies. This style of speech is special because it encourages the child to focus on the key words in a sentence as they are emphasised and repeated by the adult.

Sentences tend to be short and simplified. The child is able to work out the meaning of the sentences because the adult talks about something that is actually taking place. Adults will point to objects to draw the child's attention to them. Adopting this style of speech can particularly help children who are at the early stages of learning language. The example below shows how speech is simplified and key words are drawn to a child's attention.

SEEING THEORY IN PRACTICE

Adult is alongside a child who is playing with a farm set. The adult picks up a cow.

Adult: *Look*! Can you see the *cow*? There's the *cow*. Let's see if the *cow* can jump. Whoosh! *Look* the *cow* is jumping! *Look* the *cow* is coming to see you.

Recasting and expanding children's language

Recasting and expanding is a technique which helps children to hear a grammatically correct and fuller version of what they were trying to say. This technique can be used with all children as it is a subtle way of helping children to hear a fuller and more grammatically correct version of their speech. This technique also encourages children to communicate more as it shows them that the adult has been listening and has understood what they are trying to say. This means that this technique is particularly useful with children who have limited speech. The example below shows how an adult recasts the child's speech while also extending it.

SEEING THEORY IN PRACTICE

Child: (Letting a car go down a slide) Brrm, down go.

Adult: Yes, the car went down the slide, didn't it. It went down the slide very quickly. Shall we go and get it?

Modelling language

Before children are able to use a word, they will need to become familiar with it. Modelling language is a technique when new words or sentence structures are introduced to children. The key to good modelling is creating a relaxed situation where the child can learn words in context. The example below shows how an adult models specific vocabulary to help a child talk about size.

SEEING THEORY IN PRACTICE

Leaf printing activity.

Adult: Have you chosen a leaf yet?

Child: Yes, this one.

Adult: Can I have a look at it? Isn't it small? I think that it might be the smallest one on the table. Let me see if I can find a smaller one. (Adult then picks up another leaf and compares it to the child's one.)

Adult: What do you think? Is it smaller than your leaf? Which one do you think is the smallest?

Child: My one.

Adult: Yes, I think you're right. It is the smallest. Let's look at another leaf and see if it is still the smallest. Here is another leaf. Which one now is the smallest? Will you tell Mrs Jones that your leaf is the smallest as I am sure she would like to know.

Child: (Holding leaf to Mrs Jones) My one is the smallest.

1 What key words might the child have learnt from this conversation?

2 Why is it important for children to hear words in context?

Using visual means of supporting communication

Many children will benefit when we present information and language to them in a visual as well as spoken code. This helps children's comprehension and can also help them to remember new language.

Puppets

Many children respond positively to puppets and cuddly toys. They enjoy the characters and in some cases will talk more to a puppet than to us! Use puppets as a way of modelling language and also as a way of keeping children's attention.

Props

Using props during story and song times will help children to understand what is happening and will also help them to assimilate language more easily. Encourage children to hold and use the props at appropriate times.

Point to objects

Many children will understand more of what is being said if it is happening in the 'here and now'. This means point to objects that you are talking about and encourage children to point and to show you things as they are talking.

Picture representations

Some children will benefit from using pictures to supplement communication. You might show a picture of an apron to a child and accompany this with the

Using a puppet can aid communication skills

words 'get an apron'. In the same way, pictures might allow the child to show you what he or she needs in response to your question 'What would you like to do?'; the child might show you a picture of the type of play activity.

Commercial systems of picture representations are available and it may be useful to explore the possibility of using these with the speech and language therapist. One system known as PECS (Picture Exchange Communication System) has been used successfully with children who are reluctant to interact. Children give and also take pictures and thus learn about the 'exchange' nature of interaction. For more information on PECS, visit **www.pecs.org.uk**.

Sign representations

Some children will need to use signs alongside spoken language. Makaton is an example of a signing system that supports language. The decision to use Makaton is normally taken by speech and language therapists in conjunction with parents. The signs give the child a visual cue and thus can help them to understand and communicate their needs. Makaton is particularly helpful for children who find it hard to understand the meaning of words because of difficulties in processing abstract information. For more information on Makaton, visit **www.makaton.org**.

Literacy: skills that children need to acquire.

Developing children's literacy

Being able to read and write is another facet of communication. From an early age, children begin to find out about this type of communication and gain some of the underlying skills that are required. It is important to emphasise that formal reading and writing programmes are unnecessary and can also be unhelpful. Providing naturalisitic and playful opportunities in which to learn about reading and writing tends to have greater success in motivating and encouraging children.

To be able to read and write, children need to acquire a range of skills. Some children with special educational needs will need greater support to master these.

Language

Most children need to have a strong grasp of a language before they can master reading and writing. This means that unless otherwise advised, you should aim to work on children's speech or sign language before focusing on reading and writing.

Understand that print carries meaning

Children need to be aware of the purpose of print and that print has meaning. For some children, this realisation begins with enjoying stories and picture books, while other children may become interested in trying to write.

STRATEGIES TO HELP SHOW THAT PRINT CARRIES MEANING

- Make sure that children see you reading and writing.
- Share books with children.
- Run your finger underneath words as you are reading and writing them.
- Use opportunities to write the child's name in front of the child.
- Provide a range of writing materials and role play situations where writing is used.

Visual recall

Reading and writing letters requires children to have a good visual recall of symbols. Reading requires recognising the symbols and remembering their meaning or sounds. Writing requires children to be able to actively remember the shape of symbols. Children who cannot recognise and remember images will need support before they are ready to look at letters as these are more abstract.

STRATEGIES TO HELP VISUAL RECALL

- Encourage children to play with jigsaw puzzles, shape sorters and other resources that encourage children to observe shapes.
- Play games that encourage children to notice differences or similarities.
- Play games such as snap and picture lotto as these require children to remember pictures.

Introducing letters

Make sure that children regularly see their names, for example, in the cloakroom, at the table, on pictures and displays. Look for ways to use and hold their names, such as taking their name over to their paintings or hunting for their name in a treasure hunt. Make sure that key objects are labelled, for example, toilet, door, sand, paint. Point out key objects to children and use sensory ways of helping children to visualise letters, such as sandpaper letters, drawing letters in sand or shaving foam.

Encourage children to learn about language in a sensory way, for example, drawing letters in sand

Linking sounds to letters

Children need to be able to hear the sounds and patterns in words. This means that children's auditory discrimination will need developing.

STRATEGIES TO HELP LINK SOUNDS WITH LETTERS

- Use musical instruments with children. Can they hear the difference between rhythms, loud and soft, etc?
- Play games where children have to distinguish or guess sounds, e.g. which is the loudest sound?
- Link sounds once children are beginning to notice letter shapes.
- Play I-spy type of games.

Gross and fine motor skills

Physical development plays an important part in the development of writing. Children need to have developed gross motor co-ordination as well as fine motor skills. Children who have not acquired sufficient co-ordination may find it hard to use and control a pencil or pen. This can lead to poor handwriting habits and postures. Children can also become frustrated by their inability to control their movements.

Suggested activities

ACTIVITY 1: HOT AND COLD GAME

This game can be used to help children's auditory discrimination, but can also be adapted to encourage children who are mastering the pronunciation of particular sounds (see adaptations).

Aim: To encourage children to listen to sounds.

Resources: Musical instruments, keys, rattles, teddy or other object to hide.

Activity: Hide the teddy or another object. Ask the child if he or she can find it. Tell the child that as he or she gets nearer, you will make louder and louder sounds with a tambourine or bunch of keys, but if he or she moves in another direction, you will stop making sounds.

Possible adaptations:

Repeat the game, but ask the child to hide the objects and make the sounds.

Ask the child to hide the object, but you have to ask the child questions as to where it is hidden. Ask the child to hide the object and when you are moving in the right direction, the child makes certain sounds (these can be ones that are being worked on in speech therapy).

ACTIVITY 2: ODD ONE OUT!

This is a versatile activity that can help children in a variety of ways with their language. It can also be used to help children see visual differences (see adaptations).

Aims: To encourage children to look closely at familiar objects and to think about differences. To encourage children to use the names of familiar objects and to talk about the purpose of familiar objects.

Resources: Bag or box with familiar objects in it, e.g. household objects, toys, teddy (optional, some children may not respond to imaginative play).

Activity: Put three objects in the box or bag. Choose two objects that are either the same or that would be put together and one object that is very different, e.g. spoon, fork and a toy car. The child can take them out one by one. Using language appropriate to the child's understanding, talk about each object. Use the teddy as a stooge if the child responds well to imaginative play. Which ones are the same? Which ones go together? Which one is the odd one out? Ask the child to show the teddy which ones go together. Can the child tell the teddy what the objects are used for?

Possible adaptations:

Some children may benefit from a simple repeated script as they play this game.

Play this game with pairs of children. Repeat this game with a new odd one out object, but retain the other two objects so that children already know their names and purpose. Encourage children to choose from a selection of objects; they can see if they can fool teddy and you. Adapt this activity to help children see visual differences in symbols of pictures; put three cards in a bag or box. Can the children find two that match, e.g. two cats and one dog or two words that are the same, and one that is different.

ACTIVITY 3: FISHING GAME

Can you fish your name out of the pond?

Aims: This activity can help children to distinguish between their name and other words or symbols. It can also help children's hand-eye co-ordination and fine manipulative skills.

Resources: Cards in the shape of a fish, paper clips, baton or small stick, string, tape, magnet.

Preparation.

Write the name of the child onto several fish cards. Put dissimilar words onto other cards or other symbols. Attach a paper clip onto each card. Attach a magnet onto the baton or stick and tie it on string.

Activity: Put the fish into a pile or onto a small tray. Show the child how to fish for cards. Encourage the child to enjoy 'fishing'. Show the child the cards – which one is the child's name? Ask the child to fish and then to put the cards with his or her name on into a separate pile.

Possible adaptations:

Instead of using a fishing rod, children can 'catch' cards with their hands. If children enjoy this fishing game, it can be repeated and adapted to help children in many other ways. Pictures of animals or other objects can be stuck onto the fish – can children say the name of the object?

Pairs of words can be put onto the cards – can children find the matches? Individual letters can be put onto the cards – can children find and say the name of any of the letters? Play the game with two or more children – can they find each other's names? Use the game to teach other concepts, e.g. fishing for colours or sizes of fish.

ACTIVITY 4: TONGUE TWISTERS

This activity is particularly useful with children who are receiving speech and language support to help them with intonation and production of sounds.

Aims: It will encourage children to hear sounds in words, to hear rhymes and patterns in words and to practise certain sounds.

Resources: Props that link to the tongue twister (optional).

Activity: Make up or use some simple tongue twisters or phrases with alliteration, e.g. red robin, curly caterpillar. See if the children can repeat them. Props can be helpful as children can hold them and say the tongue twister. Using children's names as tongue twisters is also very popular. You may like to try out some of these: fiddily frogs, spinning spoons, sticky shells, brown buttons.

Possible adaptations:

Sing the tongue twisters; this can help children with stammers. Use musical instruments so that children can beat out sounds.

ACTIVITY 5: FEELY BAG

Feely bags can be used in a variety of ways with children to promote a range of language and literacy skills (see possible adaptations).

Aim: To help children use descriptive vocabulary and frame questions.

Resources: Bag with objects that will be familiar for the child, teddy (optional).

Activity: Put all the objects that you are going to use out. Check that the child knows what they are used for and their names. The teddy can be used here as the child can tell the teddy about the objects. Encourage the child to handle the objects and model descriptive words about each of the objects, e.g. 'that's quite soft isn't it?', 'that feels quite hard'. Put one of the objects into the bag without the child seeing and remove the rest. Ask the child to guess what is inside the bag. Ask the child questions about the object, e.g. 'does it feel hard?' Repeat the game with the aim of encouraging the child to tell you about the object.

Possible adaptations:

Use unfamiliar objects. Play the game with partners as a 'yes and no' type of game. Children have to ask each other questions about what is inside the bag. Encourage children to choose an object to put inside the bag to see if you can guess what it is. Play the game with pairs of objects; one inside and one outside of the bag, e.g. a spoon inside the bag, the child has to find the fork from among objects that are out of the bag. Develop children's 'thinking' language; children have to guess what is in the bag but also say why they think this.

ACTIVITY 6: WHAT WERE YOU DOING?

Most children love to look at photographs of themselves. Activities involving photographs of the child can help children to talk more freely and use the skills of recall.

Aims: To help children sequence and use the past tense.

Resources: Three photographs of the child engaged in a routine that can be put into an order, e.g. the child as he or she puts an apron on to paint, paint a picture or wash his or her hands.

Activity: This activity can be done with a teddy or other 'stooge'. Show the child the photographs. Ask the child if he or she knows who is in the photographs. Ask the child if he or she can tell you (or the teddy) what the child is doing. Can the child tell you what happened first.

Possible adaptations:

Increase the number of photographs, e.g. to four or five. Involve the child in taking photographs, e.g. the child takes pictures of the teddy doing something. Make the photographs into a book; put simple labels under the pictures.

Chapter 10

Supporting children's cognition and learning

Introduction

Psychologists are still researching how learning takes place in children and the reasons why some children learn at a slower rate than others. This is not surprising as the brain is very complicated. This means that there is no single method of helping children to learn. Indeed most practitioners find that they need to continually try different strategies to meet the needs of the individual child. While accepting that there are several theories of learning, this chapter focuses particularly on how children process information. This approach to children's learning can generate many helpful strategies for practitioners.

What is cognitive development?

In its simplest sense, cognitive development is the process by which children begin to understand the world in which they live. They learn, for example, that objects do not just disappear. They also learn to predict, reflect and reason. The notion of time, colours and being able to differentiate between objects are all examples of cognition.

The development of cognition requires that children learn to take in information, categorise it and use it to inform their thinking. As well as processing information, advanced cognition requires that children are aware of how to make the best use of their knowledge to problem solve. This aspect of cognitive development is sometimes referred to as metacognitive development.

KEY ISSUE: COGNITIVE DEVELOPMENT

There is much evidence to suggest that cognitive development is linked to other areas of development. Understanding how to support children in areas of development such as language can therefore also have an effect on their cognitive development.

The importance of the emotional climate

A good starting point when considering children's cognitive development is to be aware of the importance of who they are with and what they are feeling when they are learning. This has been dubbed the 'emotional climate'. Children and adults alike find it easier to absorb information when they are relaxed. This in part has been explained by research that suggests that when we are under stress, less memory space is made available to us. This would account for why children sometimes 'freeze' when they feel they are being tested or why a nervous child may not remember a simple instruction.

REFLECT ON YOUR OWN PRACTICE

- Remember that the emotional climate where learning takes place is more important than the 'learning outcome'.
- Begin by building a good relationship with the child.
- Adjust activities according to the child's emotional responses.

Physical development and cognitive development

There appears to be a strong link between physical and cognitive development. This is an area that is still being researched in terms of brain development, although it would appear that physical movements stimulate the brain's neural pathways. There are, for example, correlations between children who have difficulty in assimilating and using symbols and children's early co-ordination and handedness. The importance of developing children's balance, co-ordination

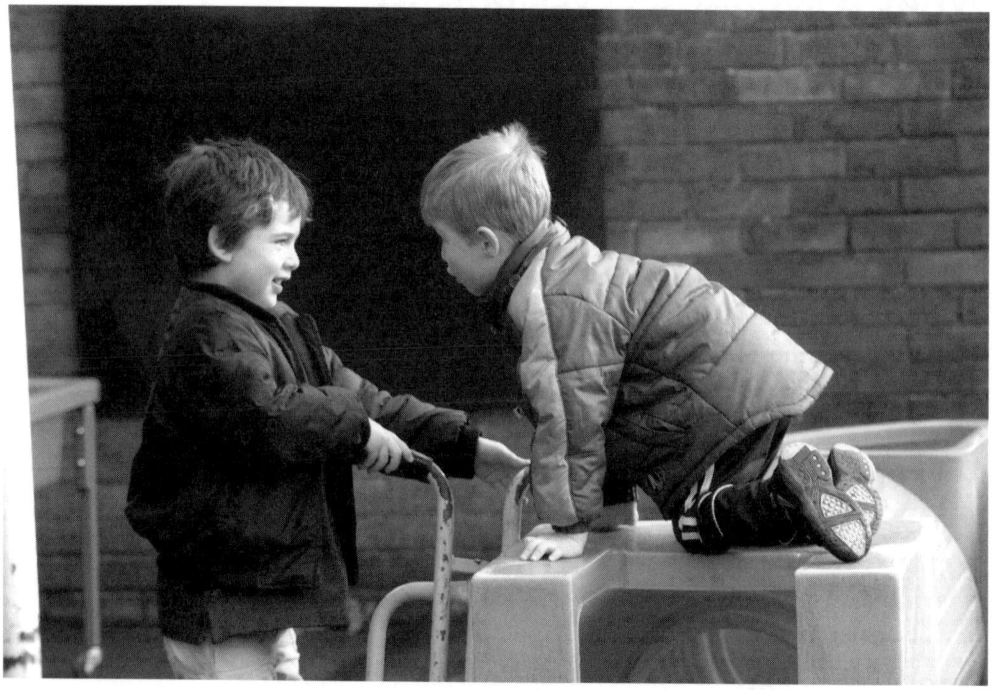

Physical activities play an important role in children's cognitive development.

and range of body movements must therefore not be overlooked. As a practitioner, this means that you should ensure that children are encouraged to take part in physical activities and that these need to be seen as having an important role in children's cognitive development. Activities that appear to be particularly beneficial include balancing, throwing and catching along with skills that encourage the brain to sequence such as climbing and crawling.

REFLECT ON YOUR OWN PRACTICE

- Give all children plenty of opportunities to develop their physical skills.
- Look for ways of making 'learning' take place out of doors and in a physical way.
- Consider adopting programmes that are designed to sequentially build children's physical skills.

Language and thought

The acquisition of language appears to make a significant difference in the way children begin to process information. It would appear that language allows us to categorise and store information more efficiently. Children who have not yet developed language may therefore find it harder to process information and organise their thoughts.

Language and self-direction

Most people mutter to themselves aloud when they are trying to think something complex through or give themselves instructions. This is an important use of language as it links to our ability to organise our thoughts and actions. As we get older, the self-direction becomes mainly internal and can be thought of as an 'inner voice'. Children also self-direct and use language in this way. At first this is always done aloud, but later children are able to think their thoughts internally. Children whose language development is atypical may often carry on needing to think aloud and it is essential that this be encouraged. With other children, you may have to help them learn to self-direct as this is an important metacognitive skill.

REFLECT ON YOUR OWN PRACTICE

- Avoid telling children who are commentating or talking aloud to be quiet; it may be their way of thinking.
- Put children who need to think aloud into smaller groups at story time.
- Model talking aloud behaviour to children; this helps them learn how to go about problem solving.

THINK IT OVER

It is story time at the end of the session. The story is about a blue balloon. Suddenly Jake shouts out 'I gotta a balloon, a big balloon. It went pop and I got it at a party and I ate lots of cake and …'. The assistant tells Jake to be quiet, not to shout out but to listen instead, and that if he cannot he will have to be taken out.

1 Was Jake listening to the story?
2 Explain why Jake shouted out.
3 How can the setting change the way it structures story time to include rather than exclude Jake?

Seeing language for thought as different from language for communication

The Foundation Stage guidance distinguishes between language for thinking and language for communication. While it may be argued that this is an artificial distinction, in terms of helping children's cognitive development it may be useful. Language for communication could be thought of as everyday routine language which sustains and builds relationships. For a child this may be phrases his or her as 'Can I have a turn?' or 'I am going to a party tonight with my friend'.

Language for thinking is different. It requires children to have the vocabulary and the grammatical structures to express thoughts and concepts. A good example of language for thinking might be 'I like this one better because it is blue and blue is my favourite colour'. In this example the child is able to use language to explain his or her preference in terms of a colour, i.e. colour is a concept.

Developing children's language for thinking

In order to help children use language for thinking it is essential that they have 'labels' for their thoughts, feelings and for objects and concepts. Labelling appears to draw children's attention to certain features which in turn helps them to develop new thoughts, for example, 'Look at this leaf. It is prickly. This one is not prickly, though, it has smooth edges'.

As well as making sure that children have the 'labels', it is also important to encourage children to use their language to show their thinking. This often requires practice, and children will also need to see this being modelled at first. The key words to use with children when they ready are 'why' and 'how'. For example this may mean saying to a child who has sorted out cars 'Can you show me how to do this and tell me what I have to look for when I am sorting the cars? That will mean I will know why they are sorted in your special way'.

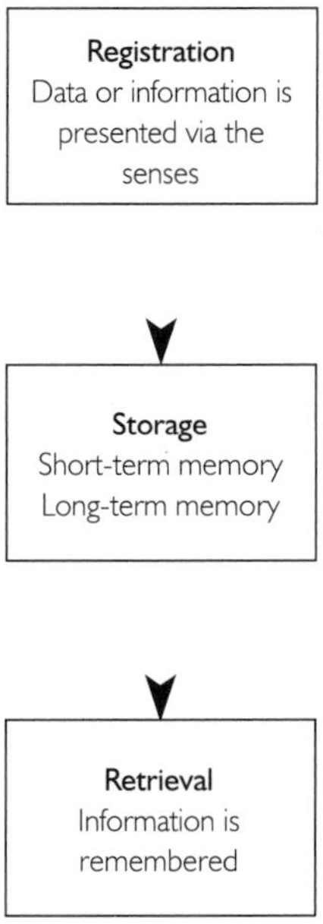

The stages involved in processing information.

Understanding how information is processed

It can be useful to consider how children take in and store information. Psychologists who are researching into this relatively new area talk about 'information processing'. Comparisons with the human brain and computers are often used in this field because of the idea that the brain is constantly inputting, handling, storing and then retrieving data in the same way that computers function. Some information processing theorists suggest that differences in cognitive development may result from the speed at which children are able to process information, and that children whose cognitive development is atypical may have difficulties in one or more areas during the actual processing. One child may have difficulties in being alert enough to respond and register information, while another child may have difficulties in retrieving information and using information.

Helping children to register information

In order to register information and for it to be stored, children need to be alert. They need to be able to focus on particular aspects of the information. This is a skill that adults tend to take for granted but is actually quite hard for children. Information processing theorists have found that as children develop they usually become better at being able to filter out information. For many children this might happen as part of the usual sequence of development, but for others such as children with Attention Deficit Hyperactivity Disorder (AD/HD) (see page 183) this will be harder.

Levels of arousal

This is the starting point. Children need to respond to the data that is being presented. Some children's level of alertness or arousal can be too low or too high. It is often when children's level of alertness is low, that we find they cannot pay attention. The activity may not be 'holding' them because their levels of arousal drop. For children to continue to concentrate, their levels of interest or arousal need to be maintained. In extreme cases of under or over-arousal, children may be given medication, either stimulants or depressants, although treating children with drugs is extremely controversial.

Attention

As well as being alert, children also need to 'ignore the irrelevant'. The brain is constantly bringing us new information from the senses. Selecting and remaining focused on the relevant information is known as selective attention. Some children find this very difficult and will, for example, turn their head to respond to a noise behind them or notice something within their reach. When this happens we may say that a child is easily distracted when, in reality, the child is having difficulty in putting aside new information that is being presented to him or her. Other children may find it hard to switch and take in new information that is relevant to them. They may try to carry on playing in the same way even though materials or playmates are no longer there.

There are many occasions when we need to do two or more things at the same time, for example, talk and prepare a meal. This means being able to respond to and take in several sources of information at the same time. The ability to divide our attention does to a large extent depend on the tasks that we are doing. The easier we find a task, the easier it is to take on another alongside it.

The ability to cope with several sources of information at once and process them is developmental. Very young children may not be able to answer a simple question while focusing on a drawing. Children with atypical cognitive development often find it hard to split their attention, so this must be taken into consideration when planning activities or giving children instructions.

Concentration

There are no hard and fast rules about how to help children concentrate, but the following strategies may be helpful.

STRATEGIES TO AID CHILDREN'S CONCENTRATION

- Consider whether the child is actually concentrating, even though not necessarily on your learning objective!
- Go to activities that are already engaging the child and look for ways of extending learning or language there, rather than taking the child away.
- Look for activities that will engage several of the child's senses at once. This can help arousal, e.g. sand, water, dough, shaving foam, cooking. The diagram below shows the different ways in which sand can engage children's senses and thus help some children to maintain concentration.

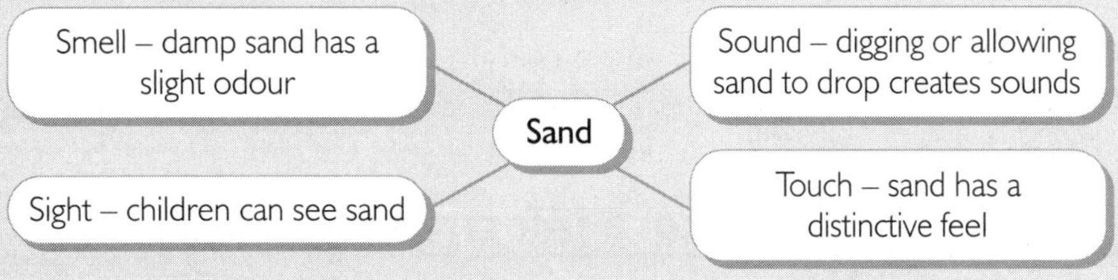

Ways in which sand can engage children's senses.

- Give children objects to handle to help them to listen and attend. Having something in their hands can help children to remain alert as this acts as another sensory boost.
- Look at the layout of the learning environment; are there too many sources of distraction for the child? e.g. in a bustling room it may be difficult for the child to filter out activities.
- Make sure that activities are appealing and perhaps have a surprise or interest element, e.g. 'What's in here? Look what teddy has brought in'.
- Avoid overloading children with too many tasks and instructions at once; look carefully at their divided attention skills.
- Think about the way and speed in which children are being presented with information. If children do not appear to be attending, change your tone of voice and if necessary slow down the pace so that children have time to register information.
- Repeat activities and once children are familiar with them, change one feature of the activity.

THINK IT OVER

Mark moves from activity to activity. Staff often try to make him sit down, but he usually prefers to stand and quickly goes off. The staff have, however, noticed that he tends to spend some time in the water tray, but because it is heavy, they only get it out occasionally. Sand is not allowed in the setting because of fears that it will scratch the floor. Today he is repeatedly pouring water out of a teapot, but a member of staff wants to do a counting activity with him.

1 Why do you think that Mark enjoys playing with the water?
2 Give one suggestion as to how counting could be incorporated into Mark's existing play.
3 Suggest other ways of providing sensory activities that may sustain Mark's concentration.

Helping children to store information

Memory is a crucial, but too often overlooked component in children's learning. If children are limited in their ability to store and retrieve information, this will limit their learning. Research and theories about how our memories work are ongoing, but it seems that children's storage and retrieval systems are not as sophisticated as most adults and that they gradually develop both strategies and systems. In particular, it seems that children's ability to 'boost' their short-term memories is limited. This might account for children who have apparently been listening, often forgetting simple instructions. Children whose cognitive development is atypical may have difficulties in 'holding' information or making the relevant connections in order to retrieve it.

Short-term memory

The short-term memory is an intermediate store of information and it is thought that the duration of memories stored is less than 30 seconds. Information that is not processed and moved along is usually lost. A key strategy that adults use to hold information is to rehearse it. We repeat instructions or telephone numbers over and over in order to hold them in our minds. Young children and older children with atypical cognitive development will not use this strategy. Another strategy that adults use is to group individual pieces of information together into 'chunks'. Instead of trying to remember all the items needed for breakfast, you may chunk the information into an overall heading 'breakfast'. It is thought that children who have difficulties with language are at a disadvantage because they are not using language to categorise in this way.

Memory codes

There appear to be three main ways in which information is encoded in our memory:

- Acoustic – information stored in a sound code.

- Visual or iconic – information stored in picture form.
- Semantic – information stored using abstract symbols, e.g. writing, words.

As adults, we tend to store a lot of information using the semantic code, for example words can trigger many memories and thoughts, but young children rely heavily on their visual code. This is thought to be the reason why your first memories are likely to be visual ones. In order for children to store information semantically, it is important that they have a good level of language. This will mean that, in general, young children will find it hard to process and retain information that is 'word based' while they will fare better if information is encoded visually or as sounds, for example, songs and rhymes.

STRATEGIES TO HELP CHILDREN STORE INFORMATION

- Use props or visual aids when telling stories or giving information.
- Show rather than tell children what they should be doing.
- Avoid presenting information just as 'talk'; look for ways of touching, feeling and seeing.
- Think about how information is being presented to children. Some children respond well to songs and remember these more than just 'words'.
- Encourage children to repeat important instructions, e.g. 'What do you do when you go to the toilet?'.
- Play games that involve memory.

Using a feely bag containing different objects can help children to store and retrieve information

Retrieving information

As well as storing information, children also need to be able to retrieve it or remember it. There are many forms of remembering and if we provide children with the right prompts, they will be able to find information.

REFLECT ON YOUR OWN PRACTICE

- Allow children plenty of time so that they can 'scan' their memories.
- Help children to find information by asking associated questions such as 'What were you wearing at the time?'. This helps children hook into their visual memory.
- Provide prompts or triggers for the child such as props – 'Do you recognise this scarf?'
- Repeat activities using the same props and in the same place.

SEEING THEORY IN PRACTICE

A nursery was finding that several children were not always following the simple instructions. Staff felt that they were poor at listening. Debra, one of the assistants, thought about how the information was being presented to the children. She realised that quite often children were being 'told' what to do rather than being shown. She introduced a puppet when giving out instructions. The puppet was a parrot and she made it squawk and flap and she used it as a stooge to show the children what needed doing. She also encouraged the children to remind the parrot what they had to do. The children loved the parrot and their 'listening' skills improved dramatically.

1. Analyse the reasons why Debra's strategy was effective.
2. Explain the link between children's ability to 'listen' and memory.
3. Why is it important that staff reflect upon their own practice?

Helping children to problem solve

As well as being able to store and retrieve information, children also have to learn how best to use it to solve problems. Being aware of the information that you have, and being able to transfer this knowledge are metacognitive skills.

Problem solving is about being able to use the information that we have acquired and use it in new situations. This is a skill that develops gradually, but some children will for a variety of reasons need support. There are specific steps in problem solving:

1. Identify the nature of the problem and what would be a successful outcome.
2. Consider what knowledge and information is available.
3. Identify strategies.
4. Consider which strategy fits best.

5 Plan how to use the strategy.
6 Implement the strategy and evaluate its effectiveness.
7 If the strategy is not effective consider how to change it.

Most adults internalise their thinking unless they are under stress or alone. To help children learn to problem solve, we can show them our thought processes. This provides good modelling. It is also important that children are given opportunities to practise the skill with carefully structured and achievable problems. This is particularly important to focus on because often children who appear slower at thinking are not given the chance to work things out, either because other children step in or because adults take over.

STRATEGIES TO HELP CHILDREN SOLVE PROBLEMS

- Teach children the steps in problem solving by going through each step with them.
- Try and elicit the process from the child by using questions.
- Model problem solving by using running commentary.
- Look for opportunities to encourage children to problem solve, e.g. 'Have we enough chairs for Katie, Denzig and you?'.

SEEING THEORY IN PRACTICE

Examples of ideas for everyday problem solving include the following:

- Jigsaw puzzles: Talk about how to look for and try out specific pieces.
- Snack time: Talk about checking that there are enough chairs, plates, etc.
- Getting dressed: What do you need to keep you warm?
- Construction play: How can you make these fit together.

Adapting information to new situations

Many children who have difficulties with their cognition find it hard to transfer and use information and skills in new situations. It may be that they find it hard to see similarities between situations. Children can be helped by sensitive prompting and also by being given tasks that have similarities.

STRATEGIES TO HELP CHILDREN ADAPT TO NEW SITUATIONS

- Talk to children about the things that they are doing that are similar to previous activities, e.g. 'Yesterday you also rolled things along, didn't you?'.
- Repeat activities, but change one feature so that while children are familiar with the core activity, they are also experiencing something that is different.

Helping children to become self-aware

In the same way that children need feedback about aspects of their behaviour, they also benefit from being given feedback about the way in which they are using information. It is all too easy for adults to concentrate solely on the task in hand, rather than the thinking that the child is putting into it. For example a child may be slow at dressing, and an adult may comment on how slow the child is rather than notice that the child is tackling getting dressed in a logical way! The danger at this point is that because the adult is focusing only on the task, the child will be disempowered by the adult who then steps in to speed the child up.

STRATEGIES TO HELP CHILDREN BECOME SELF-AWARE

- Give children positive feedback about the way that they are approaching tasks.
- Provide children with sufficient prompts, but make sure that they remain as independent as possible.

Motivation

As well as looking at the way in which we can help children to process information, it is also worth considering motivation. Children will learn better if they are motivated with the adage 'learning is caught not taught' coming to the fore here. Relevance and expected success are two factors worth examining.

Children are more likely to attempt to problem solve and concentrate if the task meets their needs and interests. This is why it important to build upon children's interests, for example, a child who enjoys playing with toy cars and lining them up is more likely to be motivated if toy cars are in some way involved.

Our expectation of success is often a key factor in whether we attempt tasks. Children who have repeated failures will not be motivated to try out new tasks, and so tasks must be suited to children's level of development and where required support must be offered.

REFLECT ON YOUR OWN PRACTICE

- Make sure that children can see the purpose of what they are doing, especially if it is an adult-directed task. Children respond well when there is a reason involved.
- Simplify and structure the task so that children experience success.
- Break down tasks into small, manageable tasks.
- Talk through the reasons why a task has not been successful and help children learn to evaluate their role or outside influences.

Learning about abstract concepts

Abstract concepts such as number and literacy can be hard for some children to respond to. As with many areas of working with children who have particular needs, there is no single strategy that will automatically work.

While some children may be able to grasp concepts quickly, other children will need a variety of reinforcing activities. The danger for practitioners is to assume that just because a child appears to understand at the time, he or she has acquired the concept. Presenting too much information too quickly can make the child lose confidence.

THINK IT OVER

Today Mahkreet managed to recognise the number 3 for the first time. His key worker is delighted because up until today, Mahkreet was not sure at all and often guessed numbers. His key worker is now planning to get him to do a worksheet about the number 4.

1. Explain why moving on to a new number may not be effective.
2. Why should Mahkreet be given opportunities to consolidate his learning?
3. Suggest three ways in which the key worker might be able to reinforce his learning.

Number

Number is an abstract concept, and before children can do 'maths', they need to be able to understand what the unit of sound and the symbol actually stands for. If you are unsure what is involved in teaching counting and using numbers, consider using the Foundation Stage guidance as a reference, and choose activities that correspond with the level of the child's awareness.

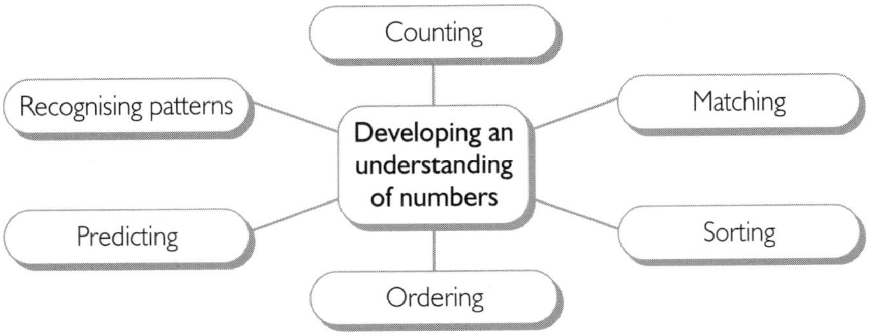

Developing an understanding of numbers.

STRATEGIES FOR HELPING CHILDREN TO UNDERSTAND THE CONCEPT OF NUMBER

- Make sure that children learn the relevance of number in their everyday lives, e.g. counting the number of chairs needed at a table or the number of children who want to play a game.
- Model ways in which you use number, e.g. count things aloud, talk about the number of objects.
- Encourage children to group materials and sort them.
- Look for opportunities for children to match items, e.g. putting a plate down where there is a plate mat, putting one piece of apple onto each plate.
- Use sensory materials such as dough, sand and water as the basis for activities about number, e.g. How many spoonfuls of sand does it take? How many pieces of dough have you got there?
- Put objects into bags; can children tell if there is more than one object in the bag?
- Look for ways of 'slipping' numbers into children's play, e.g. Would you like any extra cups in the home corner? How many would you like?
- Introduce written numbers in a variety of ways, but only when children have begun to grasp number, e.g. fridge magnets, numbers drawn in sand.
- Use games to help children use number, e.g. roll a dice.
- Avoid abstract recording, e.g. worksheets. Children will find it easier to use, see and touch real objects.

Literacy

Before children learn to read and write, they need to have developed many skills. Most children are not ready to actually learn the process of how to 'decode' until they are at least five years old, with many children really not cracking the code until they are nearer six or seven years old. This means that it is not unusual for children not to be able to recognise their names when they are just three or four years old.

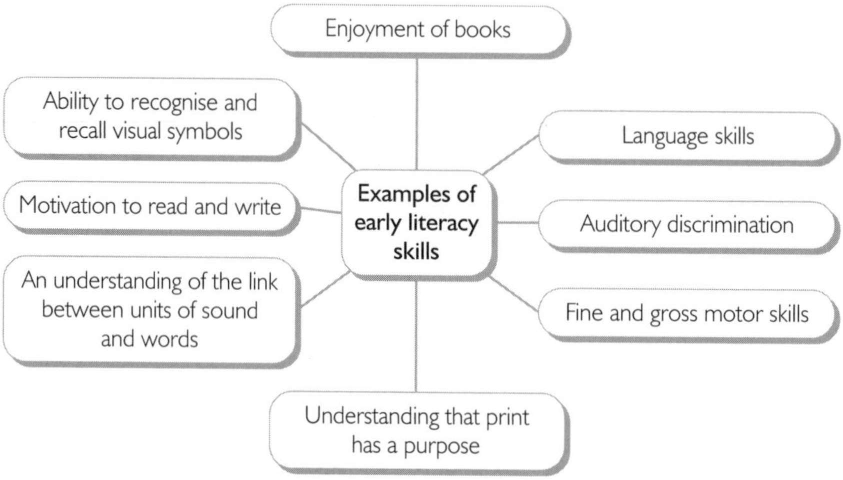

Examples of early literacy skills.

STRATEGIES FOR ENCOURAGING EARLY LITERACY SKILLS

- Share books with individual children.
- Work on children's language by modelling language.
- Provide role play opportunities for children to write, e.g. shopping lists, jotter pads, forms.
- Use picture books with children and encourage them to work out what is happening from the pictures.
- Sing rhymes and songs to children; encourage them to join in and even change words.
- Encourage children to make marks in sensory materials, e.g. shaving foam, rice, damp sand.
- Provide plenty of opportunities for children to see and hold their names. Names are generally one of the earliest words that children are able to read because they have meaning for them.

Suggested activities

ACTIVITY 1: SCARVES AND RIBBONS

This is a physical activity that can help children to recognise the shape and form of letters and can be used as a precursor to children's writing.

Aim: To help children develop visual and sensory 'maps' of letters.

Resources: Scarves or ribbons.

Activity: Begin by encouraging the children to enjoy feeling, touching and waving the scarves. You could use music for children to move and dance to. Show children particular arm movements with the scarves that link to letter shapes, i.e. a vertical movement downwards or an anti-clockwise round movement.

Possible adaptations:

Encourage children to make repeated movements such as several 'o' shapes in the air. Ask children who have some awareness of letters to make the letter shape of the initial letter in their name. Use cards with names or letters on them as cues.

ACTIVITY 2: SAME AND DIFFERENT

This activity helps children to discriminate between objects and also encourages them to use language to express their thoughts. This activity can be used with a variety of objects.

Aims: To encourage children to use language to think and to notice similarities and differences. This activity also helps children to sort and categorise.

Resources: Pairs of objects that have shared characteristics but are also different in some way, e.g. a blue pen and a red pen of a different size, a teddy and another puppet or other type of stooge.

Activity: Begin by using a teddy or puppet to bring out the two objects that you have chosen. Does the child know what they are and what they are for? Tell the child that teddy finds it hard to tell the objects apart. Can we find a way of helping him to remember what makes them different? If the child cannot see the difference or does not have the language, model the language for the child and then ask the child to repeat it back to teddy, e.g. 'We could tell teddy that this one is much bigger. Would you like to tell teddy that this one is bigger? Here take it to teddy and tell him "this one is much bigger"'.

Possible adaptations:

Choose objects that will focus children's attention of particular concepts, e.g. size, shape, colour, purpose. Repeat the activity with the same objects later in the day; can the child remember some of the language that has been modelled? Ask the child to choose two objects; 'Can you or teddy talk about them?'. Use objects that are unfamiliar to the child.

ACTIVITY 3: KIM'S GAME

Kim's game is a traditional game that can help children's visual recall.

Aim: To help children's memory and categorisation skills.

Resources: Tray, six assorted objects that can be grouped in some way, e.g. two spoons, two cars and two pencils.

Activity: Show the objects on the tray to the child. Encourage the child to hold and touch them. Encourage the child to talk about what they are for and to describe them. You may need to model language for the child. Ask the child to put them into groups or pairs. Take one object away. Can the child now work out what is missing?

Possible adaptations:

Show the child through questions how to guide his or her thoughts, e.g. There were two cars; are there two cars now? There were some spoons, are there any spoons now? Use only two objects that are very dissimilar . Encourage the child to find the hidden object and put it back where it belonged. Draw outlines of the objects first so that the child has a visual cue as to the shape of what is missing. Group objects so that it is easier for the child to identify which object is missing.

ACTIVITY 4: WHAT IS HIDDEN IN THIS SAND TRAY?

Many children respond well to things being hidden. Using sand is also a sensory activity and so the two ingredients combined can act as a way of arousing and sustaining attention.

Aims: To encourage children to find a finite number of objects. To encourage children to do some one-to-one matching.

Resources: Small tray filled with damp sand (a cat litter tray is ideal!) three spoons and three bowls.

Activity: Ask the child to put his or her hands in the sand tray. Can the child find anything that has been hidden? As the child takes out the spoons, count them one by one. Ask the child to put a spoon in each of the bowls.

Potential adaptations:

Ask the child to hide the spoons for you to find. Hide other objects such as buttons and cars in the sand tray; these can build upon a child's favourite playthings. Hide objects that can afterwards be sorted according to size, e.g. a teaspoon, a dessert spoon, a tablespoon. Hide pairs of objects, e.g. two teaspoons, two buttons, two keys.

ACTIVITY 5: THE HUNT FOR LITTLE TEDDY

This activity is a variation of the hunt the thimble game and can be adapted to provide a variety of learning outcomes.

Aim: This type of activity can help develop children's problem solving skills.

Resources: A little teddy or other object that will captivate the child's imagination or interest.

Activity: Tell the child that little teddy is playing hide and seek. Can you together work out where teddy is hiding? This activity requires the adult to show the child how to problem solve, e.g. by asking questions; 'Now where would a teddy like to hide?'. It is also important that children hear the adult's thought processes, e.g. 'I have already looked under here and he is not here, but I have not looked here'. Once teddy has been found, the activity can be repeated again.

Possible adaptations:

Encourage the child to hide teddy. You can then ask the child questions as to where he is hidden and comment on why you are looking in certain places. Limit the places where teddy likes hiding. Encourage the child to think about what he or she knows about teddy. Use other objects that will help children to problem solve such as a large object that will not be able to fit into many spaces.

Chapter 11

Supporting children's behaviour and social and emotional development

Introduction

Being able to socialise, feel part of a community and understand how to behave appropriately are important skills for children. Children whose behaviour and social and emotional development are atypical are often 'excluded' by both adults and other children. Understanding the reasons behind children's behaviour and also ways in which we can foster children's emotional and social development is therefore essential. This chapter focuses on ways in which we can understand and promote children's behaviour and social skills.

Guiding children's behaviour

Learning and showing appropriate behaviour is a part of children's overall development. Some children who have special educational needs may need particular help in this area. The key to managing children's behaviour is to first understand it in order to develop effective strategies.

Promoting positive or 'wanted' behaviour should always be the focus in settings and so a good starting point for everyone in a setting is to consider what actually is 'good' or wanted behaviour. Defining the types of behaviour that we wish to encourage in children can be difficult, but in essence comes down to forms of respect.

KEY ISSUE: WHY IS OBEDIENCE DANGEROUS?

Many staff at first may believe that 'good' behaviour is about children doing as adults tell them. This is a dangerous road to travel in relation to child abuse. 'Obedient' children who associate being good with simply obeying adults are potentially vulnerable children and could be easy prey to abusers. We also ideally want children to be considerate of others because they know that this is the right thing to do rather than just to please an adult.

Forms of respect.

Punishment is not effective

It is now recognised that simply punishing children is not effective. The best approach towards encouraging children to show considerate behaviour is to adopt a pro-active and positive approach towards children. There are many reasons why punishing children does not work:

- It creates a negative atmosphere for all of the children in the setting.
- It is reactive and does not get to the reason behind the behaviour.
- It can make children feel that they are 'bad' and lose confidence.
- It does not encourage children to take responsibility for their actions.
- It can make some children repeat unwanted behaviour in order to gain adult attention.

Learning appropriate behaviour

No child is born understanding what is and what is not appropriate behaviour. Children's ability to understand how to show appropriate behaviour gradually develops alongside other areas of development. For children who have atypical patterns of development, this may mean that they will need support in showing appropriate behaviour.

KEY ISSUE: DEVELOPMENT OF APPROPRIATE BEHAVIOUR

Understanding the links between behaviour and other areas of development is essential as children who have specific developmental needs will not necessarily show behaviour that will be expected for their age or stage of development.

Communication

Being able to communicate effectively allows us to express our needs, explain ourselves and express emotions. Communication also allows us to respond to what others are saying or showing us through their body language. Most children have learned the basic skills of communication by the time they are three years old, and this often marks the start of more co-operative and appropriate behaviour.

Children who for a variety of reasons find it hard to communicate their needs or to receive messages from others can become very frustrated, and aspects of their behaviour may be similar to much younger children, such as tantrums, biting, snatching.

REFLECT ON YOUR OWN PRACTICE

Consider whether any unwanted behaviour is exacerbated or even caused by a child's difficulties in communicating in your setting. If so, part of the strategy to support the child's behaviour will need to include ways of helping him or her to communicate more easily.

CASE STUDY

Jodie is nearly four years old. She is a bright and lively child. Staff at the pre-school have been concerned by her aggressiveness towards other children. She often snatches objects and has occasionally bitten other children. Together with Jodie's parents, staff are now working on her speech as this was showing signs of delay. Her parents have also made an appointment to check out whether Jodie is fully hearing.

Physical development

There are many physical skills that are taken for granted, yet enable children to be independent and to join in with the play of other children. This can mean that some children who have difficulties with controlling their bodies can become frustrated or become reliant on adult support.

REFLECT ON YOUR OWN PRACTICE

Observe carefully a child who may have difficulties in co-ordination and physical movement. How accessible are the activities? Are staff on hand to support the child and to give him or her encouragement? What activities are being planned in order to help the child maximise his or her physical potential? Consider too, if certain play activities or routines have a competitive element that may causing problems, for example, first child outdoors gets first choice of the toys.

CASE STUDY

Rayan occasionally throws objects across the floor for no apparent reason. His key worker is watching him while he is playing with some building bricks. She notes that he seems to know where he wants the bricks to go, but cannot always manoeuvre them to fit together. She also notes how frustrated he becomes when another child takes bricks from a pile and puts them together effortlessly.

1. Explain why Rayan may be throwing objects.
2. Why is it important that children are closely observed?

Cognitive development

Most children gradually learn to remember any rules or boundaries and eventually to apply them in different situations, for example, not to climb on the furniture. They also begin to understand the reasons behind some of the boundaries, i.e. climbing may cause accidents and damage the furniture. Children also begin to understand that their actions may have consequences, i.e. that if they throw sand, they may be taken away from the sand pit.

Some children with learning difficulties may not be able to reason and process information in the same way as other children. It may appear as if they are deliberately testing adults or have not listened to what has been said to them.

REFLECT ON YOUR OWN PRACTICE

Consider how instructions or how behaviour is managed in your setting. Some children cannot process multiple instructions and need to be given them one at a time. Some children also find it hard to process words and remember them so will do better with visual symbols or actually being shown what they should do. They may also need gentle reminders at the start and during activities. In some cases, children will need very close adult supervision as they are not thinking through the consequences of their actions.

Social and emotional development

Playing co-operatively alongside other children is a gradual skill that most children gain when they are between three and four years old. In the same way, children learn to wait to have their needs met and to be aware of others. There is a variety of reasons why some children's social and emotional development is delayed or impaired. The result may be children who find it hard to take turns, co-operate and negotiate with others. They may also become frustrated if children shy away from playing with them.

It is important to provide opportunities for children to play alongside each other

THINK IT OVER

Consider if children need adult support to be able to play with others. They may, for example, need an adult to play with them so that they learn the skills of how to take turns, or they may need an adult alongside them to gently 'coach' them. In some cases, children may need close supervision.

Understanding how children learn behaviours

Many psychologists believe that most behaviours, both wanted and unwanted, are learned rather than being instinctive. It is essential that all staff understand that many behaviours are not consciously learned, for example, a child does not necessarily know that he or she is behaving in a certain way to get adult attention.

There are three theories that can help us to understand how children learn wanted and unwanted behaviour.

1. Conditioning

Conditioning theories are based on the idea that children learn to repeat certain behaviours if they have been rewarded or reinforced. Look at the examples below to see how this theory works.

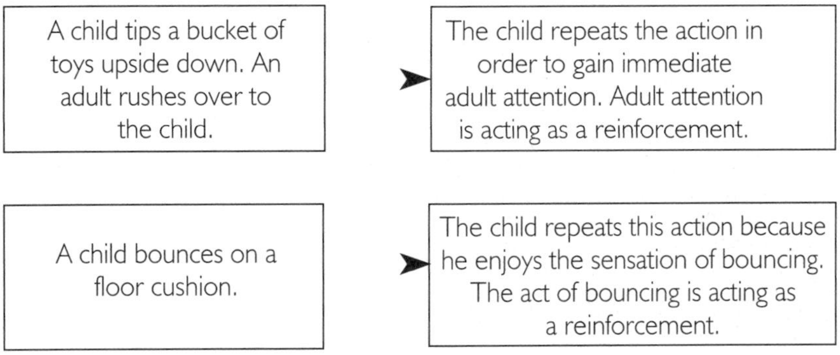

Conditioning theory.

Types of reinforcement

The range of reinforcers is vast. In some cases, behaviour is being reinforced by different reinforcements, for example, a child who throws a toy on the floor may get adult attention, enjoy the feeling of power and may also be fascinated by the sound of the toy hitting the floor.

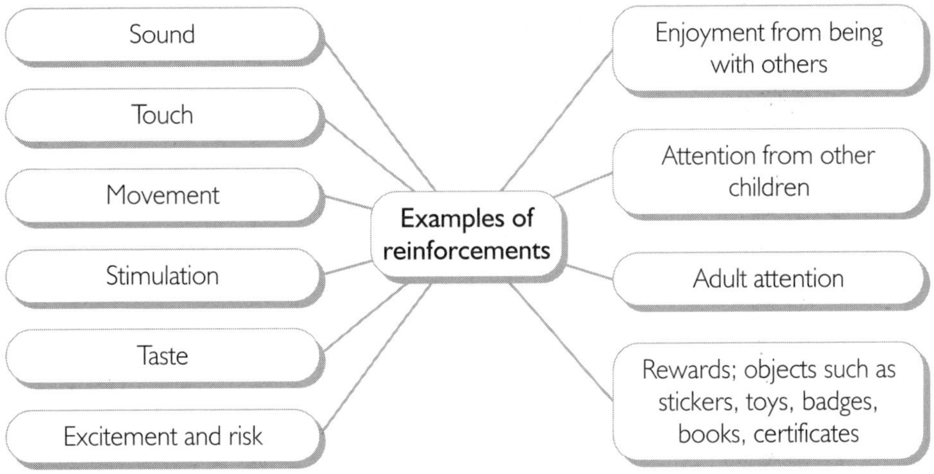

Examples of reinforcements.

If an action is being reinforced because the action itself is providing some pleasure or excitement, the child is likely to find it hard to stop. You are likely to have two choices:

- Provide a distraction that will equal or surpass the amount of reinforcement the child is getting from the unwanted behaviour, e.g. show the child another activity or way of playing with an object.
- Consider whether the object or the child needs to be removed to avoid further temptation.

THINK IT OVER

Kate is playing in the sandpit. She lets sand run through her fingers and then scoops some and throws it onto the floor. It makes a light flicking sound. The girl next to her laughs and they both look at each other and smile. A few moments later, Kate throws sand again.

1 Can you work out the ways in which Kate has been reinforced for her action?

2 How can Kate be helped to show wanted behaviour?

Adult attention as a powerful reinforcer

Most adults do not realise that their attention is so powerful that in some cases children are showing unwanted behaviour just to gain adult attention. Adults often mistakenly believe that if they are being negative and disapproving, the attention given to a child will not act as a reinforcement. For many children, this is not the case and they actually seek out adult attention by deliberately showing unwanted behaviour.

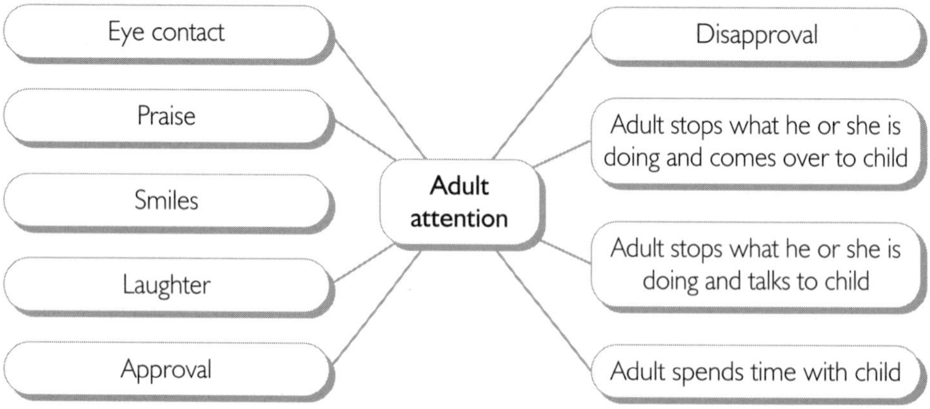

Adult attention as a powerful reinforcer.

It is always worth identifying any reinforcements that a child may be gaining when they show unwanted behaviour. Key questions might include the following:

- What adult attention is given to the child?
- How long does this attention last?
- What is the child's reaction to this attention?

- Does the child get as much attention when he or she is showing wanted behaviour?

Reinforcements are stronger if they are immediate

It has been found that a child is more likely to repeat actions that have been reinforced if the reinforcement happens during or very soon after the action.

A child is praised while he or she is tidying away.	➤	The praise acts as reinforcement. The praise is 'stronger' because it has been given during the action. The child is more likely to repeat this behaviour.

Immediate reinforcement.

Understanding how habits are formed

Habits are formed when children have been frequently reinforced for their actions. Habits that are particularly difficult to address are those that have been intermittently reinforced, for example, sometimes the child has gained a reinforcement and other times he or she has not. A child may sometimes get to keep a toy that he or she has snatched, but sometimes not. The child may automatically snatch because he or she learned that sometimes it is possible to keep the toy.

REFLECT ON YOUR OWN PRACTICE

Consider how behaviour is managed in your setting. Consistency when tackling unwanted behaviour is essential and it is useful if everyone, including parents, agrees to work together and use the same strategies.

Using primary and secondary reinforcers

Reinforcers can be primary or secondary. Primary reinforcers meet a need or desire, while secondary reinforcers lead us to a primary reinforcer. A good example of a secondary reinforcer is money. Money in itself is of no use, but we can use it to buy something that will give us pleasure. Star charts or putting marbles in a jar are examples of secondary reinforcers. The aim is that children get a star or a marble and when they have enough of them, they are traded in for something that each child wants, such as a toy, a certificate, etc.

Young children or children whose cognitive development is impaired prefer primary reinforcers such as praise, stickers, etc. This is because they can immediately see the value of them. Secondary reinforcers require children to be able to understand that they will eventually lead to something that they want.

KEY ISSUE: STAR CHARTS

Star charts and similar methods of building up children's wanted behaviour can be very effective, but consider whether the child is old enough or cognitively able to see the connection between the token and the eventual reward.

STRATEGIES TO PROMOTE POSITIVE BEHAVIOUR

The following are some key points that help us not only to understand why children repeat behaviours but also how we can change or promote positive behaviour in children:

- Reinforce wanted behaviour immediately after or at the same time as it is being shown.
- Remember that instant primary reinforcers such as praise, smiles and signs to show approval will be strong reinforcers.
- Consider whether the unwanted behaviour is being reinforced by the action itself, e.g. the child is enjoying the sensation.
- Look at the way in which unwanted behaviour is being managed and consider whether or not the child is gaining adult attention.
- Consider ignoring unwanted behaviour so that a child does not get adult attention.
- Make sure that more positive adult attention is being given for wanted behaviour than 'negative' adult attention for unwanted behaviour.
- If you need to intervene when unwanted behaviour is being shown, limit the extent of adult attention.
- Consider avoiding eye contact and restricting the amount of time spent with the child.

2. Children learn by watching others

As well as learning behaviour by being reinforced, children also learn by copying others. This process is known as modelling. Children are particularly influenced by adults, especially those who are close to them.

There is a huge onus on all adults working with children to be good role models as children will be constantly learning about appropriate behaviour from them. This means reflecting on how you act and the messages that the child is learning, for example, if you wish a child to learn to ask permission before touching someone else's toys, it will be important for you to remember to do the same when you join in children's play.

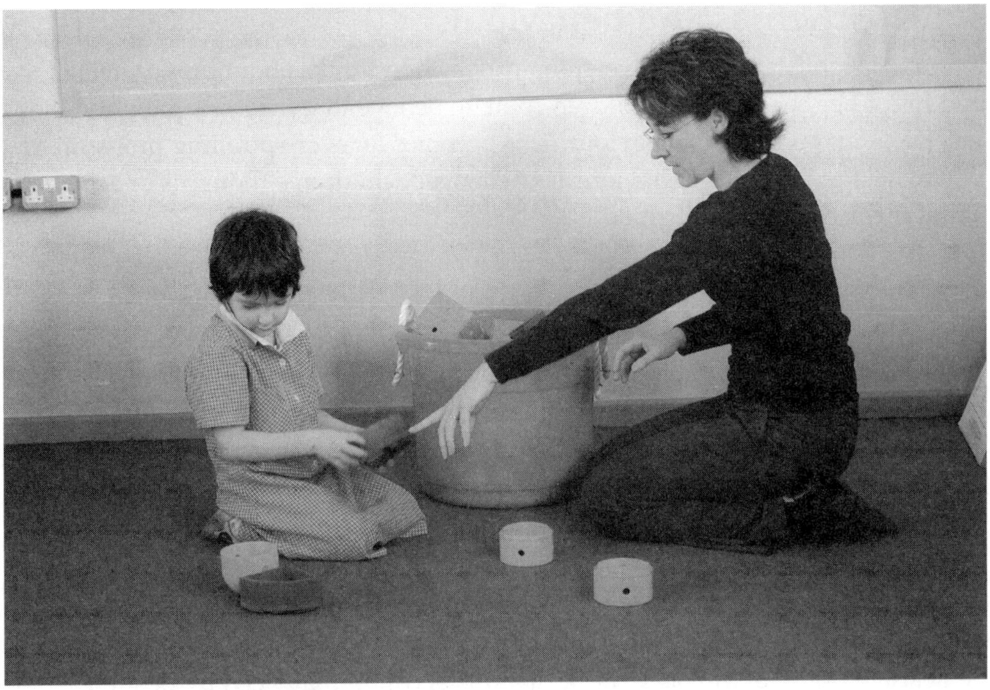

This adult is asking the child if she can use the bricks. The child is learning about asking rather than snatching toys.

Modelling and reinforcement

The theories of reinforcement and modelling are complementary rather than competitive. Children who see a behaviour, imitate it and then are in some way reinforced for it, are likely to repeat it.

Sometimes a child will copy another child, especially if he or she sees that there is some form of reinforcement involved, for example, one child begins to bang his or her fists on the table, another child might do the same.

Some children who find it hard to socialise appropriately will benefit from having an adult show them how to do it. The adult will need to play with or alongside the child showing him or her how to take turns, listen to others and join in.

SEEING THEORY IN PRACTICE

Consider whether any unwanted behaviour that a child is showing has been modelled to him or her. Then consider how this behaviour is being reinforced. Provide alternative behaviours that the child could model and positively reinforce these.

3. Self-schemas and behaviour

There is a significant link between the way a child thinks about him or herself and his or her behaviour. If children come to believe that they are 'naughty' they will show inappropriate behaviour. This becomes an ever-spiralling problem, as when the inappropriate behaviour is challenged, children's thoughts or schemas about themselves are confirmed.

It is useful to understand how children develop schemas about themselves. Children are not born knowing about themselves. They learn about themselves primarily through the reactions of others. This is sometimes called the 'looking glass effect'. Children who regularly receive negative messages will begin to believe that they are incapable of gaining adult approval and behaving appropriately. This is why positive behaviour strategies are considered to be more effective than simply disciplining and punishing children.

Adults have an important role in helping children believe that they are 'good'. Challenging inappropriate behaviour must be done in ways that are positive and the child must understand what they need to do in order to behave appropriately. It is also important that adults think about the number of times that children may be hearing 'don't' or 'no' and check that this is counterbalanced by positive messages.

Self-schemas are slow to change

Once children have developed schemas whereby they see themselves as being 'naughty' or 'difficult', it can be hard for them to see themselves in any other way. They can get used to behaving in certain ways and become comfortable with the results. For staff trying to change the way a child sees him or herself, it is therefore important to be patient and persistent. A child's behaviour may improve but then after a few days appear to get worse. This may be the child finding it hard to believe and accept the new 'them'. By reverting back to inconsiderate behaviour, the child can test out his or her new schema to see how strong it really is. The danger for staff is that they can feel that the new strategy is not working and they too revert to their previous ways of handling the inconsiderate behaviour!

REFLECT ON YOUR OWN PRACTICE

Are there any children you work with who are likely to hear more negative messages than positive ones during a session? Consider carrying out a tally chart and noting how many negatives to positives a child is hearing over a session. Changing the balance can change a child's view of him or herself.

Understanding that adults develop schemas about children

As well as children developing schemas about their behaviour, adults guiding children's behaviour also develop schemas or expectations about children's behaviour. Once we believe that a child is 'difficult' or 'is bound to be aggressive', this can shape our behaviour towards him or her. Research shows that when adults have positive and strong expectations of children, they are likely to mirrored by the child.

Taking a pro-active approach to guiding children's behaviour

While it is important to understand how children learn about behaviour and how certain behaviours are reinforced, we also need to have some practical ideas as to how to guide children's behaviour. The key here is to take a pro-active approach and aim to prevent children from learning inconsiderate behaviour. A good starting point when taking a pro-active approach is to stand back and consider what is happening and why.

Observing children

In many cases, observation of a child's behaviour will provide a good understanding of what is happening and why. It is also likely to provide some clues as to how best to support the child. Observations can also provide us with a way of seeing the effectiveness of any strategies that have been put into place.

There is no one standard way of observing children. Different types of observation simply provide different types of information. This means that you need to start by thinking about the information that you need. In some cases, an informal observation may suffice, as by simply spending time closely watching a child, you learn more about the child's needs. The questions below may help to focus your thoughts when observing a child.

- How well does the child appear?
- Does the child appear to be seeking adult attention?
- Are adults unwittingly reinforcing unwanted behaviours, e.g. giving attention for unwanted behaviour?
- How does the child respond to adults and other children?
- Are there any children in whom the child appears particularly interested?
- What activities and equipment does the child appear interested in?
- Are there any areas of the child's development that appear to be delayed?
- Is the structure and routine of the setting causing periods of inactivity for children?

The types of observation methods have been described in Chapter 4, page 40 and include event samples, target child observations. Once observations have been carried out, it is essential that staff and perhaps parents consider what information has been gathered. Settings that are good at guiding and modifying children's behaviour are able to be objective and analytical about the way in which staff are meeting children's needs as well as focusing on the child themselves.

Observations may reveal that part of the difficulty lies in the way the child is responding to the curriculum, routine or environment. This means that you will need to consider how best to change these elements in order to meet the child's needs. This can be hard as it requires being objective, but can provide immediate answers and therefore strategies. Some behaviours such as wandering, lack of concentration, spoiling other children's play can result from a child being either over stimulated or under stimulated.

- What play activities or resources engage and interest the child and are these available for them?
- Are the activities suitable for the child's stage of development?
- Are the activities enjoyable and achievable for the child?
- Is the length of an activity 'fixed' or can a child finish when he or she has lost interest?
- Are the activities and equipment accessible and sufficient?
- Are there periods in the routine when children are expected to wait?
- Does the child need frequent changes of activities or resources and if so, does this happen?
- Does the child need a strong routine in order to feel secure and if so, does the child need reminding of the routine?
- How can the layout be changed? e.g. if children are running, can furniture be moved?
- Does the child need quiet areas if he or she is sensitive to noise and over excitement?

Giving children clear guidance

Another pro-active approach to supporting children's behaviour is to give them clear guidance. Children may need to be reminded or told what they should do before they start an activity. This should be done in a positive way, for example, 'Can you remember where the apron goes when you have finished painting?'.

Guidance needs to be given in ways in which the child can understand and process. For some children, guidance needs to be given in small pieces, as too much information at the same time is hard for them to process. With children who find it hard to process the spoken word, visual guidance might be helpful, i.e. actually showing the child where the apron goes. Where possible, reasons for the guidance should be clearly explained: 'If you put the apron away, other children will find it easily'.

Giving children feedback

Feedback helps children to learn which aspects of their behaviour are appropriate. Just praising children can make them believe that good behaviour is about pleasing adults. A pro-active approach is therefore to give children plenty of feedback about what they are doing and why it is important; 'You waited for Harry to finish his turn on the slide. That was good because he could get up safely'.

Supervision and attention

A pro-active approach may mean changing the way in which staff are deployed in a setting. Time spent reacting to an unwanted behaviour is better spent preventing the unwanted behaviour from occurring in the first place. It is not unknown in settings for staff to be on the look out and 'waiting' for the first incident to occur, when this time would be better used by engaging the child directly. Consider monitoring the time that is being spent on reacting to behaviours and consider instead providing the chid with the same amount of adult time but in a positive context.

- What level of support does the child need and is this being received?
- Does the child need an adult to help him or her play alongside or with other children?
- What situations are likely to cause the child to show unwanted behaviour and are staff actively looking to guide the child?
- Are staff reacting to incidents rather than looking for ways of distracting the child or diffusing a situation before it can build up?
- How are children gaining adult attention and time?

Change the elements of a situation

Taking a pro-active approach can change patterns of behaviour. Being pro-active means changing elements of a situation so that the child cannot use his or her normal responses. For example, a child in a nursery always tries to climb onto the table at lunchtime. Usually the staff react to this by taking the child off the table and telling her not to do this again. A pro-active approach would be to set out a picnic rug outdoors. The child no longer has a table on which to climb and staff can give the child a plate of food to carry outside.

Specific challenging behaviours

Biting, pinching and hair pulling

These behaviours are common, particularly with children whose language is limited or delayed. Sometimes they begin as exploratory behaviours with children just enjoying the feeling of using their senses. They can also sometimes be a child's way of showing frustration or claiming possession of an object and can give children a sense of power. Unfortunately, the sensory element means that children can gain pleasure from the act itself. This means that they can quickly become a habit as the child is getting instant reinforcement. Significant adult attention can also create situations where children bite, pinch or pull hair in order to get an adult to react to them quickly.

At the time of an incident

Keep calm! Over reaction is likely to teach the child to use these behaviours as a way of getting immediate adult attention. Consider avoiding direct eye contact with the child and focus your attention on the victim. This is not what the child will necessarily be expecting and so avoids future situations where the child acts in this way in order to get immediate adult attention. If you feel that the child poses an immediate threat to the other children, either remain with the child or take him or her over to another place where he or she can play quietly. Avoid referring to or talking about the incident.

Preventing another incident

It is important that these behaviours do not develop into habits. The problem is that many children will quickly want to bite or pinch again, having had strong sensory and other reinforcements. This may mean playing alongside the child until the end of the session so that the child is getting plenty of adult attention, without needing to bite or pinch again. During this time, the child should be praised and given rewards for any wanted behaviour that he or she shows. Once the session has finished, it will be important to talk to the child's parents as the child may try again at home. Over the next few days, staff will need to remember that the urge to bite or pinch is likely to remain strong and so good supervision and plenty of positive attention is essential.

SEEING THEORY IN PRACTICE

Are these behaviours originating because a child is finding it hard to communicate his or her needs? If this is the case, working on ways of helping the child to express him or herself will be essential. It is also important to build choices into activities and routines so that children are not left feeling powerless and potentially frustrated.

Disrupting others' play and work

The reasons why some children deliberately appear to sabotage other children's work and play are complex. Discovering the reason behind such behaviour is essential as the answer to how to handle the behaviour will be there. In terms of immediate reaction, avoid confrontation and avoid being negative. Distraction can be a useful tool here, especially where a child is not really aware of the way in which he or she is causing others distress. Where children are able to reason,

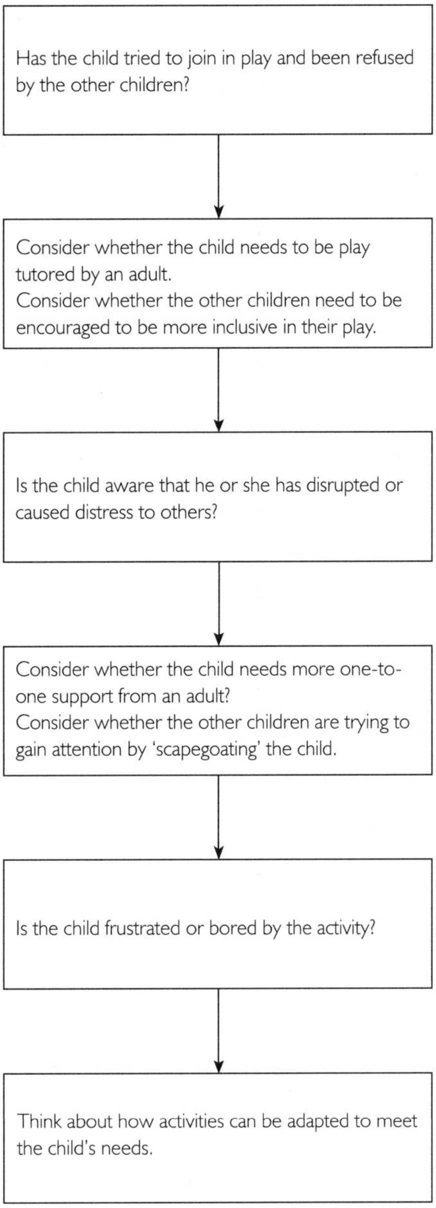

Disrupting others' play and work.

explain how the child can change his or her behaviour rather than tell the child what he or she should not be doing.

Snatching, not taking turns and not sharing

These types of behaviour are often linked to children's social and cognitive development. Some children have great difficulty in waiting for their needs to be met and are therefore extremely impulsive. A child may see another object and try to take it with little understanding of the other child's feelings or rights.

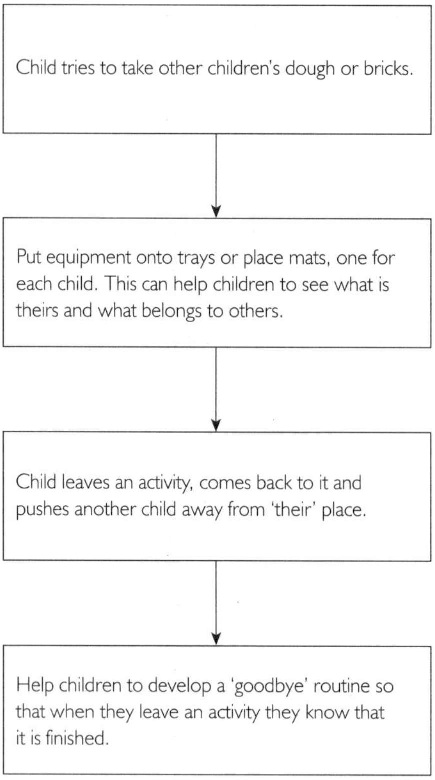

Snatching, not taking turns and not sharing.

Children who are at this stage of development will need close supervision and may respond to play tutoring. Some children will also respond well to clear guidance and feedback.

Supporting children's emotional and social development

In Chapter 8, we looked at the importance of how we work with children. The themes of self-esteem and empowerment were considered. Children also have a basic emotional need to be loved and accepted by others. This forms the basis of social interaction. There are many reasons why some children find it hard to socialise with others or to gain acceptance. Helping to support and integrate these children is essential, as children gain developmentally from being in each other's company. In addition, there is also evidence to show that being isolated in childhood can lead to depression later on in adult life. It is therefore not sufficient to 'accept' that a child does not appear to have friends.

Links between social development and other areas of development

There is a strong link between children's emotional development, their social development and their ability to show appropriate behaviours. The three are so closely interwoven, that it is hard to consider one without the other. Children who feel secure, have high self-esteem and have a sense of belonging are able to engage appropriately with others, while children who have a deficit will find it harder to show socially accepted behaviours. The starting point for helping many children will therefore lie in making sure that their emotional needs are being met.

Ways of supporting children's social development

Adults have a key role in helping children to socialise and engage with others. We need to start by making sure that we create the optimum conditions for children to socialise.

Creating a feeling of belonging for all children

All children need to feel that they belong in a setting. Creating a good emotional climate for all children is essential if we wish children to interact freely. Young children are not able to choose where they go and the company they are with. Children who find themselves socially isolated are therefore 'trapped' in a setting unless adults take responsibility for creating a pleasant and warm environment.

REFLECT ON YOUR OWN PRACTICE

- Do children know each other's names?
- Are children encouraged to help each other?
- Are opportunities available for children to play in a range of group sizes?
- Do you have a 'group' song?
- Are children encouraged to greet each other?
- Are there opportunities such as parties for children to celebrate together?

Consider the cues that children are picking up

The way we talk to children and acknowledge them will influence how other children relate to them. Some children quickly become labelled by other children based on how they perceive adults relating towards them. A child who is seen as 'naughty' is more likely to be excluded from the play of others, while a child who is frequently positively acknowledged is more likely to be included. The way in which children pick up cues from adults means that sometimes children become scapegoated by other children. They may come and tell us what 'Johnny is doing'.

Withdrawing children from a room to work individually therefore needs to be carefully considered in this context. While children may benefit from individual attention, it is worth considering whether this one-to-one attention can take place within the room, and where possible alongside or involving other children.

THINK IT OVER

Consider the ways in which you are guiding children's behaviour:

- Think about the way activities are structured. Are messages unwittingly being sent out about a child's capability?
- Avoid situations where children are encouraged to 'tell tales' on others.

Be flexible with groupings

Children tend to play with children that they have come to know. Settings that have inflexible groupings can unwittingly create barriers to children knowing and finding out about each other.

THINK IT OVER

Consider how and when you use groups. Make sure that activities are planned that create opportunities for children to come together in different ways.

Avoid disciplining children by splitting them apart from friends

In some situations you may find that children show unwanted behaviour when they are together. Usually behaviour is deemed to be boisterous or aggressive when adults take this decision. Splitting children apart may seem like the obvious answer, but it is worth considering the effects on the child. Are they likely to be able to join in with others' play or will they be socially isolated? To help children, a better approach may be to incorporate others into their play or to distract and engage them in more acceptable and appropriate play.

Create opportunities for group co-operation

The toys, equipment and style of activities can be important in helping children to play. Certain activities such as role play, construction and cooking can foster co-operative or parallel play. It is also important to check that there are sufficient resources, as where materials are scarce, children often become predatory and competitive.

REFLECT ON YOUR OWN PRACTICE

- Think about the activities that are available; will they encourage parallel or co-operative play?
- Use parachute games with children.
- Sing rhymes and action songs so that children feel part of the group.
- Plan parties.
- Play party games, but change the focus so that they are not competitive, e.g. hunt the thimble, one child has to look for it, but the other children help them by telling them if he or she is 'hot' or 'cold'.

Teaching children the skills of play

It can be helpful for children to learn to play at first with an adult. Look for games where children have to take turns or co-operate as part of the enjoyment. Give children feedback as to why they are playing well, for example, 'When you waited for your turn, it made me enjoy the game more'. Introduce other children into any game and where possible gradually take a step back. Thinking about activities that have an 'appeal' factor can also be helpful; planting seeds, cooking and carrying out 'grown up tasks' can be useful.

Helping children to join others' play

Some children need to learn how to join in or approach other children. This is a sensitive area and in the first instance it can be worth modelling how they might do this. When children are playing, join in by at first observing them and then playing alongside them, but not disrupting or taking over their game. Use phrases such as 'May I use this, if you have finished' rather than taking materials. These modelled behaviours are important for children to learn. Quite often children try to 'take over' a game or become aggressive rather than trying quietly to blend in. Children may also need to learn how to positively recognise others ideas and play, for example, 'That's a good idea' or 'Your tower is going to be really big'.

It is also important if we are to encourage children in the group to admit rather than refuse entry to children who want to join in that they see adults doing the same. It is not unusual for a child to come alongside an adult who is already engaged with a child or group and be told 'It's not your turn yet'.

Some settings have successfully adopted a slogan within their setting of 'We all play, we don't turn away' and have reinforced it with all the children. This can help very young children learn to let others play alongside them.

Suggested activities

ACTIVITY 1: HELP TEDDY TO REMEMBER

Puppets and stooges such as a teddy can act as non-confrontational ways of reminding children about the boundaries in the setting.

Aim: To help children remember boundaries and the reasons for them.

Resources: Teddy, puppet or other stooge.

Activity: Tell the children that teddy loves to come to the setting because he loves watching them play. He wants to learn how to play safely, but we will need to tell him how. Can the children remember anything that they should or should not do when playing in the sand? Encourage the children to tell teddy the reasons behind what they are saying.

Possible adaptations:

Encourage children to take teddy to play with them so that they can show teddy how to play safely. Use teddy as the stooge to help children talk about playing safely in a variety of contexts.

ACTIVITY 2: WHO IS IN THE SAME FAMILY AS YOU?

This type of traditional party activity can help children to get to know each other and can create a feeling of belonging.

Aim: To help children socialise with each other in a fun way.

Resources: Cards with pictures of animals, e.g. four dogs, four cats, four ducks.

Activity: Give each child a card with an animal on. Remind the children of the animals and sounds that they can make. Tell the children to walk around the room and see if they can find their family. It is important that this is not a competitive game; competition can create barriers as some children quickly focus on 'winning' rather than on playing and enjoying.

Possible adaptations:

Put children into larger or smaller groups. Play the game so that 'pairs' of animals hunt for the rest of their family; this allows an adult to join up with a child and thus help him or her discreetly. Use sound cues such as film canisters filled with rice. Play a game where children have to whisper their partner's name to find them.

ACTIVITY 3: DEN MAKING

Many children respond well to feeling independent. Den or tent making can encourage children to come together because they have the same focus.

Aim: To help children co-operate and feel part of a group.

Resources: Sheets, boxes and anything else that will lend itself to being used in making a den.

Activity: Show small groups or pairs of children the materials and ask them if they would like to make their own den, play area or 'home'. Lend adult support when required but avoid taking over.

Possible adaptations:

Adults can play alongside children.

ACTIVITY 4: BOUNCE THE BALL

Parachute games can help children feel part of a group as a collective effort is required to make the games work.

Aim: To encourage children to be part of a collective game.

Resources: Small parachute or large circular table cloth, small football.

Activity: With a group of around eight children, take out the parachute or tablecloth. Encourage children to raise and lower it. Give children time to enjoy feeling the breeze on their faces; try lifting and lowering the parachute quickly as well as slowly so that children gain some control. Introduce a ball onto the parachute and encourage the children to send the ball up into the air.

Possible adaptations:

When children are able to gain control of the ball, they can see how long they can keep the ball bouncing without it falling off. There are plenty of other parachute games, for example children can take turns to run in and out from under the parachute.

ACTIVITY 5: TEDDY NEEDS SOME FRIENDS

Teddy or puppets can help children to think about how to join in play with others. This activity can be done with groups of children to help them learn the slogan 'We all play, we don't turn away'.

Aim: To help children learn how to join in a game.

Resources: Teddy, other cuddly toys.

Activity: Tell the child that teddy is not feeling very special today. He wants to join in with his friends. Tell the child that you are going to talk to his friends to find out what is going on. Take out one of teddy's friends. Tell the children that teddy often tries to take over the game and if he doesn't get his own way will spoil the game by pushing someone over. Ask the child to show teddy how to join in a game. At this point you may give suggestions to help the child. Ask the child to talk to teddy's friends to explain to them why it is important to let other children join in.

Possible adaptations:

Encourage the child to use small world people to model how to join in play. Consider using stickers in the setting to remind children that 'We all play, we don't turn away' is important.

ACTIVITY 6: TEDDY'S RICE

This type of non-competitive activity can encourage children to play alongside each other and help children to get to know each other.

Aim: To help children socialise in a non-competitive way.

Resources: Rice, food colouring, tray, plastic bag.

Activity: Colour the rice by putting rice into a plastic bag, add in some drops of red food colouring and shake the bag. Once the rice has been coloured, spread the rice out to dry; it can be dried off quickly in a low temperature oven. Repeat this again with green food colouring. Put the green rice into a tray so that there is plenty for children to hold and feel. Sprinkle some grains of red rice into the tray, enough so that they are easy to see. Ask the children if they can see that there is some red rice in the tray. Leave the tray out so that children can go over at any time and sort out the rice. This will encourage children to drop in and out of the activity. The repetitive nature of the activity allows the children to talk easily to each other.

Possible adaptations:

Encourage two children to help you prepare the rice. Put in several colours of rice. Put in larger objects such as seeds or beans to make it easier for children who will otherwise find it hard to find the rice.

Chapter 12

Supporting children's sensory and physical development

Introduction

Children's sensory and physical development is an important area, although it is easy to take it for granted. Children who have a sensory impairment or whose physical development is atypical will need extra support in order to enjoy experiences and to benefit from the learning environment. Increasingly, research is showing that children's sensory and physical development is linked to their cognition and ability to process information. This chapter looks firstly at ways of supporting children who have a sensory impairment and then goes on to look at ways of promoting children's physical development.

Understanding why sensory development is important

Our brain relies on our senses to bring in information. Children learn about themselves and their world from the sensory information that they receive. Children who have an impairment affecting one or more of their senses will therefore not be receiving a range of information. This can affect the way they think, learn and remember and therefore has an impact on their cognitive development.

As well as sensory information being important to cognition, it is also linked to children's physical development. The feedback and information gained from our senses informs the movements and responses that we make. To lift a cup, for example, requires that we are able to adjust our hand movements according to the visual and tactile information that is sent to the brain. This can mean that a child who has a sensory impairment may also show atypical physical development and will need additional support.

A good starting point is to understand that sensory information sent to the brain helps children to remain alert. This is essential in order for children to concentrate. Children who have difficulty in concentrating often have difficulties in either receiving sensory information or processing it. In terms of supporting children, this means that activities that are multi-sensory are usually more effective in helping children to remain alert and concentrate.

Touch

Most people take their sense of touch for granted, yet for some children, their sense of touch may be over or under developed. As touch provides the brain with a rich source of sensory information that helps the brain to remain alert, this can mean that children may appear to be easily distracted or find it hard to settle.

Children who are over sensitive to touch (tactile defensive)

Some children's tactile receptors can be over sensitive. Touching paint or sand or other sensory activities may make them distressed. These children may refuse to take part in 'messy' activities or wear particular clothes. This is known as tactile defensiveness.

Understanding why some children react in this way is important as it is otherwise too easy to dismiss their fears. It would appear that the brains of children who are tactile defensive are instinctively adopting a protective approach, sometimes dubbed 'flight or fight' response. This is a primitive reaction designed to keep us safe, for example, we automatically remove our hands from flames or something that we are unsure of. While we all retain the protective instinct, most of us have also gained the ability to override this instinct in order to use our sense of touch to explore objects in our world and to discriminate between things. Given the choice of two peaches to eat, we may touch them both and then choose the softest.

Children who cannot use their sense of touch effectively are therefore missing out because they are not learning about the properties of materials and gaining the ability to discriminate and notice similarities and differences.

Supporting children who are tactile defensive

To help children who are tactile defensive we need to look for ways of helping the body suppress its instinctive desire to withdraw the hand. Firm touches and pressure are usually more successful in doing this. A child may become very distressed if asked to gently touch sand, but may respond if asked to clutch and grasp wet sand firmly. Confidence and support are also an important part of working with children. Adults must understand their fears and build their confidence gradually.

The following ideas are suggestions only and if you are working with a child who is tactile defensive, you may also wish to seek further ideas from your local SEN advisory team.

STRATEGIES FOR SUPPORTING CHILDREN WHO ARE TACTILE DEFENSIVE

- Do not dismiss children's fears.
- Do not force children's hands into things; this can make them feel panicky.
- Avoid making an 'issue' out of their reluctance to handle things; some children can then learn to use this as an attention seeking device.
- Ask parents about materials that the child enjoys at home.
- Choose activities and games that encourage children to touch large scale things with pressure, e.g. bouncing on a trampoline, trampling on wet sand, wearing wellington boots, wringing water out of fabric.
- Look for materials that are firm for children to explore, e.g. dried beans, marbles.
- Encourage firm movements using tools, e.g. cutting dough with knives, printing into wet sand with forks, drawing with sticks.

  Consider putting sand or dough into a plastic bag so children can play with it through the plastic.
- Introduce more tactile materials such as cornflour and water only as children become more confident.
- Model language so that children can learn to express what they are feeling.
- Look for ways of helping children to remain in control, e.g. they can wipe their hands on a towel any time when playing in sand. The knowledge that they can do this can help children to gain confidence.

Children who under react to touch

Some children find it hard to remain alert and are easily distracted because they are not reacting sufficiently to the sensory information provided by their tactile receptors. They may constantly fiddle, touch and feel objects around them and may find it hard to keep their hands to themselves. Some children may also put things into their mouths beyond the age that might be expected; at around two years, most children use their hands increasingly rather than their mouths to explore objects. It is thought that these children are under reacting to touch and that they are effectively 'boosting' the amount of sensory information by constantly touching and using their mouths.

Supporting children who under react to touch

There is a real danger that children who under react to touch are labelled as being 'naughty' or 'difficult'. Understanding that they find it hard not to boost their sensory input is therefore very important for everyone working with children. It means that you will need to increase the sensory level in activities and look for ways of helping them to gain the stimulation that they seek in more positive ways.

STRATEGIES FOR SUPPORTING CHILDREN WHO UNDER REACT TO TOUCH

- Provide daily sensory activities.
- Build upon children's interests and deliver the curriculum in ways that appeal to them, e.g. if a child plays well in the water tray, you may play a 'roll the dice' game where a child fills up a bucket of water by putting in the number of scoops shown on the dice.
- Engage individual children by talking to them, showing them things and giving them things to hold; left to their own devices, these children will find it hard not to touch others and objects around them. They may also put objects into their mouths.
- During quiet times, such as story time, give the child something to hold and explore, e.g. a piece of dough, a shell or a ribbon. This means that he or she can 'legitimately' fiddle.
- Do not take fiddling as a sign that a child is not listening; many adults doodle when on the telephone.

CASE STUDY

Marvin is four years old and seems to be a constant fiddler. He finds it hard to sit still and constantly prods, pokes or pinches objects and other children. The staff at the nursery have worked hard at positively reinforcing 'wanted' behaviour, but still notice that he finds it hard to stay focused on any single activity. After attending a training course, one of the staff decided to try to increase the amount of sensory stimulation in activities. She noted that Marvin responded well and that if he had a piece of dough in his hand, he would concentrate for longer periods.

1. Why might the dough help Marvin to concentrate?
2. Suggest three sensory activities that might help Marvin to concentrate.

SEEING THEORY IN PRACTICE

The following are examples of tactile activities:

- **Gloop**: Mix cornflour with water to form a sticky paste that can flow.
- **Sand:** Wet or dry sand can be used with children. Put sand into small trays so that children can play with it by themselves.
- **Water:** Use warm water as well as cold water. Add in food colouring, glitter or ice cubes for a change.
- **Cold cooked spaghetti:** Cooked pasta such as spaghetti can help children to explore. Consider colouring the spaghetti. (This is not suitable for children with Coeliac's disease.)
- **Dry coloured rice:** Add a few drops of food colouring to dry rice and use this to help children make marks and scoop.
- **Brushes:** A selection of brushes, e.g. paint brushes and make-up brushes, can be put out for children to explore. Children can stroke their hands with them or use them to brush other materials such as sand, water or rice.

Vision

Vision is an important source of information for the brain and there are many reasons why children may have an impairment. It is important that practitioners understand and look for children who are not fully seeing, as this can affect their hand-eye co-ordination and, later in their school years, their ability to learn to read and write. Early identification that children are not fully seeing can make significant differences to children's learning and socialisation.

Indicators that a child may have a visual impairment

- Reluctance to look at objects or shows no interest in things that other children are doing.
- Frowns in order to focus.
- Moves whole head to look at objects.
- Complains of headaches.
- Draws and paints very close to the paper.
- Shows little interest in watching television, videos or using computers.
- Rubs eyes or has eyes that are often red.
- Has frequent accidents caused by bumping into others or falls over objects.
- Has poor spatial awareness.
- Avoids tasks or becomes frustrated with tasks requiring hand-eye co-ordination.
- Is slower to react and notice what others are doing.
- Easily distracted and becomes tired and loses concentration more quickly than other children.

Visual discrimination

Being able to notice similarities and differences is an important skill. The brain must use the visual information being given. Visual discrimination is part of the process of learning to read. While some children readily look at objects and inspect them closely, other children need to gain the skills of doing so. Activities to help children's visual discrimination also build up their hand-eye co-ordination. Children will benefit more fully if adults also model language so that children can connect what they are seeing with words.

Early years practitioners should provide opportunities for children to practise visual discrimination skills

STRATEGIES TO HELP CHILDREN'S VISUAL DISCRIMINATION

- Put out buttons for children to sort. Which one is their favourite?
- Use magnifying glasses to allow children to inspect objects in more detail, e.g. shells.
- Mix up objects and see if children can separate them, e.g. oranges and satsumas.

Supporting children's physical development

There are many reasons why a child's physical development may be atypical, and we have already seen that there is a significant link between children's sensory skills and their movements. While it is not possible or desirable to 'fast track' children's development, we may be able to help children by building on their existing skills and stimulating them to make particular movements. Building children's confidence in particular is essential as many children quickly lose interest in activities that they do not enjoy or find frustrating. There are many components in physical development including balance, gross motor skills and fine motor skills. Co-ordinated movements require sensory and physical integration.

Before looking at some of the component parts of physical development, it is worth noting that children whose physical development is atypical may be unwittingly discriminated against. Other children may not wait for them to 'catch up' when playing games, or adults may repeatedly reward children who are first to fasten up their coats or move to the next activity. As many games and activities require increasing levels of physical skill, this means that children can quickly lose confidence and also lose out on friendships. Being aware of the way in which physical skills are often 'prized' in settings and putting into place support for children is therefore an essential part of putting 'inclusion' into practice.

Balance and spatial awareness

Children's sense of balance is determined by movement receptors in the inner ear and in their muscles, and works in combination with their vision. Children also need to have adequate muscle tone, as to remain balanced requires tiny shifts in weight-bearing positions. Spatial awareness is about understanding where you are in relation to your environment. A good sense of spatial awareness prevents you from bumping into other objects. The combination of information from movement receptors and vision is used by the brain to develop a feeling of where you are. The more experiences children have of moving, the more easily the brain learns to process the information and make necessary adjustments.

REFLECT ON YOUR OWN PRACTICE

Children who require mobility aids need to experience the world from different heights and angles as otherwise they will find it hard to develop the same level of spatial awareness as others. If you look at most children during a day, they may spend time in a variety of positions.

Ask a physiotherapist or occupational therapist about changing the levels for children with mobility needs e.g. lying on the floor or raising a work area so they can look downwards for some of the time.

Helping children to develop a sense of balance and spatial awareness

The starting point if you have concerns over a child's balance or spatial awareness is to talk to the parents. It may be that the child has a visual impairment or that there is an underlying medical condition. Help might also be sought from a physiotherapist if concerns remain. Children who have experience of falling over quickly lose confidence and so the starting point for any activities is enjoyment. Begin by checking that an activity is achievable for a child and then gradually make it more challenging.

THINK IT OVER

Make a list of the equipment and materials that you have available in your setting that would help children to develop a sense of balance and spatial awareness.

Activities to help children develop a sense of balance and spatial awareness

- Pushing a pram or shopping trolley. Can the child stay on the path? Make the path gradually more challenging, e.g. narrower, and introduce bends and curves.
- Obstacle courses.
- Move across different textured surfaces.
- Follow-my-leader type games.
- Trampolining.
- Jumping or stomping on large bubble wrap.
- Stop-and-go type of games, e.g. when you hear a clap you must stop.

Gross motor movements

Gross motor movements refer to whole limb movements such as throwing or kicking a ball. These movements are linked to children's balance and spatial awareness.

Climbing and crawling

Climbing and crawling require balance as well as sequencing and gross motor skills. The sequencing in particular is thought to help children's later acquisition of reading. Look out for children who have passed directly from sitting to walking or who have 'bottom shuffled' or 'rolled'. These children will benefit from climbing and crawling activities.

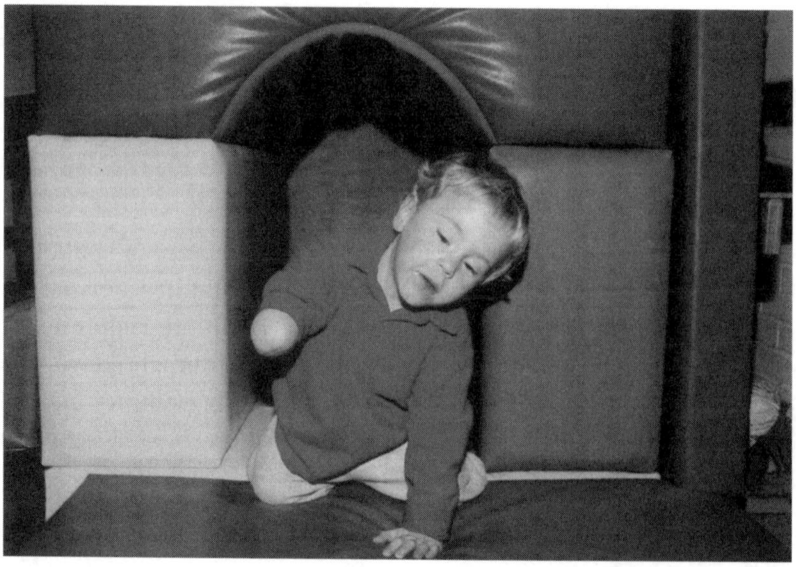

Crawling in a soft play area promotes children's development of spatial awareness

Climbing and crawling activities

- Play tunnels and tents for children to crawl through.
- Pretend games where children crawl as animals.
- Climbing and crawling over cushions and large foam blocks indoors.
- Crawl through and into large cardboard boxes that children can make into dens.

Jumping

Jumping movements strengthen the legs as well as help children to gain spatial awareness. Children who find it hard to keep still often benefit from jumping movements before being expected to stay still. Note that some children appear to be fearless and will jump from heights that are unsafe. It is thought that some of these children are not gaining enough sensory information about where they are in relation to the ground. Increasing the amount of movements these children make is therefore useful, but close supervision will be essential.

Jumping activities

- Trampolining: children who are unsure can sit down on the trampoline while you gently bounce it. This helps them to experience the sensation. They can then move to a crawling position before eventually standing and holding on to a bar.
- Hopscotch.
- Stepping from hoop to hoop.
- Jumping down from a low step; increase the height as children become more confident.
- Jumping on large cushions.
- Jumping on giant bubble wrap.

Throwing and catching

Throwing and catching skills can help gross motor development and also teach children other skills such as judging speed, time and distance. Throwing is easier than catching, as catching requires that a child can judge the speed of the oncoming object and continue to track it while also preparing and moving the hands.

The key to throwing and catching is to go at the child's pace and to build on his or her confidence. Vary the items that children throw and catch. Balloons, 'Beanie Babies' and scarves are often easier for young children to manage. Look too at the size of the object that children are using; large, soft items can be easier to catch than smaller items.

Throwing and catching activities

- Roll the ball: sitting down, children roll a ball to you and then stop it when it comes back to them.
- Balloons in bags: put balloons in bags; this gives them a little more weight and makes them easier to aim and catch.
- Paper balls: encourage the child to scrunch up paper into a ball and throw it.
- Bubbles: blow bubbles into the air; can the children squash them?
- Passing games: pass the ball and gradually increase the distances.

Fine motor movements

Hand movements are referred to as fine manipulative or motor skills. The development of fine manipulative skills is important as babies and children use their hands to explore their world and grasp things within their reach. Gaining control of their hands is also important for children, as many everyday tasks that make children independent of adults require the use of hands, for example, dressing, toileting, pouring drinks, etc. As children get older their fine manipulative skills become increasingly important as they are needed in order to write and manipulate tools such as scissors. Children who have poor fine manipulative control may avoid tasks where control is needed, and this can affect their learning and development.

Hand preference

Hand preference is biologically determined and many three year old children have a clear preference for using one hand for skilled movements. Older children who have not developed a hand preference are more likely to have difficulties with their fine motor movements and also in learning to read and write. While it is important to seek advice from educational psychologists and physiotherapists, the following suggestions might be helpful.

STRATEGIES FOR SUPPORTING HAND PREFERENCE

- Encourage plenty of two-handed activities where one hand is holding an object and the other carries out more skilled movements, e.g. holding a cup in one hand and putting beads into it with the other. Repeat the activities but vary the materials so that some pattern is established.
- Provide plenty of activities where children have to reach diagonally across, e.g. put a glue pot slightly off centre so that children have to reach to dip the spatula in.
- Observe carefully the way in which children use their hands. Are they consistently using the same hand for the same purposes? For example sometimes a child may cut with the right hand but choose to draw with the left. In such cases it is best not to interfere unless the child would be more accurate with the other hand.
- Consider pairing a child who shows slight left-hand preference with an adult who is left handed. Sometimes children awkwardly use their right hand because they are copying a right-handed adult.

Building strength in the hands

Children need to develop strength in their hands so that they can control them more easily. Many everyday tasks require a certain amount of strength, for example, pulling on socks, opening screw top lids or holding onto a rung of a climbing frame. The reasons why some children may not have sufficient strength in their hands can vary, and can include a child's previous reluctance to touch things. Building strength in children's hands must be done through play activities that children enjoy. This will help them to concentrate for longer periods and will also give them confidence. The key to successful activities is to gradually change one feature to make them slightly more challenging. Look out for activities that will encourage children to repeat movements, as in the repetition the muscles in the hand are strengthened.

Activities that increase hand strength

- Put out a range of plastic bottles or containers with screw tops that have something inside that a child might want, e.g. a message or a small toy. Gradually tighten the lids so that more strength is required.
- Look for activities that encourage children to push or pull, e.g. pushing a wheel barrow, pulling a wooden cart with bricks.
- Put sponges out in the water tray. How much water can the child squeeze out?

Using two hands

There are many activities that require children to use two hands at the same time, for example, holding a toothbrush while putting toothpaste onto it or washing a plate with a sponge. Look for activities that are fun and at first do not require a large degree of accuracy. Consider also the size of items, for example, it is harder to glue a sequin onto a piece of paper than a large bead.

Activities that require two hands

- Dressing a large teddy or doll.
- Holding a mixing bowl and stirring the mixture.
- Making a sandcastle.
- Folding paper.
- Using a hole punch to punch holes in paper.
- Winding up a clockwork toy.
- Hanging up clothes using pegs or a coat hanger.

Developing children's hand-eye co-ordination

Using the information from your eyes to inform hand movements is the basis of hand-eye co-ordination. There are a variety of reasons why children may have some delay in this skill, for example children who have a visual impairment that was previously undetected may have some delay in this area. Children will need some simple activities that encourage them to use their hands and eyes together. Begin with large objects and scale down as children become more skilled. As with other activities, children must feel that they are being successful and enjoy what they are doing.

Activities that require hand-eye co-ordination

- Threading beads, buttons or pasta tubes.
- Picking out seeds from a tray of rice.
- Catching bubbles.
- Jigsaw puzzles.
- Pouring drinks from a jug.

Helping children to use scissors

Learning to use scissors is a process. Children need to begin by having enough strength in their hands to manipulate the scissors and then need to be able to open and close them. The first movement that most children make is snipping. To help children gain satisfaction by being able to snip easily it is worth beginning by putting out thin strips of dough or heavy paper. Once the child is able to snip across, you can increase the width of the strips. It is important to remember that children need to be given heavy paper, as thin paper is harder to cut. Most children will need plenty of practice before they are able to cut along lines or cut out circles. Begin by drawing lines onto patties of dough. Children can then cut across the dough. They can also make their own lines to follow. Introduce wavy lines and once children become more accurate you can introduce circles. It is essential that children enjoy using the scissors, as the more they use them, the more skilled they will become. This means looking for materials that children will enjoy cutting and focusing on the feeling of cutting rather than the end product. Alternatives to putting out dough include spaghetti or jelly.

Helping children's pencil grip

Children who are not holding their pencils in a 'lateral pencil grasp' are showing that their hands are not yet developed sufficiently. Many children who are trying to write will actually tense their bodies and their hands in order to gain control; this is reflected in their pencil grasps and their writing position. Instead of tracing and formal writing, they should be offered a range of activities that will strengthen their hands and help them to be more co-ordinated. A classic mistake, therefore, is to continue to make children practise handwriting, when in reality, children will benefit far more from going back a few steps and practising larger movements with their hands.

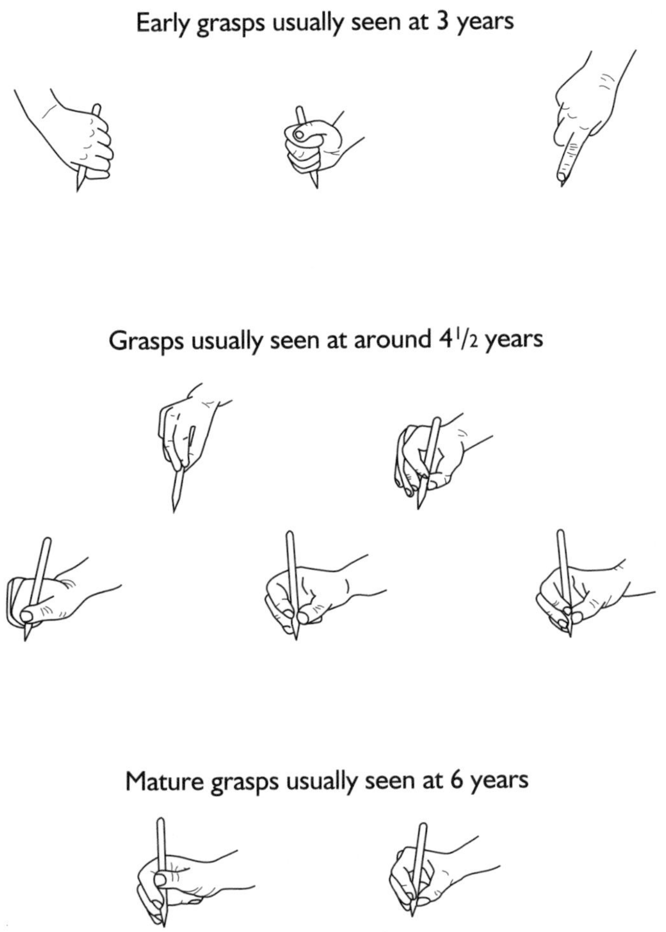

Variety of pencil grasps.

Activities that strengthen children's hands

- Making patterns and shapes in wet sand.
- Painting and chalking on a large scale.
- Drawing shapes and patterns in gloop.
- Writing on a large white board with a marker.
- Finger painting.
- Making marks and movements with fingers in shaving foam.

Suggested activities

ACTIVITY 1: OBSTACLE COURSE

Obstacle courses help children to plan their movements as well as providing them with particular movements. Obstacle courses can be adapted in terms of complexity and so are very versatile.

Aim: To develop children's balance, perceptual skills and 'stomping' movements.

Resources: Plastic hoops, chalk, a teddy.

Activity: This obstacle course can be done outdoors. Being outdoors can help children feel a sense of freedom.

Draw parallel lines with chalk onto the ground; these act as pathways for children to walk or run along. Lines can be made wide or narrow depending on the level of skill of the children. The pathways are broken from time to time with hoops that the children have to 'stride into'.

Begin by showing children the obstacle course; you might consider going along it with the teddy to show children what to do. Encourage children to go round the obstacle course; perhaps the teddy can urge them on!

Allow children to repeat the course as each practice will develop fluency of their movements. Adjust the course if necessary to change the level of skill required.

Possible adaptations:

Make obstacle courses indoors and play music with a strong beat to encourage strong movements. Change the difficulty of the obstacle course by making the pathways more curved. Add in equipment that will encourage children to climb, such as cushions or beams.

ACTIVITY 2: PAINTING WALL

Creating a painting wall can help in developing children's writing skills.

Aims: To develop children's grasp and arm movements using a sensory medium. This activity will also help children to see a range of colours while helping with early letter formation.

Resources: Plastic sheeting, lining paper, masking tape, small tray, large paintbrushes, rollers, red, blue, yellow and white ready-mixed paint.

Activity: Begin by taping the sheets of plastic to a wall. This can be outdoors or indoors. Tape a long strip of lining paper to the plastic. Put a squirt of each of the paint colours onto a small tray and provide large paintbrushes. Ask the children to take a brush, dip it into some paint and make circles. As children keep dipping into other colour paints, they will mix colours.

Possible adaptations:

Encourage children to make other marks, such as wavy lines, vertical strokes from top to bottom. Repeat the activity using crayons, markers and felt tips. Encourage children to produce large paintings. Use rollers instead of paint brushes.

ACTIVITY 3: CUTTING DOUGH WITH SCISSORS

This sensory activity can be helpful for children who are tactile defensive as the cutting action is a 'firm' movement. This activity is especially useful for developing scissor skills and building the muscles in the hand. It works well because it does not focus children on an 'end product' and so children who normally avoid using scissors are more likely to spend time enjoying the feeling of cutting.

Aim: To develop children's grasp and arm movements using a sensory medium.

Resources: Left- and right-handed safety scissors, dough (a stretchy dough can be made by adding coloured water to self raising flour and leaving it for a few hours).

Activity: Put out the dough and scissors on the table. Roll the dough into sausage shapes and begin to cut the dough. Most children will model the dough in the same way that they see adults do. Use this opportunity to talk and listen to children. What are they pretending that they are cutting?

Possible adaptations:

Use different types of dough and adjust the stiffness of the dough. Provide plasticine for a more rigid feel. Provide cold cooked spaghetti for children to cut. Make patties and draw a line on them – can children cut along the line?

ACTIVITY 4: SQUEEZE AWAY THE CHALK LINES

This activity helps strengthen children's hands and also encourages them to make marks. It is a fun outdoor activity that does not have an end product.

Aim: To develop children's grasp, hand-eye co-ordination and also give them opportunities to make large marks.

Resources: Washing-up liquid bottle or container with a spray nozzle filled with water, jumbo chalks.

Activity: With the jumbo chalk encourage a child to draw a line onto a wall. Show the children how they can squeeze water out of the bottle and aim it at the chalk line. Encourage children to make their own marks with the chalk and then erase them with water.

Possible adaptations:

Use paintbrushes so that children paint with water and erase the line.

ACTIVITY 5: THREAD AND CATCH THE KEYS

This activity helps children to track objects and also helps their hand-eye co-ordination. This activity can be played with more than one child.

Aims: To develop children's hand-eye co-ordination and also help them to track objects as they move.

Resources: Bunch of keys or other item that can be threaded and then moved along a long piece of string or cord, length of string or cord approximately 1– 2 m.

Activity: One end of the string or cord needs to be tied to a pole or attached to a wall at about 30 cm from the floor. The other end of the string is given to the child. Can he or she thread the bunch of keys onto it and then watch it as it travels along the string? As the child lowers or raises the string, the keys will move backwards or forwards.

Possible adaptations:

Look for other objects that can be threaded onto the cord or string. Play a game where one child threads the object and the other child has to try and catch it before it reaches the end of the string.

ACTIVITY 6: FLYING BIRDS

This activity helps children to track objects and also helps their hand-eye co-ordination. It encourages spatial awareness and gross motor movement.

Aims: To develop children's hand-eye co-ordination and also help them to track objects as they move. This activity also develops children's whole arm movements and spatial awareness.

Resources: Music for children to move to, a selection of square scarves.

Activity: Play the music and show children how to make their square scarf gently rise and fall. They might be able to do this in time with the music. Play a game with the children where they imagine that the scarf is a bird. Can they make their 'bird' fly up high, but also swoop down and around?

Possible adaptations:

Play a game where one child tries to catch another child's bird. Encourage children to throw the scarves. Play games where you wear a tail (the scarf) and children have to run behind you and take the tail from you. Encourage children to make anti-clockwise and vertical downward movements with scarves. This will help them to get a feeling for letter shapes.

Part 3

Meeting the needs of children with specific impairments or conditions

This part of the book is designed to give you some background information about the type of specific needs that some children may have. It has been written in response to many practitioners' requests to have information about how they might meet the needs of children with particular impairments or conditions. It has not been written with diagnosis in mind. Concerns about children's development must be raised with parents so that a professional referral and subsequent diagnosis can be made.

Any written information about impairments and conditions can only be generalised, as each child is very much an individual and two children with the same 'diagnosis' are likely to have very different responses, likes and dislikes. The focus of this part is therefore to help you consider how best to work with parents and to flag up some of the questions that you will need to focus on in the setting to meet the child's needs.

- **Name of the impairment or condition:** This section tells you about the impairment or condition.
- **Incidence and diagnosis:** This section gives you a backdrop to the condition or impairment.
- **Health and development**: This section gives you a summary of how the condition or impairment usually affects children. Note that this is a generalised summary. You will need to talk further with parents.
- **Information that we may need from parents**: These questions should help you to find out from parents how best to meet the child's needs.
- **Getting it right for the child**: This is a summary of practical information that settings might find useful when thinking about how best to meet the child's needs.
- **Key questions**: Use these questions as a checklist to help you think about how your setting will adapt its practice to meet the child's needs.
- **Some day-to-day questions**: Use these questions as a regular checklist and add to this list to help you remember the everyday needs of this child.
- **Contact**: This gives you the name, address and website of a leading support group. You should also ask parents if there is a local group which can also provide you with further information.

Chapter 13

Summary of conditions and impairments in children

Asthma

Asthma is a condition that affects breathing. During an asthma attack, the airways of the lungs tighten and become inflamed. This causes excess mucus to be produced by the body which again has the effect of narrowing the airways. While most asthma attacks leave a child struggling for breath and feeling frightened, occasionally attacks can be fatal which means that asthma should be taken seriously.

Incidence and diagnosis

According to the National Asthma Campaign, asthma in children is on the increase; one in seven children is currently diagnosed with the condition.

Health and development

Asthma does not cause any learning difficulties in children, although children can lose confidence in their own abilities as a result of being made to feel 'different'.

Information that we may need from parents

- What type of medication does your child have?
- Are there any known triggers? (See table below.)
- How do you manage the child's asthma at home?

Getting it right for the child

It is essential that inhalers for children are accessible and given promptly. Children are often encouraged to 'take control' from an early age for this condition. Feeling in control can actually lessen the chances of a child having a strong attack, as when children panic, their airways are more likely to become tense. This means that staff need to listen to children when they say that they are breathless or need their inhalers.

There are different types of medication and it is useful if staff understand that they work in different ways:

- Relievers – these are inhalers that contain fast acting drugs that quickly open the airways. They are usually in blue containers. Relievers can be life saving and so they should always be accessible and staff (and the child) should know where they are at all times.
- Preventers – these inhalers contain drugs that help the airways to become less sensitive to potential triggers. They are often in brown or white containers and most children will take these at home.

As well as the 'classic' type of inhaler, with a mouthpiece, there are also devices called spacers or volumatics which send out the drug as a mist for children to inhale. Spacers are often used with children under five years.

Managing an asthma attack

At the first signs that a child is becoming breathless, action needs to be taken to prevent a serious attack:

- Remain calm and reassuring, but react quickly.
- Give the child their reliever inhaler; this should be named and already near the child.
- Encourage the child to find a comfortable position.
- Talk to the child while monitoring the effect of the inhaler.
- If the inhaler is having no effect after 5 to 10 minutes, call 999.

Once the attack has finished, the child may still remain shaken and frightened. It is important to reassure the child and acknowledge his or her feelings. Praise the child for the way in which he or she coped. Remember to record the attack and pass this information onto parents at the end of the session.

Removing triggers in the environment

To help children, we should be aware of the triggers in the environment and take steps to remove or limit them.

Triggers	Preventative action
Dust mite – thrives in dusty environments	Remove cushions with feathers in them. Put soft toys in the freezer for 6 hours before washing at 60°C. Make sure the setting is regularly dusted. Wash curtains regularly – if possible install blinds.
Viral infections – coughs and colds	Keep rooms well ventilated. Reinforce good personal hygiene routines. Provide disposable tissues and check that children's noses do not need blowing.
Air pollutants	Avoid aerosol spray products while children are present. Ask parents whether any chemicals act as triggers. Avoid air fresheners. Reinforce a no smoking policy in the setting at all times.
Pollen	Keep windows closed during hay fever peak times if setting is near fields or gardens. Check with parents if there are any flowers or grasses that can trigger an attack and avoid bringing them into the setting.
Fur	Keep cats, dogs and other animals away from the setting if a child is allergic to fur.
Mould	Have any damp walls or areas within the setting treated or sealed.
Emotion	Make sure that children are reassured if there are likely to be changes to routines. Create a calm atmosphere within the setting. Use a key worker system so that children feel secure.

Finally, it is important to understand that asthma should not affect a child's learning or ability to participate. Physical activities can be planned that have 'rests' in them, for example, 'It's time for the tricycles to come back to the garage to be checked' or 'Let's see if we can now walk really slowly'.

Key questions

- Have parents brought in a spare 'reliever' inhaler that is named?
- Do staff understand that the child has asthma?
- Does everyone know what to do if the child has an attack?
- Are there any triggers such as cuddly toys, feathers or chemicals in the environment?

Some day-to-day questions

- How well is the child today?
- Is the child's inhaler accessible?
- What is the expiry date of the inhaler?
- Are activities planned to allow the child to pace him or herself?
- Is there good ventilation in the setting?
- Are the child's records accessible and emergency contact details up to date?

Contact

National Asthma Campaign
Providence House
Providence Place
London N1 ONT
www.asthma.org.uk

Attention Deficit Hyperactivity Disorder

Attention Deficit Hyperactivity Disorder also referred to as Hyperkinetic Disorder was first recognised 100 years ago, but has only recently been more widely accepted by the medical community. Children with this disorder find it difficult to sit and concentrate and have unusually high levels of activity and impulsivity. While research is still ongoing into this disorder, many researchers believe that the high levels of activity are a result of the brain not processing sensory information in an effective way.

Incidence and diagnosis

It is estimated that between 3 and 5 per cent of children and adolescents have this condition, but accurate figures are hard to gauge. Research into the causes of this disorder are still ongoing, but there appears to be more than one cause or trigger, including intolerance to foods, brain damage and also genetic susceptibility.

Diagnosis in young children is not easy as many children show impulsive behaviours and high levels of activity. Children with AD/HD will show persistent and sustained levels of activity and impulsivity over time. A child who is perfectly fine in one setting but not in another is likely to have behavioural difficulties rather than AD/HD.

Treatment once a diagnosis is made is variable and reflects the different thoughts about the possible causes of AD/HD. This means that some children may be following additive free diets while others may be given drug therapy such as Ritalin. Behavioural modification programmes are also offered. Many young children with AD/HD appear to outgrow the condition in later childhood.

Health and development

Concentration

Children appear to lack concentration and may run around and find it hard to settle to one activity. This prevents them from learning skills such as fine motor skills.

Social development

The difficulty in concentrating means that children may not be long enough in one place to join in and play a game. Other children can also be fearful of children who show apparently 'disruptive' behaviour. If the child is often being 'reprimanded' other children may decide to tell tales and scapegoat the child.

Emotional development

There is a danger that children with AD/HD can become depressed and have low self-esteem. They may see that their parents and other adults become frustrated with their behaviour and they may confuse this with not being liked or loved.

Information that we may need from parents

Many parents can feel worn out by their children and frustrated by professionals who often imply that this disorder has its roots in the parenting of the child. In young children, it is unlikely that a firm diagnosis has been made, and so parents are also likely to be working hard to get some support for their child. This means that working with parents and building a good relationship with them is very important. Parents need to feel that we are taking their needs and those of their child seriously. Positive parenting and consistent attitudes between home and setting will not in itself eliminate AD/HD, but may help significantly. While the causes of AD/HD are uncertain, it can be hard for parents to decide what approach to take with their children. It is important that we respect that there is more than one view of AD/HD and work with the parents.

If parents have not referred their child for a hearing and vision test, it may be useful to suggest that they do so, as a child who is not seeing or hearing well might also show lack of concentration and aggressive frustrated behaviours.

Getting it right for the child

There is no single approach or way of helping children with AD/HD, although it is essential that staff remain positive and look for ways of acknowledging wanted behaviour. Many practitioners find that multi-sensory activities can help young children and that observing the child carefully can provide clues as to activities that might interest and 'hold' him or her.

The following guidelines have been found to be helpful, although it is also important to understand that strategies that might be effective for one child may not work so well with another. Other professionals who work in your local area, such as the educational psychologist, may also provide you with other strategies:

- Create calm atmospheres and react calmly to the child.
- Look for positive moments with the child and make sure that these are shared with the parents.
- Praise and acknowledge the child's good behaviour as much as possible.
- Keep to strong routines and structures within the setting.
- Avoid situations where the child is 'waiting'; being still will be extremely difficult for them.
- Make sure that activities are open ended and that a child can 'leave' them if his or her concentration wanes.
- Avoid confrontations and look for ways of making tasks such as tidying into games.
- Avoid long explanations; get your message across simply.
- Provide adult initiated activities for the child, but make sure that the child is given choices and responsibilities within them.
- Remind children of any boundaries before they begin an activity.
- Look for ways of absorbing and engaging the child, e.g. short 'jobs' such as putting out beakers, helping with sorting books can be effective.
- Use visual cues and props rather than relying on 'telling' the child.
- Provide frequent feedback as to how well the child is doing.
- Consider the use of stickers and other ways of visually giving children positive feedback.
- Consider looking at changing the layout to provide areas where the child is less likely to be distracted.

Key questions

- Who will work as the child's key worker?
- How will behaviour be managed to avoid stigmatising the child?
- How will positive aspects of the child's behaviour be identified and celebrated?

- How can the routine of the setting be adapted to ensure that the child is supervised and is engaged?

Some day-to-day questions

- What sensory activities have been planned for the child?
- How well is the child today?
- Are there any changes to the routine today? How will these be managed?
- What has the child achieved today that can be celebrated with the parents?

Contact

Hyperactive Children's Support Group
71 Whyke Lane
Chichester PO19 7PD
www.hacsg.org.uk

Autistic spectrum disorder (autism and Asperger's syndrome)

Autism affects children's ability to form relationships and communicate effectively with those around them. The extent to which children are affected can vary enormously. Two forms of autism were identified in the 1940s: Kanner's syndrome and Asperger's syndrome (although it is now recognised that there are many subgroups). The term autistic spectrum disorder (ASD) is used to reflect this wide range, with Asperger's syndrome being included in the spectrum.

Incidence and diagnosis

The incidence of ASD among children is not at present known, but some current estimates suggest that it can affect around nine in every 1000 children. The cause of autistic spectrum disorder is not completely known although there appears to be some genetic disposition with more boys being affected than girls. Diagnosis does not currently take place until a child is at least two years old and often much later, especially if the signs are subtle, as social development can be delayed in children for a variety of reasons. Increased awareness of Asperger's syndrome has in some cases led to adults realising that they have this condition.

Health and development

The extent to which children are affected by ASD varies enormously. This means that you will need to get to know the child and seek information from parents and other professionals who have been involved with the child.

There are three ways in which children are affected by ASD to varying degrees. They are often referred to as the triad of impairments:

- Social interaction.
- Social communication.
- Imagination.

Social interaction

Most children, once they have reached the age of three years are able to play alongside and with other children. They notice the reactions on other's faces and adjust their behaviour accordingly. It is thought that children with autistic spectrum disorders have difficulty in recognising and imagining other's feelings. This means that social interaction is difficult for children with autism. In cases where a child is severely affected, he or she may not be interested in playing with other children at all, while children with Asperger's syndrome may wish to join in, but do not always show appropriate behaviour, for example, they may pinch or hug another child, but not for any particular reason.

Social communication

Language is used for a variety of purposes, but it is also an important tool to communicate with others. Children with autism will find it hard to use language to socialise and are limited in their ability to use non-verbal language such as facial expression and gestures. The amount of language used by children with autistic spectrum disorder varies with some children finding it difficult to communicate at all, while others may have a good vocabulary but talk inappropriately and find it hard to listen and think about what others are saying. Children may for example repeat phrases that they have heard over and over again although they are not being used meaningfully. Many children also have difficulty in expressing their feelings and getting their needs met.

Imagination

The ability to imagine is very significant. It allows us to guess what others may be thinking or feeling. It also allows us to predict what may happen and is connected to our ability to make sense of what is happening to us. Children with autism are limited or unable to think imaginatively. They therefore often show stereotyped and repetitive play and behaviours. They may also play with unusual items such as vacuum cleaners or parts of toys such as just the wheels in a construction set. It also means that they are unable to consider the consequences of their actions, and so safety for themselves and others is a real issue. Limitations of imagination also mean that children who have some social language will often take things literally and so phrases such as 'it's raining cats and dogs' will be taken as such. Changes in routine are also difficult for children with autism as they find it hard to understand and predict what is going to happen for them next.

Information that we may need from parents

- How do they communicate with their child?
- What strategies do they find helpful to manage their child's behaviour?
- What play does their child enjoy?
- Is the child receiving support from the speech and language team in your area?

Getting it right for the child

No two children who have been diagnosed with an autistic spectrum disorder will be the same. This means that your first step is to get to know the child, their strengths as well as areas that are particularly difficult for them. Parents should be helpful in this respect as they will usually have by trial and error found out what works best for their child. Some parents may also be trying out one of the many programmes designed for autistic children, including music therapy, and if so, you will need to find out if the programme needs following in your setting.

A key worker will be essential to give the child some one-to-one attention and also to forge links between the child and other children. Close supervision may also be needed if the child repeatedly shows aggressive or inappropriate behaviour towards others. Safety is a further reason why close supervision is required. Remember that children lack the ability to predict the consequences of their actions. This may include 'escaping' from the setting or running the taps in the washbasins. Staff will need to understand that these types of behaviours are not wilful or deliberate, but a result of this condition. Patience, calm and a sense of humour are very much needed with children who can at times present challenging behaviour.

Changes to routine will also need to be considered and thoughtfully managed; again it may be wise to draw upon parents for advice. In terms of communication, there are a range of strategies that may be useful including the Picture Exchange Communication systems (PECS) and Makaton.

It is also important to encourage the child to play. This can be done in a one-to-one situation with the adult putting in a clear structure. A story with accompanying puppets can help some children to play symbolically.

Key questions

- Who will act as the child's key worker?
- Does everyone within the setting understand that this child will find it hard to socialise and will need to be supported?
- How will the safety of the child be ensured?
- What does the child enjoy doing and how can this be built upon?
- Is there a speech and language programme that can be followed?

Some day-to-day questions

- Are there any changes to routines that may create difficulties for the child?
- Are activities designed to allow the child to interact with another child with close supervision from an adult?

Contact

National Autistic Society, 393 City Road, London EC1V 1NG
www.nas.org.uk

Cerebral palsy

This is a general term to describe disorders that prevent the brain from controlling muscles and movements in the body. There are several causes of cerebral palsy including birth injuries, maternal infection in the first few weeks of a pregnancy, head trauma and genetic disorders. There are three main types of cerebral palsy with some children having a combination of two or more.

- **Spastic cerebral palsy:** This form of cerebral palsy creates stiffness in the muscles which in turn decreases the amount of movement that is available. This is the most common form of cerebral palsy and can affect different areas of the body.
- **Athetoid cerebral palsy:** This form of cerebral palsy creates jerky, irregular movements because muscles rapidly change from tense to floppy. Children will be unable to control these movements. Speech is also affected by this form of cerebral palsy because of difficulty in controlling tongue and breathing movements. There may also be some hearing problems.
- **Ataxic cerebral palsy:** This form of cerebral palsy causes difficulty in maintaining balancing and judging spatial awareness. Hand movements and speech can also be affected, although most children with just this form of cerebral palsy are likely to be mobile.

Incidence and diagnosis

It is thought that one in 400 children have some form of cerebral palsy. Some children will be diagnosed at birth, while others will be diagnosed during their first year as their motor development will not be progressing.

Health and development

The extent to which a child may be affected can vary enormously with some children having only slight indications of cerebral palsy. While children with cerebral palsy may have difficulties with motor co-ordination and speech, it is important not to assume that they will have learning difficulties. The huge variance between children means that it is essential to gain information about the child from parents and also to get to know the child.

Children's physical development will be affected with many children requiring mobility aids such as standing frames, walking aids and wheelchairs. Gross and fine motor control are affected in varying degrees.

Spatial awareness

Some children will be able to see, but find it hard to process the visual information. This results in children having poor spatial awareness and they may appear to be 'clumsy', for example, a child may reach out to grasp a cup, but his or her hand may go slightly to one side causing the cup to fall over.

Touch

Some children's sense of touch is affected. This means that some sensations can be unpleasant or distressing. Close observations of a child's reactions when introducing sensory play materials such as sand or water will be essential.

Communication

Some children's speech is affected and they will usually be seen by speech and language therapists. You will need to find out how to support this work.

Toilet training

Constipation is common among children and toilet training can be delayed or difficult to achieve.

Feeding

Some children can have difficulty in feeding as the muscles in the throat and mouth can be affected. Advice as to how to help with feeding should be sought from parents and/or physiotherapists.

Some children may also have one or more of the following:

- Epilepsy (see also page 211).
- Hearing impairment.
- Visual impairment.

Information that we may need from parents

As no two children will have the same requirements, it is essential to gain as much information as possible from parents. Be ready also to ask parents to show you how they manage any care needs of the child.

- What does your child enjoy doing at home?
- What mobility needs does your child have?
- What care needs does your child have, e.g. toileting and feeding?
- How do you manage these needs at home?
- Is the child receiving any physiotherapy and is there a programme that should be followed?
- Is the child receiving any speech and language support and if so, how can this be supported in the setting?
- Does your child have a hearing or visual impairment?
- Does your child have any medication that needs administering in the setting?
- Are there any professionals who work with your child who we should be in contact with?
- Are laxatives or toilet training strategies used at home?

Getting it right for the child

Cerebral palsy affects children in so many different ways that it is essential to learn as much as possible about the individual child. This information should come from parents and also from other professionals who support the child and their family.

Once information is available, it is essential for everyone to consider how to include the child in the day-to-day activities of the setting. A good deal of flexibility and creativity is often needed and this may include the use of information and communication technology (ICT).

Empowering the child by encouraging him or her to make choices and to be independent is often essential as it is not uncommon for carers to 'take over' and to 'baby' the child. The term 'spastic' is no longer used to describe cerebral palsy. Talking about a 'spastic' child is offensive.

Key questions

- Who will liaise directly with the parents and other professionals?
- Who will act as the child's key worker?
- What resources and equipment do parents and physiotherapists recommend?
- Do members of staff need lifting and handling training?
- Do members of staff need to learn how to feed the child?
- Do staff know how to keep the child physically comfortable?

Some day-to-day questions

- Have activities been planned to meet the needs of this child?
- Are the necessary resources and equipment available?

Contact

SCOPE
6 Market Road
London
N7 9PW

www.scope.org.uk

Coeliac disease

Coeliac disease is a condition affecting digestion. Children with coeliac disease have an intolerance of gluten. Gluten is a protein that is found in cereal grains such as wheat, barley and oats. When gluten is eaten, the body reacts and the small intestine becomes inflamed and the lining is damaged. The inflammation, while causing symptoms such as diarrhoea and vomiting, also prevents the body from absorbing the nutrients in the food such as vitamins, iron and calcium. This can leave the child malnourished, and weight loss usually indicates that the child has the disorder.

Incidence and diagnosis

Coeliac disease was once thought to be rare and detected only in childhood. It is now thought to affect one in 1000 people and adults are increasingly being diagnosed with the condition. Symptoms include weight loss, anaemia, diarrhoea and vomiting. An intestinal biopsy is normally carried out to confirm the condition. Once a diagnosis has been made, gluten has to be excluded from the diet.

Health and development

Once a diagnosis has been made and the child is on a gluten free diet, there should be no effects on the child's health and development, although it is important to ensure that the child feels positive about him or herself.

Information that we may need from parents

- Would you like to bring food in for your child or is there a diet sheet that we can follow?
- Are there any immediate signs that your child has had gluten?
- What would you like us to do if your child inadvertently eats food or dough containing gluten?

Getting it right for the child

Children must be given food that is gluten free. Some parents will prefer the child to bring in food so as to lessen the risk of gluten being inadvertently given. It is also important to supervise children at meal times as other children may offer some of their food containing gluten to the child. As gluten is found in most types of play dough, it will be important to supervise the child when he or she is playing in case the child eats some.

As well as ensuring that the child avoids gluten, it is also important that children are not made to feel different. This may mean altering the foods that are served at snack time so that the child does not have to have different snacks all the time, such as slices of apple instead of a sweet biscuit or rice cakes instead of crackers.

Key questions

- Is everyone in the setting aware that this child has Coeliac's disease? (A photo of the child with a note in the kitchen to remind staff that a child has the condition can be a useful strategy and is often suggested by parents.)
- Does everyone understand the dietary needs of this child?
- Who will act as the child's key worker and liaise with parents regarding food and other requirements?
- Are emergency contact details for the child easily accessible?
- How can the meals and snacks of the setting be altered so that the child's dietary needs can be integrated?

Some day-to-day questions

- Has the child brought in food and snacks?
- Are cooking activities gluten free?
- If dough is being used how will this be supervised?

Contact

Coeliac UK
PO Box 220
High Wycombe
Bucks HP11 2HY
www.coeliac.co.uk

Cystic fibrosis

Cystic fibrosis (CF) is an inherited condition in which abnormally thick mucus is produced by the body. This in turn creates difficulty with lung function and also with digestion. Medical advances have significantly prolonged children's lives over the years, although children still need medical treatment and physiotherapy.

Incidence and diagnosis

Cystic fibrosis is a genetically inherited disease. Children will only have the condition if both of their parents are carriers of the abnormal gene. It is estimated that one in 20 people of northern European ancestry will have the gene. Detection of the condition can occur shortly after birth if the baby's pancreas has already been blocked by mucus, otherwise failure to put on weight, frequent bouts of coughing and vomiting may be noticed in the baby's first year. Confirmation of the condition usually follows a 'sweat test' and possible blood tests.

Health and development

This condition does not affect children's capacity to learn, but repeated absences due to infections and the physical toll that this condition has on children can affect their opportunities to play and learn.

Lung infections

Children with CF are prone to repeated lung infections that can damage the lung and create difficulties in breathing. Daily physiotherapy is used to help loosen the mucus in the lung which the child then coughs up. Young children are also taught to learn to control their breathing so that they can maximise their lung function. As well as regular physiotherapy, children also take antibiotics to fight off infections.

Difficulties with digestion

The abnormally thick mucus that is produced as part of this condition prevents the pancreas from working effectively and the body lacks enzymes that are used to process and break down food. Replacement enzymes are therefore given to children before each meal.

Growth

Many children with CF are under weight and have delayed growth. This is caused by the body's difficulties in absorbing food properly added to the strain of repeated lung infections.

Information that we may need from parents

- What physiotherapy does your child require during the session?
- How would you like this to take place?
- What are the signs in your child that he or she may be unwell?
- What would you like us to do if we suspect that your child is poorly?
- What nutritional requirements does your child have?
- What types of food and snacks does your child enjoy?
- What type of medication does your child have?
- How does your child feel about CF?
- What activities does your child enjoy?

Getting it right for the child

It will be essential for staff to work closely with parents and also to listen to and observe the child. Children may not feel like joining in some activities as they are feeling tired or may want to engage in play that is comforting and repetitive. Early signs that a child is poorly and is fighting an infection must be taken seriously. It will also be important for parents to be aware of the amount of food that the child has had in the day.

Meal and snack times

Making sure that children are gaining sufficient nutrition is essential. All foods provided should be nutrient rich to make sure that the child will gain enough calories, vitamins and protein. It is also important for children to have regular snacks and drinks. Avoiding making the child feel 'different' will be important and so looking for ways for other children to have snacks might need to be considered. Children will also have medication to take before and at meal times. It is essential that a member of staff takes on responsibility for this.

Preventing infections

It will be important to have good hygiene routines in the setting to avoid cross infection. Children will need to be reminded to wash their hands frequently and good ventilation will also be essential. Measures such as those required for children with asthma (see page 181) should also be put into place.

Coughing

One effect of the constant mucus production is a persistent cough. Children are encouraged to spit out the mucus as soon as they are able rather than to swallow it. This means that a ready supply of tissues should be with the child and that adults in the setting understand that the cough is not 'put on'.

Emotional needs

As well as getting the physical care needs right for the child, children will also need to be given emotional security and opportunities to play and develop. While this is a potentially life threatening condition, children still need enough freedom and play in order to develop and fulfil their potential. This means encouraging children to enjoy being outside and joining in physical activity at their own pace. Repeated absences will mean that good settling in and key worker systems need to be put into place. Looking for opportunities for children to keep up friendships, especially when they are absent will be important. Children can send drawings to each other, or the setting can send postcards to the child.

Some children can also be aware that they are growing at a slower rate than other children. This means activities such as measuring each other's height may not be appropriate. Role play can help the child to express their feelings and so it may be helpful to create hospitals and homes in the role play area.

Key questions

- Who will be the child's key worker?
- Who will liaise with parents regarding physiotherapy, amounts of food that the child has had, etc.
- Is everyone in the setting aware of the effects of this condition?
- Where will any medication be stored?
- Who will be responsible for giving the child medication?
- Who will ensure that the child is eating snacks and meals?
- How will the risk of cross infection be managed in the setting?
- Is there a quiet area where the child can nap or have physiotherapy if required?
- Are emergency contact details for the child easily accessible?

Some day-to-day questions

- Has the child brought in his or her medication?
- How well does the child seem?
- Does the child need to rest more today?
- Has the child been eating well?
- Are tissues to hand for the child?

Contact

Cystic Fibrosis Trust
11 London Road
Bromley BR1 1BY
www.cftrust.org.uk

Diabetes mellitus

Diabetes is a condition in which the body is unable to regulate the amount of sugar in the blood stream because the body is either not manufacturing sufficient quantities of a hormone called insulin or the body is not processing the insulin effectively. Symptoms of diabetes include thirst, frequent urination, weight loss, tiredness and irritability. The condition, if left untreated, can be fatal, but this is extremely rare and treatment is highly effective. There are two types of diabetes:

- **Type 1: Insulin dependent diabetes** – this is the type of diabetes that children under 11 years are likely to have. This type of diabetes is partly controlled by regular insulin injections (as the pancreas is not manufacturing any insulin) but can also be controlled by diet and exercise. As children get older, they are encouraged to self-inject and monitor their own blood. This helps them to take responsibility for managing their diabetes.
- **Type 2: Non dependent diabetes –** this type of diabetes is controlled by diet, exercise and sometimes tablets or insulin. It usually occurs in people over 40 years old.

Incidence and diagnosis

Diabetes UK estimates that 1.4 million people have been diagnosed with diabetes, with a further 1 million who do not know that they have the condition. Diabetes in young children is however quite rare. It is thought that around 20,000 children have the condition, although this number is on the increase. Diagnosis is usually made from a urine or blood sample.

Health and development

Diabetes can be properly controlled and should not cause any additional heath problems for children. It should not create any learning difficulties, although children may need emotional support.

Hypoglycaemia

Children with diabetes develop hypoglycaemia when the level of glucose in their blood is too low. This can occur rapidly and can be frightening for the child and other children. There are many reasons why a child may have hypoglycaemia but common causes include the following:

- Lack of food – the child may not have eaten sufficiently or is late having the following food.

- Insulin level – the dosage of insulin may not be correct.
- Additional demands on the body – vigorous exercise such as swimming, running or stress can cause the body to metabolise glucose more quickly, thus creating a shortfall.

Signs that a child has hypoglycaemia include the following:

- Sudden or gradual lack of colour.
- Irritability.
- Tiredness.
- Hunger.
- Shakiness.
- Unconsciousness.

Treatment is actually simple as the child needs to take in fast acting carbohydrate such as a sugary drink, sweets or glucose tablets. If the child has become unconscious an ambulance needs to be called as an injection of glucose will be required. Once the child is feeling better, he or she will need to eat some slower burning carbohydrates such as a sandwich, cereals or pasta. Parents must be informed that a child has been hypoglycaemic in order that they can adjust the insulin dosage or seek professional help.

Hyperglycaemia

Hyperglycaemia develops when children's glucose levels are too high. While the condition should not be left for long periods untreated, its short-term effects are less severe than when there is insufficient glucose. Hyperglycaemia often occurs when children have colds, flu or are feeling unwell. The body's metabolism therefore changes and this means that the usual dose of insulin needs to be changed.

Some of the symptoms such as tiredness and irritability are the same as hypoglycaemia but the key difference tends to be the slower onset, although this may not be sufficient a sign for you to tell the difference. As the signs of hypoglycaemia and hyperglycaemia are very similar, but with very different results (the child with hypoglycaemia may become unconscious), Diabetes UK suggests that it is always best to err on the side of caution and take steps as if the child has hypoglycaemia.

Information that we may need from parents

- How does your child cope at home with diabetes?
- What are the signs that your child is hypoglycaemic? (This is important as signs can vary enormously from child to child.)
- How can we contact you if the child becomes hypoglycaemic?
- At what times does your child need snacks?
- What type of food should we keep in stock in case your child forgets to bring in a snack or you would like us to prepare it?

- What quantity/type of foods should be given to your child and what should be avoided?
- What would you like us to do if your child refuses food or snacks?
- What type of information about the child's food and drink intake would be helpful to you?
- Will your child need an insulin injection while he or she is with us?
- Will your child's blood sugar level need monitoring?

Most children's insulin levels are monitored and controlled by parents at home. However, if there is a need for children to have an insulin injection while in the setting or to have their blood sugar level monitored, it will be essential for parents or other professionals to train staff. If children are to eat food and snacks provided by the setting, it is also essential that parents advise the setting as to the quantity as well as the type of foods that should be given.

Getting it right for the child

It is essential for everyone working with a young diabetic child to be observant and to listen to the child. They must understand what they should do if the child is becoming hypoglycaemic. Avoiding hypoglycaemia is essential, as not only is this frightening for the child, it may also have some longer-term effects on the child's health.

The dosage of insulin in relation to food often depends on the type of activity that a child has done and will be doing. To help parents adjust dosages, it is important to let parents know what the child has been doing as well as any vigorous physical activities that might be planned, such as swimming or going on long outings. Parents will also need to know if the child has eaten less than usual as this will affect the amount of insulin that is required.

As well as making sure that the child's physical needs are met, it is also important that children feel good about themselves. Children with diabetes can feel very 'different' and so it is a good idea to look for ways of integrating your main snack and lunch times with those of the child's wherever possible. If this is not possible, consider encouraging the child to choose 'snack' partners who can sit with the child. Sharing a snack is not a good idea as it is important that the child gets sufficient food, but a snack partner can have a separate snack.

Finally, it is also important that staff think about cooking activities and any parties that involve food as children with diabetes may be unwittingly excluded. Plan cooking activities, parties, etc. in a way that will allow the child to make foods that he or she can eat.

Key questions

- Is everyone in the setting aware that this child has diabetes? (A photo of the child with a note in the kitchen to remind staff that a child has diabetes can be a useful strategy and is often suggested by parents.)

- Does everyone understand the dietary needs of this child?
- Are staff aware of the importance of regular foods and snacks for this child? (Consider an alarm or timer for the key worker.)
- Does everyone know what they should do should the child become hypoglycaemic?
- Who will act as the child's key worker and will liaise with parents regarding food and other requirements?
- Are emergency contact details easily accessible?
- What system will be in place to alert parents to a change in the normal routine of the setting that might affect the child's energy requirements, e.g. going on an outing, swimming, etc.
- How can the routine of the setting be altered so that the child's dietary needs can be integrated?

Some day-to-day questions

- How well is the child looking?
- Will the child be engaging in any vigorous physical activity that requires extra energy?
- Has the child brought in food or snacks?
- Does everyone know what time the child needs snacks, drinks and food?
- Who will be letting parents know about the child's food and drink intake over the day?
- If children are to be taken out of the setting, e.g. on a trip or walk, has a sugary drink or high carbohydrate food been packed in case the child becomes hypoglycaemic?

Contact

Diabetes UK
10 Parkway
London NW1 7AA
www.diabetes.org.uk

Down's syndrome

Down's syndrome is a genetic condition (meaning present from birth) caused by the presence of extra genetic material. There are three types of Down's syndrome although by far the commonest type is Standard Trisomy 21 in which a child has an extra copy of chromosome 21. The extra genetic material causes a range of characteristics that were first documented in 1866, although not linked to DNA until 1956. These include specific physical characteristics as well as learning difficulties and some medical conditions. While children may share physical

The Down's Syndrome Association provides a guide for teachers and learning support assistants (reproduced with kind permission).

characteristics such as an enlarged tongue, children with Down's syndrome are very individual and will have varying needs.

Incidence and diagnosis

Down's syndrome affects about one in 1000 children. It is not yet understood why an extra copy of chromosome 21 sometimes occurs, it is however known that the incidence of Down's syndrome is higher among older mothers. The condition is usually diagnosed at birth by the presence of several physical characteristics including facial shape and poor muscle tone. Some women know as a result of an amniocentesis test during their pregnancy that they are expecting a child with Down's syndrome as the test is routinely offered to women over the age of 35 years.

Development and health

Learning difficulties

All children with Down's syndrome will have some form of learning difficulty, although the extent will vary enormously and a child can be stronger in one area of development than in another. Communication and language is often delayed and some children may need to use Makaton or a picture exchange system to help them to communicate. Progress is made very much at the child's own pace, although stimulation and a good play environment are essential.

Conductive hearing loss

Children with Down's syndrome are prone to hearing loss as a result of physical differences to the inner ear that are exacerbated by colds, infections and the higher level of ear wax produced by children with Down's syndrome. This means that children may not always be able to hear properly which in turn affects their language development. This means that staff need to be aware of whether or not a child is hearing properly and if necessary to adapt the activity accordingly. It is also important that ear infections are detected as early as possible and so signs that a child is in pain or is rubbing his or her ears need to be taken seriously.

Visual impairment

Many children with Down's syndrome may have some form of visual impairment, including squints, long and short sightedness. These are usually corrected by the wearing of glasses and so checking that a child has his or her glasses is important. It is also worth considering whether a child who has Down's syndrome is seeing properly as although regular eye checks are usually carried out, long sightedness can develop gradually as a result of the eyes compensating for a squint.

Heart problems

A third of children with Down's syndrome have some form of heart condition, although the severity ranges enormously with some babies requiring surgery early on in their lives. It is a good idea to work with parents in order to modify activities to make them appropriate.

Respiratory and other infections

Many children with Down's syndrome are prone to chest and other infections. These are usually treated with antibiotics but may result in the child being frequently absent. Good hygiene routines in the setting are very important so as to avoid unnecessary cross infections. It is also important for staff to look out for signs that a child is unwell and then to contact parents.

Information that we may need from parents

- What type of activities does the child enjoy at home?
- Are there any key words, gestures or signs that the child uses?

- How well can the child adapt to changes in routine?
- Does the child wear glasses or have any visual impairment?
- Does the child have a hearing impairment or is prone to temporary hearing loss because of ear infections and/or glue ear?
- Does the child have any medication that should be given or held by staff?
- In cases where a child has a heart condition, are there any activities that should be avoided or adapted?
- Are there any particular signs that we should be aware of that may indicate that the child is unwell?
- What stage of 'toilet training' has the child reached?

Getting it right for the child

Remember that children with Down's syndrome develop and learn in much the same way as any other children, although their progress is likely to be slower. Walking, toilet training and talking will often be later than for most other children. No two children with this syndrome will share exactly the same characteristics. This means that it will be important to assess each child's stage of development when providing activities and resources, rather than to consider the child's chronological age. It will also be important to repeat activities where a child has enjoyed them so that he or she gains in confidence and understanding.

In terms of children's emotional development, it is important to consider how the setting will help the child if he or she has frequent absences due to illnesses. Such absences can lead to the child showing separation anxiety when he or she returns unless the child has established a strong attachment to one particular member of staff (a key worker.) To cope with such absences, it may be worth considering a flexible approach to the sessions that can be attended. This avoids situations where a child loses out because he or she is ill on the day that the child is down to come in, but are better on a day when the child is not scheduled to come in.

Key questions

- Who will act as the child's key worker?
- How will we help this child to settle in after any absences?
- Who will be responsible for any medication and where will this be kept?
- Are we planning activities that can be adapted to suit this child's stage of development?
- How can we encourage this child to develop self-help skills?
- Are the hygiene measures taken in the setting sufficient to eliminate the risk of unnecessary infections?

Some day-to-day questions

- Has the child brought his or her glasses into the setting?

- Is the child hearing fully?
- Is the child looking well?
- Does the child need any medication?
- Are the other children 'mothering' this child and preventing him or her from becoming self-sufficient and developing self-help skills?
- Are we remembering this child's stage of development when dealing with any unwanted behaviour?

Contact

Down's Syndrome Association
155 Mitcham Road
London SW17 9PG
www.dsa-uk.com

Duchenne muscular dystrophy

There are 20 known types of muscular dystrophy with Duchenne being the most common in children. Muscular dystrophies are genetic conditions that cause cells in the muscles to break down and gradually be lost. This causes increasing loss of movement and can eventually reduce life expectancy.

Incidence and diagnosis

Duchenne muscular dystrophy only affects boys and is quite rare with around 100 boys a year being born with the condition. Failure to meet the expected milestones of walking are often the first indications that a boy has the condition, unless the condition is already known in the family. A blood test is then carried out to confirm the condition.

Health and development

Although the condition mainly affects a boy's health, some boys do have slight difficulties with speech and language although these are not usually severe.

Mobility

The gradual loss of mobility is one of the main features of this condition, although young children are still likely to be mobile but may need assistance or extra time in order to move. Children may be able to climb stairs on all fours or need the banisters. The weakness in the muscles also means that children may fall down or need to sit down. To counteract the deterioration in muscle strength, most children will have a programme of physiotherapy and be encouraged to remain physically active.

Nutrition

It is important that children with muscular dystrophy do not become overweight as this makes it harder for the body to move. This means that you should check with parents if the child has particular nutritional needs.

Information that we may need from parents

- What mobility needs does your child have?
- Are there any adaptations or equipment that would be useful for your child?
- Are there any activities we will need to adapt to help your child participate?
- Does your child have a physiotherapy programme that we should adopt?
- Does your child become frustrated and if so, how do you help him?
- Are there any general or specific signs that you would like us to look out for?
- Does your child have any specific nutritional needs?

Getting it right for the child

This can be a distressing condition for parents and carers as little by little they see the strength in their child ebb away. Giving children a good quality of life is therefore essential and the focus of work should be to look for ways of helping the child to join in everyday activities alongside other children. This may mean changing the layout of equipment to allow the child to move to it more easily. The way that the condition progresses also means thinking about what the child's future needs will be and how best to meet these. Ramps might need to be installed or activities moved to a different place to allow for access. Thinking ahead prevents situations where the child is faced with not being able to join in.

Key questions

- Who will be the child's key worker
- Who will be responsible for ensuring that any physiotherapy is carried out?
- What activities does the child enjoy?
- How can we plan activities that will take into account the child's physical needs?
- What adaptations to the setting are required?
- Are emergency contact details for the child easily accessible?

Some day-to-day questions

- How well is the child?
- Are activities planned that allow the child to participate?
- Will the pace of the day allow the child to rest?

Contact

Duchenne Family Support Group
37a Highbury New Park
Islington
London N15 2EN
www.dfsg.org.uk

Dyslexia

Dyslexia is a specific learning disorder causing persistent difficulties in processing information that mean a child's ability in reading, writing and spelling can be affected. While it is not fully understood, it would appear that the brain finds it hard to process certain types of information. This means that an older child or adult with dyslexia may have excellent language, knowledge and creative skills but find it hard to process symbolic information. Dyslexia and dyspraxia are often linked disorders, although some children with dyslexia may not have any apparent difficulties in controlling their movements.

In children's early years, it is not appropriate to diagnose dyslexia, as formal teaching of reading, writing and spelling is not suitable for children under six years old. However, it is possible to notice some tendencies such as a child not having developed a clear hand preference or struggling with word order. Where children are showing dyslexic tendencies, increasing activities that encourage balance, control and movements have been shown to be beneficial as it is thought that these types of activities stimulate the brain's information pathways. As such, physical activities and a play-based approach to learning is emphasised in the Foundation Stage curriculum.

Contact

British Dyslexia Association
98 London Road
Reading RG1 5AU
www.bda-dyslexia.org.uk

Dyspraxia

Dyspraxia is a developmental disorder that affects children's control and co-ordination of movement. The term dyspraxia is relatively new and replaces previously used terms such 'clumsy child syndrome'. Some children with dyspraxia may also have other learning difficulties such as dyslexia or speech and language disorders. The cause of dyspraxia is not fully understood, but it would seem that the brain is not processing information effectively.

Incidence and diagnosis

The incidence of dyspraxia is hard to calculate because the extent to which it can affect a child or adult can vary enormously. The Dyspraxia Foundation estimates that dyspraxia affects between 2 and 10 per cent of the population, with boys up to four times more likely to be affected. Diagnosis is usually made by an educational psychologist.

Health and development

The extent and way in which dyspraxia affects children can vary enormously and some of the signs of dyspraxia are the same as other disorders such as Fragile X. It is important to remember that while children may have difficulties with their movements, their overall intelligence is usually average or above average.

Gross motor and locomotive skills

Children are often slower to reach the developmental milestones and may not follow the expected sequence of development. It is not uncommon to find that a child has not crawled as a baby but has bottom shuffled or gone straight to standing. Young children may find it hard to throw or kick a ball. Their running and movements may look jerky and they may often trip over or bump into others. Children with dyspraxia may find it hard to sit still as sitting still actually requires co-ordination and control.

Fine motor skills

Some children with dyspraxia may have difficulties in making movements that require co-ordination such as threading beads, cutting food and may actively avoid activities that require a high level of manual dexterity. Older children may find it hard to produce legible handwriting.

Concentration, language and thought

Some children with dyspraxia may also have related difficulties in other areas of their development, notably language and thought. They may find it hard to speak coherently and sequence events. Children may also find it hard to concentrate. This may be as a result of the brain receiving too much or too little sensory information.

Tactile defensiveness

Some children with dyspraxia are very sensitive to touch. This is called tactile defensiveness (see Chapter 12, page 162). They may not enjoy playing with sensory materials such as sand or may object to having their hair combed or teeth brushed.

Behaviour

Children may show 'inappropriate' behaviour. This can be a result of frustration or as a way of avoiding situations where they think that they may fail. A child, for example, may run around the setting rather than pick up the bricks as the child knows that he or she will be slower than other children. It is also worth remembering that children may find it hard to sit still as this requires a good level of co-ordination. Looking for ways of shortening the time that children have to sit still in situations such as meal times and story times is therefore important.

Information that we may need from parents

- What activities does your child enjoy at home?
- Are there any specific movements or activities that we should adopt in this setting?

- Does your child have any specific areas of difficulty, e.g. dressing, climbing?
- How do you support your child at home?
- Does your child receive any speech therapy?

Getting it right for the child

It is often parents who first notice that their child's physical development is atypical and so listening to parents and supporting them is an important part of getting it right for the child. In children's early years, parents may still be trying to get recognition and support for their child. Listening to parents and working with them is therefore essential.

For the child, it is important to look for ways of developing fine and gross motor skills in enjoyable ways that will give the child confidence. This means that it is good practice to build on children's interests so that they may gain fluency of movement through play. Consider carefully the physical 'stage of development' of the child when planning activities as it is important that children continue to master sequentially fine and gross motor movements. Avoid the notion of 'fast tracking' their development as this can exacerbate children's difficulties. A child who is not interested or able to hold a pencil should not be 'forced' to do so. Instead other activities such as drawing in shaving foam or making shapes in a rice tray will be more developmentally appropriate. Children may also need a little extra time to complete tasks that require physical movements, so it is a good idea to avoid situations where children who are first and fast to do things are praised. This can lead children with dyspraxia to 'give up' and look for other ways of gaining attention.

In the same way, it is important to remember that the child may have difficulty in sitting still for story times, etc. Look for ways of making story times interactive so that the child does not have to sit still and be quiet. Some children with dyspraxia also find it hard to concentrate and organise their thoughts. Looking for ways of providing information in a sensory and active way is therefore important. You may also need to look out for activities that have an element of repetition in them so that children naturally know what to expect and can practise movements. Parachute games encourage children to repeat the same arm movements and shelling peas requires children to continually open pods so they can count the number of peas each time.

Helping children to concentrate

Some children with dyspraxia find it hard to concentrate and are easily distracted. Breaking down tasks into smaller components can therefore be helpful. Consider ways of minimising distractions for the child, i.e. carry out activities in areas where other children are not 'walking by'. Also ensure that activities are interesting and relevant for the child.

Emotional needs

Children with dyspraxia can develop low self-esteem. They know what they want to achieve but find it hard and frustrating to make their bodies work for them. Children who have started the primary phase of their education may begin to notice that their handwriting, paintings or ability to dress themselves is not the same as other children. This can lead to frustration and feelings of inadequacy. Some children also begin to believe that they cannot learn and are 'stupid'. This in turn can lead to children showing inappropriate behaviour.

There is also a danger that some children can become over reliant on adult support as adults can unwittingly take over activities such as dressing or feeding to speed the child along. This stops children from using and developing everyday skills and thus independence. To help children build a positive view of themselves, it is therefore important for adults to allow children enough time to complete tasks and also to adapt activities to ensure that children are working at their developmental level.

Key questions

- Who will be the child's key worker?
- Is everyone in the setting aware of the difficulties that the child may have in co-ordinating movements?
- How will the planning of activities and routines take into consideration the child's needs?
- How will the child be encouraged to take part in activities that require fine motor skills?
- Are staff aware that they will need to think about the way in which they praise and acknowledge children? e.g. if they praise children for putting their coats on quickly, this child may begin to feel a failure.

Some day-to-day questions

- What activities have been planned to promote this child's motor skills?
- Do activities take into consideration the child's interests?
- Are activities planned that are developmentally appropriate to avoid frustration?
- Is an adult available to offer support and encouragement?
- Are any specific activities planned which will support any ongoing physiotherapy?

Contact

British Dyspraxia Foundation
8 West Alley
Hitchin
Herts SG5 1EG
www.dyspraxiafoundation.org.uk

Eczema

Eczema, also known as dermatitis, is part of a group of skin conditions. Skin becomes dry and itchy and when a child has severe eczema the skin may become raw, cracked and bleeding. There are many different forms of eczema:

- **Atopic eczema** – this is the commonest type of eczema. It is thought to be inherited and is triggered by allergens in the child's environment which cause the body's immune system to over-react.
- **Allergic contact dermatitis** – this type of eczema occurs when the body's immune system begins to react to a substance that is in direct contact with the skin. The allergic reaction often occurs gradually and repeated contact increases the intensity of the reaction.
- **Irritant contact dermatitis** – this type of eczema occurs when the body comes into contact with chemicals, e.g. in detergents.

Incidence and diagnosis

Eczema is a very common condition. It is thought that up to one in 5 children may have some type of eczema, although the severity can vary enormously. While there is no cure for eczema, the National Eczema Society estimates that 60–70 per cent of children will be free of symptoms by their mid-teens. Symptoms include soreness, dryness of skin and itchiness. Most children see a GP who may then refer them to a specialist dermatologist.

Health and development

Concentration

Eczema does not cause any learning difficulties but some children can find it hard to concentrate properly.

Tiredness

Eczema can interrupt sleep as the itchiness can keep the child awake. This may mean that the child will feel tired and this may be reflected in his or her behaviour. Children may be irritable or find it hard to concentrate. Some children may also be prescribed anti-histamine tablets which can cause drowsiness.

Social and emotional development

Some children may not feel good about the way that they look and this can prevent them from socialising. It is important therefore to look for ways of boosting children's self image.

Information that we may need from parents

- How is the child's eczema being managed?
- Are there any creams or medication that the child needs in the setting?
- Are there any known triggers?

- Are there any materials in the setting, such as sand or dough, that may irritate further or dry out the skin?
- Does the child have any dietary requirements?
- What would the parents like the setting to do if the child begins to scratch uncontrollably?

Getting it right for the child

Eczema can be extremely distressing for children. The itchiness can become unbearable and so it is unfair to tell children not to scratch. Working with parents to find ways of helping the child is therefore important.

Emollients

These are creams that help to moisturise the skin. They can also help with the itchiness. As with any form of treatment, it is essential to find out from parents how and when the cream can be applied. Make sure that the child's hands and your hands are clean. Bacteria are easily introduced into inflamed parts of the child's skin. Avoid any cross infection by making sure that each child with eczema has his or her own labelled pot of cream. Apply or help the child to apply the cream very gently. Rubbing can irritate the skin and cause further itching.

Topical steroids

These creams contain steroid drugs and are used when children have severe eczema. These creams will be applied at home, but where a child spends time in full day care, staff may be asked to apply them.

- Only use topical steroid cream when asked to by parents.
- Check that the cream is 'in date'.
- Read any instructions given on the tube carefully.
- Wash your hands thoroughly before and after applying the cream.
- Apply the cream sparingly and only to the area of skin affected.
- Make sure that steroid creams are properly labelled with the child's name.
- Do not use steroid cream on any other child.

Antihistamines

These drugs are given to children to help them sleep and to reduce the itchiness. They are usually given at home. They can make children feel very drowsy.

Antibiotics

Some children may have antibiotic cream or medicine to take if they have an infected area of skin.

- Read the instructions on the packet carefully.
- Store them in a cool place.
- Make sure that the cream or medicine is labelled with the child's name.

Bandaging

Children may wear bandages that contain soothing paste, sometimes known as 'wet bandages'. Bandages are usually applied at home. Check with parents whether there are any activities that will interfere with the bandages.

Removing triggers in the environment

The triggers for eczema are similar to those for asthma (see table on page 182) . In addition, stress can play a huge part for many children. This means providing a calm and relaxed environment and observing children closely for the first signs of any distress.

Key questions

- Who will be responsible for liaising with parents on a day-to-day basis?
- Are staff aware of the symptoms and effects of eczema?
- Who will be responsible for administering any medication or treatment?
- How will the child's dietary needs be met?

Some day-to-day questions

- How well is the child today?
- Has the child slept well?

Contact

National Eczema Society
Hill House
Highgate Hill
London
N19 5NA
www.eczema.org

Epilepsy

Epilepsy is a neurological condition that results in a person having recurrent seizures. The seizures are caused when the brain's normal pattern of electrical activity is temporarily disturbed. Epilepsy is a complex condition as there appears to be several types. There are also over forty types of seizures. Seizures can, however, be grouped into two broad categories: generalised and partial.

Incidence and diagnosis

Epilepsy is thought to affect one in 133 people and so is a relatively common neurological condition. The majority of people with epilepsy have their first seizure before the age of twenty. There are several reasons why a person may develop epilepsy, including brain damage sustained during birth or as a result of an injury to the head, complications from diseases such as meningitis but also as part of a chromosomal disorder. However, in many cases, the exact cause is unknown. Diagnosis is not always easy and information needs to be gained about what happened during a seizure. When epilepsy is suspected, referrals are usually made to a neurologist. A range of tests may then be performed including an EEG which measures brain activity and an MRI scan which provides pictures of the brain. Once diagnosed, anti-epileptic drugs are usually prescribed. These are usually efficient, but can cause side effects (see below).

Health and development

Epilepsy alone will not necessarily cause any learning or health difficulties, although sometimes the drugs that a child is taking may have some side effects. This is important to remember as some children with epilepsy do not always fulfil their academic potential.

Seizures

While seizures can be grouped into two broad categories, there are many different types of seizures. You should talk to parents about the form in which their child is likely to have any seizure. The form a seizure takes depends on the part of the brain that is being affected.

Partialised seizures (local focal)

In partialised seizures, brain activity begins or is involved in one area of the brain. The child's experience of the seizure will therefore be determined by the area of the brain that is being affected. Some seizures begin as partial seizures and then spread to other areas of the brain causing a secondary generalised seizure.

Simple partial seizures

In simple partial seizures, the child remains, or is at first, conscious. There may be motor activity such as twitching or unusual sensations in the limbs depending on the area of the brain that is being affected.

Complex partial seizures

Children having a complex partial seizure may appear to be dazed or show repetitive automatic movements such as fumbling with clothes, mumbling or chewing. They may be able to respond or reply, but afterwards will have little memory of the seizure.

Generalised seizures

Children having generalised seizures will lose consciousness as the wide areas of the brain are being affected. Some of these types of seizures can be dramatic with the child falling to the ground such as in tonic clonic seizures, although with some children generalised seizures can take the form of absences.

Tonic/clonic

These types of seizures are often the most recognised among the general public.

In the first part of the seizure (tonic) the child becomes stiff and falls to the ground. The seizure continues but changes (clonic) with the child's muscles relaxing and then tightening rhythmically. This causes convulsing movements. Once the seizure is over the child will need to rest. They may be drowsy and have a headache.

Absences

Absences are common in young children. The child loses consciousness for a few seconds. They may appear to be staring aimlessly or look blank. These types of seizures often go unnoticed, but the child may have missed out on instructions or appear to be puzzled.

Possible side effects of drugs

Finding the right dosage and drug for children can be difficult in the early days. It is important to recognise the side effects that some drugs can cause and report these to parents.

Drowsiness

Some medication causes children to be drowsy. If this is the case, allow children to rest and sleep as their body indicates. Overtiredness can trigger epilepsy in some children.

Memory and concentration

Sometimes medication can affect a child's ability to concentrate as brain activity is being slowed down. It is important to notice changes in the level of attention and concentration that a child shows as this can indicate some changes in the brain's activities.

Overactivity

Some children are affected by the medication by becoming more active and restless. This again should be noted and talked through with parents.

Information that we may need from parents

- Is your child's epilepsy fully or partially controlled by medication?
- Are there any side effects of this medication on your child?
- Are there any triggers that may cause a seizure?
- What type of seizure does your child have?
- How long do they normally last and what form do they take?
- How much rest does your child usually need afterwards?
- Would you like to be contacted immediately if your child has a seizure?
- Are there any activities that need limiting or modifying?
- How does your child feel or what does he or she understand about having epilepsy?
- Does your child have any other medical condition?

Getting it right for the child

Firstly, it is useful to understand that there is still widespread ignorance about epilepsy. This dates back hundreds of years when people with epilepsy were thought of as being in some way possessed by the devil or suffering from mental illness. In reality, most children with epilepsy lead straightforward, normal and active lives as having epilepsy, in itself, does not create any further health or learning difficulties. To get it right for the child, it is important to gain information from parents about the frequency of any seizures and any effects of medication. It is also important for all staff to provide a supporting, calm and reassuring atmosphere so that if a seizure occurs, the child does not feel stigmatised. It is also known that stressful situations can for some children trigger seizures.

Where children have repeated seizures, it is also important for staff to be able to correctly describe the type of seizure and what happened. This is particularly important if a child is in the process of being diagnosed.

Managing risks

It is essential that children are not cocooned and that whilst some precautions may need to be taken, children are not prevented from activities such as swimming, climbing and riding tricycles. For most children, simply supervising closely, yet unobtrusively, will be sufficient. For children with high levels of unexpected seizures, you should take advice from parents. In some cases protective headgear is worn so that children can still take part in activities.

What to do if a child has a seizure

Many practitioners are concerned that they will not know what to do if a child has a seizure, although in reality little, if any, First Aid is often required. It is, however, useful if all members of staff or adults working with the child know how to place children in the recovery position.

Remember to:

- Remain calm and stay with the child
- Guide the child away from any danger
- Cushion the head if the child is falling
- Place the child in the recovery position when the seizure has finished
- Stay with the child until they have regained consciousness
- Be aware that a child may have lost bladder or bowel control in some instance and respond sensitively.

Do not:

- Move the child unless they are in danger
- Attempt to restrain or hold the child
- Give the child any drink until they are fully conscious

When to seek emergency help

You should phone for an ambulance if:

- it is the child's first seizure
- the seizure is generalised and continues for longer than 5 minutes or if the seizure is longer than the usual for the child
- another seizure occurs when the child has not yet gained consciousness
- the child has been injured as a result of the seizures.

Correct language

The word 'fit' is no longer used as it is often used in relation to someone being angry or violent. The term 'seizure' or 'epileptic seizure' is preferred. The terms 'petit mal' and 'grand mal' are outdated as it is now known that there is a multitude of different seizures.

Key questions

- Does everyone in the setting know that the child has epilepsy?
- Does everyone know what to do if a seizure occurs?
- Is everyone aware of any side effects of the medication?
- Does everyone understand that epilepsy should not be seen as a barrier to many everyday activities?
- How will risks be managed in the setting?

Some day-to-day questions

- How well is the child?
- Are there any changes to the child's level of concentration, memory or signs that they are drowsy?
- Does the child need extra supervision or protection in order to engage in any physical activities?
- Are emergency contact details available?

Contact

National Society for Epilepsy
Chesham Lane
Chalfont St. Peter
Bucks
SL9 0RJ
www.epilepsynse.org.uk

Epilepsy Action
www.epilepsy.org.uk

Fragile X

This is an inherited genetic condition which is called 'Fragile X' because the X chromosome is slightly damaged. It results in most of the affected children having some form of learning disability. Boys are more seriously affected than girls as girls usually have another undamaged X chromosome that appears to mitigate the effects of the other damaged chromosome. Fragile X is the most common form of inherited learning disability, although it was not recognised until the late 1970s.

Incidence and diagnosis

Fragile X affects about one in 4000 boys and one in 8000 girls. Diagnosis can be difficult unless one of the child's parents already knows that his or her family is affected. Once suspected, however, diagnosis can be made from chromosomal testing.

Health and development

There are marked differences between girls and boys with Fragile X syndrome. Generally, boys are affected more severely and show more challenging behaviour.

Behaviour

Boys particularly show unwanted and challenging behaviour as they can be impulsive, overactive and irritable. They can also have aggressive outbursts.

Physical development

Children can have difficulties with their hand-eye co-ordination and may at times appear to be 'clumsy'. Children with Fragile X syndrome may also have poor spatial awareness.

Cognitive development

Boys and girls can find it difficult to concentrate, but boys will have particular difficulties. Their attention span can be limited according to the type of activity presented. There can also be difficulties in understanding and remembering new information with children seeming to have difficulties in situations where there is too much going on, i.e. over stimulation.

Communication

Speech can be disorganised and fast. It is common for children to repeat themselves and also to echo back what has been said to them. This is thought to help them process the information more easily.

Emotional and social development

Some children show characteristics that are often associated with autism, such as avoidance of eye contact, repetitive speech, hand biting and resistance to changes in routines. Most children are however affectionate and interested in social interactions although sometimes shyness and inappropriate social responses such as hand flapping create barriers for them. Between 10 and 30 per cent of people with Fragile X syndrome can develop epilepsy.

Information that we may need from the parents

- What does the child enjoy doing at home?
- What type of strategies do parents use to manage the effects of Fragile X?
- Does the child have epilepsy and if so does the child have any medication?
- Does the child have any medication to help with any over activeness?
- Does the child have any particular ways of communicating that we should be aware of?

Getting it right for the child

It is very important to provide close supervision and be very patient with children, especially boys who have Fragile X syndrome. It is important to remember that they are not being deliberately difficult or aggressive. Staff will need to make sure that they focus on the child rather than on the behaviour.

Activities will need to be carefully thought through so that children can 'leave' them easily if their concentration wanes, for example a shorter game or short story. New activities or 'exciting' days such as trips out or parties may provide too much stimulation for the child and so good preparation will be required to help the child adjust.

Key questions

- Who will act as the child's key worker?
- How will the child be supervised during the session without 'smothering' him or her?
- Are there any areas where close supervision will be essential to avoid accidents?
- Who will be responsible for any medication and where will this be kept?
- Are all staff confident that they know what to do if the child has an epileptic seizure?
- What strategies will be used to develop the child's communication and language skills?
- How will we avoid situations where the child may be over stimulated?

Some day-to-day questions

- Have we planned activities and this session remembering that this child finds it difficult to concentrate?
- Is there likely to be too much excitement in this session?
- Are activities planned that will help the child to process information at his or her own rate?

Contact

The Fragile X Society
53 Winchelsea Lane
Hastings
East Sussex
TN35 4LG
www.fragilex.org.uk

Hearing impairment

Hearing impairment is a generalised term that covers any amount of hearing loss whatever its cause. Hearing impairments are not always permanent and the amount of hearing loss can be categorised according to its severity as mild, moderate or severe.

There are two types of hearing impairment: sensorineural and conductive. Sensorineural impairments are caused in the inner ear or beyond, while conductive impairments occur when there is some type of blockage or obstruction in the outer ear that prevents sounds from being fully received. Some children can have both types of hearing impairment and this is referred to as a mixed impairment.

- **Sensorineural hearing impairment**. This type of hearing impairment tends to be permanent and occurs for a variety of reasons including premature birth, genetic factors and diseases such as meningitis and mumps. Sensorineural hearing impairments prevent sound information from being processed effectively.
- **Conductive hearing impairment**. This type of hearing impairment is common among children and not always permanent. Blockages such as ear wax or fluid build up in the Eustachian tube and prevent sound from being fully registered.

Incidence and diagnosis

There are many causes of hearing impairment and the levels of incidence therefore vary considerably. According to the National Deaf Children's society 840 babies a year are born with a permanent hearing loss, 80 per cent of children under eight years will at some time be affected by 'glue ear' (a conductive hearing impairment caused by a fluid build up in the Eustachian tube), and one third of acquired deafness is a result of meningitis.

Diagnosis of a hearing impairment is usually made following parents' or carer's observations that a child is not responding or speech is not developing as expected. Unfortunately, many children are not identified as having a hearing loss promptly, especially where they have a conductive hearing loss or where their hearing loss is mild to moderate. Once a child is referred to a GP a hearing test will identify the nature and the significance of the hearing loss.

Health and development

Hearing impairments do not affect children's level of intelligence, but may create a barrier to learning if steps are not taken to help the child access information.

Language

Children's language is likely to be significantly delayed unless their hearing impairment has been diagnosed and steps are taken to support the child. This is why early diagnosis is essential.

The impact on children's language development depends on the level of the hearing loss, how quickly it has been identified and whether the child has been able to hear at any time. Children who have an acquired hearing loss, for example, from contracting meningitis, may have already acquired a good level of speech, but children who have never been fully hearing may not be using the spoken word to communicate. The decision as to the best strategy to help the child to communicate is usually taken by speech and language therapists in conjunction with parents. This may mean that some children will be encouraged to use a sign based language while other children may be encouraged to lip read and to use the spoken word.

Behaviour

Some children with hearing impairments may show inappropriate behaviour. In some cases this is due to frustration caused by being unable to communicate their needs or being unable to understand what is happening. Understanding that behaviour reflects a child's unmet needs is a useful perspective for adults to take, as once the child's needs have been fully met, the number of incidents of inappropriate behaviour lessens.

Social and emotional development

Some children whose hearing impairment is not diagnosed quickly may have missed out on opportunities to socialise with other children. This can mean that they may need to be shown how to interact with others as some children with a hearing impairment will have adapted to playing alone.

Information that we may need from parents

- What type of hearing impairment does your child have?
- How does your child's hearing impairment affect his or her daily life?
- Does your child receive any speech and language support?
- Would you be happy if we contacted this service to gain further advice?
- What strategies do you use to communicate with your child?
- Does your child use a hearing aid?
- What advice have you been given about how best to use the hearing aid?
- What type of activities does your child enjoy doing?
- Are there any activities that can cause your child to become frustrated?

Getting it right for the child

Your starting point should be talking to parents. They will be able to advise you as to the communication strategy that they are using with the child. While many children will be using speech as the main communication method, some children may be learning British Sign Language if they have a profound hearing impairment. Note that British Sign Language is not the same as Makaton. Makaton is a visual signing system and not a complete language. It is used with children whose cognition makes it harder to understand abstract symbols. If the child is learning British Sign Language, it will be important for members of staff to learn it as well to support the child. A few signs alone will not be sufficient to develop and support the child's emerging language. It is also important that everyone in the setting is aware of the signs that a child is not fully hearing as early identification is essential.

The key to helping all children with hearing impairments is to consider the way in which we are communicating with them. It is important that we create the best possible environment to maximise their hearing and also to help them understand what is happening.

Do's

- Check that you have the child's attention before talking.
- Maintain good eye contact with the child.
- Identify the topic of conversation early on.
- Use a normal pace of speech, but make sure that you speak clearly.
- Be expressive and use good intonation in your speech.
- Make sure that the lighting in the setting is sufficient so that children who are lip reading or relying on facial cues can see you.
- Use props and visual aids to reinforce your communication with children, e.g. show the child an apron rather than talk about one.
- Use props to support story time and make sure that the child can see the pictures.
- Emphasise key words in your speech.
- Use meaningful facial expressions and gestures to support verbal messages.

Don'ts

- Obstruct your face, e.g. put your hand over your mouth.
- Exaggerate your facial movements or speech.
- Shout or speak in a loud voice.

As well as being able to communicate effectively with the child, it is also important that you are able to listen carefully to the child. Many children may have speech patterns that are atypical or may not be speaking as clearly as other children of their age. Children who are not feeling listened to will quickly become frustrated and may withdraw. Show the child by nodding, paraphrasing and smiling that you understand what is being said. Allow children plenty of time; avoid competitive situations where children shout out. Make sure that children have some time working with an adult by themselves or in small groups.

Supporting children who wear hearing aids

Hearing aids amplify wanted sounds. Advice about supporting children who wear hearing aids should be gained from parents and the audiologist who supports the child. The following general pieces of advice may be helpful:

- Always make sure that the hearing aid is in the correct ear. Children who have bilateral hearing impairments may have two hearing aids; they must be put in the correct ear.
- Handle hearing aids gently; they are sophisticated pieces of equipment.
- Check that the battery is not flat; try to have spare batteries in the setting.
- Check that the earpiece is not covered in wax; this is normally removed by washing the mould with warm soapy water.

Key questions

- Who will be the child's key worker?
- Is staff training required to learn British Sign Language?
- How will everyone become aware that this child has a hearing impairment?
- Is the lighting sufficient in the setting?
- Who will take responsibility for implementing any speech and language programme for the child?
- How will quiet areas be created within the setting?

Some day-to-day questions

- How well is the child hearing today?
- Is the child's hearing aid functioning properly?
- Are spare batteries available?
- Does everyone working with the child understand how best to communicate?

Contact

The National Deaf Children's society
15 Dufferin Street
London EC1Y 8UR
www.ndcs.org.uk

Hydrocephalus

Hydrocephalus occurs when the cerebrospinal fluid that is produced in the brain is unable to flow freely away. This causes a build up of fluid and thus pressure in the brain. This in turn can cause permanent brain damage although the extent is variable. There are several causes of hydrocephalus including spina bifida, meningitis and brain haemorrhage. Hydrocephalus is treated by inserting a shunt into the brain which allows the fluid to drain. The shunt is usually permanent. Signs that the shunt is not working include vomiting, dizziness, visual disturbances and drowsiness. If any of these signs are apparent, the parent should be contacted immediately and emergency medical attention should be sought.

Incidence and diagnosis

Hydrocephalus is usually diagnosed at or shortly after birth, although it can occur later as a result of conditions such as meningitis or brain tumours. Premature babies and babies with spina bifida will be closely monitored and these are two common causes of hydrocephalus. Head circumference measurements may indicate a large head to body ratio and the fontanelle may show signs of swelling. Once diagnosed, the insertion of a shunt is immediate as otherwise this condition can become fatal.

Health and development

The extent to which children are affected by hydrocephalus varies enormously and depends on the amount of damage caused to the brain.

Blockage of the shunt

The shunt is invisible as it is completely inserted into the child's body. It can however become blocked and this can be potentially life threatening. Signs that the shunt is not working effectively include headaches.

Physical development

Children may have poor hand-eye co-ordination and poor gross motor skills.

Learning difficulties

Some children may have difficulties in reasoning and may need plenty of reinforcement activities with the focus on providing visual information. While many children's IQ scores are lower if they have hydrocephalus, this is not always the case and it is important not to assume that a child with hydrocephalus will have learning difficulties.

Memory and concentration

Children may have difficulties with short-term memory and concentration. Frequent reminders may be required and instructions given one at a time. Poor short-term memory can also mean that behaviour is difficult to manage as children may forget what they should be doing or even why they have been told to stop certain behaviours.

Social and emotional development

Many children dislike any change in routine and find change hard to cope with. As short-term memory can be affected, children may not remember why changes are happening. Children can also have 'seemingly' irrational fears and dislikes.

Noise sensitivity

Some children are very sensitive to every day noises such as vacuum cleaners and washing machines. They may become very distressed, although the reason why this should happen is not known

Information that we may need from parents

- Does your child have any fears or strong dislikes?
- Have you noticed any difficulties with memory?
- What type of strategies do you use at home to overcome short-term memory difficulties?
- Does your child find it hard to cope with changes in routines?
- Whom should we contact if we suspect that the shunt is not working properly?
- Are there any activities that your child should not take part in? In addition to activities, are there specific movements your child should not do e.g. forward rolls?

Getting it right for the child

As many children have difficulties with their short-term memory, it is essential that all staff understand the implications of this. It can mean that a child will quickly forget any instructions and will need to be told and reminded over and over again. Staff will need to understand that this is not because the child is being 'difficult' and remain patient and calm. Strong routines are also suggested as children feel more secure.

Because of their poor concentration and short-term memory difficulties, some children will need extremely close supervision, and even one-to-one attention to avoid accidents. Behaviour strategies such as time out will not be effective as the child will quickly forget why they are having time out. As the ability for some children to manage and retain information is limited, visual and sensory activities are more likely to be successful. Advice should also be sought from parents as to whether there are any vigorous physical activities that may cause the shunt to dislodge and if so, everyone in the setting should be aware of these. Finally, it is essential that everyone is familiar with the signs that the child's shunt is not functioning as this can prove fatal.

Key questions

- Who will act as the child's key worker?
- Does everyone in the setting know the signs that the shunt is not working properly?
- How will activities be presented to ensure that the child can concentrate and take in information at their level?

Some day-to-day questions

- Are there any signs that the shunt is not working effectively?
- Are there any vigorous physical activities that the child should not engage in?
- Is the routine likely to be disrupted and how is this being managed?
- Are there sufficient activities that are of a sensory and visual nature?
- Are staff and helpers aware that the child may have difficulties in remembering information?
- Is there adequate supervision / one-to-one assistance to prevent behavioural incidents and / or accidents?

Contact

Association for Spina Bifida and Hydrocephalus
42 Park Road
Peterborough PE1 2UQ
www.asbah.org

Sickle cell disorders

Sickle cell disorders are a group of genetically inherited blood disorders that affect red blood cells in the body. The haemoglobin in the red blood cells is abnormal and changes the shape of the red blood cells. Haemoglobin is important because it carries oxygen around in the body. Children with sickle cell disorders are likely to have bouts of severe pain caused by the abnormal shaped blood cells becoming blocked in small blood vessels. They are also likely to be anaemic because their levels of haemoglobin are reduced as the red blood cells that are affected by the condition are unable to survive as long as normal red blood cells.

Incidence and diagnosis

Sickle cell disorders are inherited as it is a genetic condition. For a child to be affected by the disorder, both parents must carry the faulty gene. The term sickle cell trait is used where only one parent has the gene. In this case, the child will not be affected by the disorder but will carry the gene. In the UK, sickle cell disorder primarily affects children and adults whose families once originated in the Caribbean and Africa. There are currently around 6000 adults and children with sickle cell disorders.

Health and development

Anaemia

Children with sickle cell disorder are often anaemic. This results in lethargy and extreme tiredness. Children may need to rest frequently and may have difficulty in concentrating. A diet high in folic acid is often recommended as a way of helping with anaemia.

Pain and 'crises'

Sickle cell disorders create pain as the abnormal blood cells become blocked or trapped in small blood vessels. These blockages cause pain in the arms, legs, back and stomach. Severe episodes of pain are known as 'crises'. Sickle pain can happen anywhere and at any time, although there are some triggers such as the child fighting an infection, becoming dehydrated or cold. The onset of a crisis is usually gradual but can result in a child needing to be hospitalised. It is therefore important to contact parents when a child reports being in pain.

Priopasm

Priopasm occurs in boys during a crisis. The penis becomes stiff because the red cells become blocked. It is rare in boys under six or seven years old. It is painful yet some boys may not mention the pain because they are embarrassed. It is important that medical attention is sought because it can lead to later impotence.

Infection

To avoid infection, most children with sickle cell disorder are given antibiotics on a daily basis.

Learning

Sickle cell disorder has no effect on children's ability to learn, although frequent absences due to crises or to attend check ups may mean that the child can miss out.

Information that we may need from parents

- What should we do if the child complains of being in pain?
- Will your child need any medication during the session?
- Are there any particular triggers that may cause a crisis?
- Does your child have any favourite drinks?

Getting it right for the child

It is essential for everyone to understand that this condition may affect the child's levels of activity and listening to the child and responding to his or her needs is important. A child who complains of pain must be listened to as this might be the onset of a crisis. In the same way, a child who wants to sit quietly or have a nap should not be discouraged.

Keeping children warm and dry

The condition becomes worse when children are cold and when the weather is damp. Sudden drops in the child's temperature can trigger a crisis. It will be important therefore to make sure that your setting is adequately heated and also to encourage the child to stay indoors when it is particularly cold and damp. Swimming is therefore not advised unless the water is very warm and the changing rooms are heated. Some children can also be sensitive to cold drinks and food and so this may need to be discussed with parents.

Encouraging children to drink

Children with sickle cell disorders need to maintain their fluid levels. It is important that they do not dehydrate. This means that they should be encouraged to take frequent drinks and instead of having set times for drinks, it may be advisable to have drinks on 'stand by' for the child. The risk of dehydration increases in the summer and so particular attention needs to be paid to checking that a child is drinking enough. As a consequence of increased fluid intake, the child will also need to use the toilet or have his or her nappy changed more frequently.

As well as managing the physical needs of the child, it is also important that the child feels emotionally secure. A young child will benefit from having a key worker who will be able to recognise the child's feelings, fears and also any signs of a crisis because he or she has got to know the child well. A key worker will also be important to help the child settle in after any absence.

Key questions

- Who will be the child's key worker?
- Who will ensure that the child is regularly offered drinks?
- Is everyone in the setting aware of the effects of this condition?
- Where will any medication be stored?
- Who will be responsible for giving the child any medication?
- Does the planning for the child include periods of rest as well as activity?
- What area in the setting can be used to help the child rest or nap if required?
- Are parents' emergency contact details accessible?

Some day-to-day questions

- What is the weather like?
- What activities are planned for the day? How will these be adjusted to suit the child's needs?
- How is the child feeling?

Contact

Sickle Cell Society
54 Station Road,
Harlesden
London NW10 4UA
www.sicklecellsociety.org.uk

Spina bifida (see also hydrocephalus)

Spina bifida is a congenital disorder that occurs early in pregnancy. The vertebrae in the spine do not form properly, leaving part of the spinal cord exposed. As the spinal cord serves as the passage for messages to be passed to and from the brain from the limbs, any blockages can result in loss of sensation and loss of use of the limbs. Hydrocephalus often accompanies spina bifida at birth.

Incidence and diagnosis

The numbers of people with spina bifida varies regionally, although the mildest form, spina bifida occulta is thought to be present in one in 10 people. The cause of spina bifida is still being researched although a mix of genetic and environmental factors appear to be at work. An increased intake of folic acid before conception and during the first 12 weeks of pregnancy is currently recommended as a preventative measure. Diagnosis of spina bifida is often made during routine ultra sound examinations and also at birth.

Health and development

The way in which children might be affected by spina bifida depends on the type that they have. Note that a proportion of children who have spina bifida cystica will also have hydrocephalus.

Spina bifida occulta

This type of spina bifida is the commonest and the mildest form of spina bifida. It rarely causes any disability. Although rare, a few children with spina bifida occulta may have difficulties in controlling their bladders and bowels and this usually reveals itself during toilet training. Parents are usually advised to seek medical help if after the age of three years a child is not making any progress.

Spina bifida cystica

This is so named because a cyst or blister is formed on the spine. There are two forms of this type of spina bifida:

- **Meningocele –** the nerves are not usually badly damaged and are able to function, therefore there is often little disability present. This is the least common form.
- **Myelomeningocele (meningomyelocele)** – this is the most serious and more common of the two forms of cystic spina bifida. The spinal cord is damaged or not properly developed. As a result, there is some paralysis and loss of sensation below the damaged region. The amount of disability depends very much on where the spina bifida is and the amount of nerve damage involved. A significant proportion of children with this type of spina bifida will also have hydrocephalus.

Depending on the extent of the paralysis, many children will need mobility aids. Children may need support to sit and stand. Young children are sometimes able to crawl, but as they become older and heavier, they may need a wheelchair.

It is common for children with this form of spina bifida to remain incontinent and therefore liaising with parents as to how to meet the child's needs is essential.

Information that we may need from parents

- Does the child have hydrocephalus? (If the answer to this is yes, refer also to the section on page 221).
- Does the child have any mobility needs?
- How does the family meet these needs at home and have they any preferences in the setting? (Some children crawl at home, but parents may not wish their child to crawl in the setting.)
- Does the child have a physiotherapy programme or movements to improve circulation and prevent any pressure sores?
- Does the child have a special diet?
- What are the child's toileting needs?

Getting it right for the child

It is important to understand that spina bifida in itself will not cause learning difficulties in children. It is the added complication of hydrocephalus that may cause learning and behavioural difficulties. This means that it is essential to find out whether or not the child has hydrocephalus.

Children with spina bifida myelomeningocele are likely to need equipment or support to be mobile. This does not necessarily imply a wheelchair, as many younger children can get around by using a standing frame or even by crawling. The mobility needs of the child will therefore need to be discussed with parents, and their advice may need to be sought as to how to avoid pressure sores that can occur if mobility is reduced. Adaptations to activities and/or the environment may need to be carried out on a daily basis so that children can fully participate, for example bringing activities down to the child's level. It will be essential to look for ways of empowering children as it can be easy for adults and other children to overcompensate and 'help' a child with mobility needs. This can prevent a child from becoming independent and gaining in confidence.

Key questions

- What are the mobility needs of the child?
- Are any adaptations required in the setting?
- Who will be responsible for ensuring the personal hygiene needs of the child are met?
- Where will the changing of nappies/pads take place and meet the child's needs for privacy?
- Who will be responsible for ensuring that any physiotherapy exercises or movements are carried out?

- Who will be responsible for ensuring that the child's dietary requirements are met?

Some day-to-day questions

- Are the activities accessible for the child?
- Are there sufficient nappies, pads and other personal hygiene items?
- Are there any signs that pressure sores are beginning to form?
- Are the other children treating this child as an 'equal'?

Contact

Association for Spina Bifida and Hydrocephalus
42 Park Road
Peterborough PE1 2UQ
www.asbah.org

Visual impairment

Visual impairment is one of the terms used when a person cannot fully see, although recently the Royal National Institute for the Blind has found that many of its members prefer the term 'sight problems'. There are many degrees of visual impairment, although it is rare to find complete blindness where an adult or child cannot perceive any differences in light. The term 'blind' is used when a person's visual acuity is below 6/60, which means that they can see at 6 metres what a sighted person can see at a distance of 60 metres or where the field of vision is significantly restricted. This is sometimes called tunnel vision.

There are many causes of visual impairment, including genetic factors, diseases and damage to the eye or optic nerve. In some cases, the eye and optic nerve are healthy, but eye movement is irregular, while for some children the shape of the cornea causes refractive errors such as long or short sightedness.

Incidence and diagnosis

It is hard to calculate the number of children with visual impairment, but it is thought to be around 20,000. The speed of diagnosis depends on many factors including the severity of the impairment. Routine health checks often detect that a child is not fully seeing and children are then referred to a specialist.

Health and development

Visual impairments do not cause learning difficulties in children, but can affect their learning if undetected.

Gross and locomotive skills

Children with visual impairments may not have gained confidence in their movements. Vision is used to support spatial awareness and young children tend to move in order to explore the world that they see. Sighted babies will try to reach out for objects that are within their grasp or take their first steps when attempting to reach something out of range.

Children with visual impairments may be reluctant to run or move quickly. They may bump into objects, find it hard to negotiate stairs and find it hard to make co-ordinated movements such as kicking a ball.

Fine motor skills

Many fine motor skills involve the use of hand-eye co-ordination. Children may have developmental delays in areas such as feeding and dressing themselves, doing jigsaws or playing with small toys and pieces of equipment.

Behaviour

Some children may have learned inappropriate behaviour as a result of frustration. They may, for example, push toys or activities away or find it hard to concentrate on activities.

Language

Non-verbal language is an important part of communication. Children who cannot see others' responses may have delayed language. They may not make eye contact or they may, not show the usual range of expressions as most babies 'mirror' back the expressions that they have seen.

Information that we may need from parents

- What is the nature of your child's visual impairment?
- Does your child wear glasses? If so, when does he or she need them?
- Is your child happy to wear glasses or does he or she need encouragement?
- How have you adapted your home to suit your child's needs?
- What activities does your child enjoy at home?
- Are there any activities that your child does not enjoy?
- Are there any vision exercises or activities that your child should do?

Getting it right for the child

It is important first of all to find out about the extent of the child's visual impairment from parents and if necessary from other professionals. This will mean that adaptations to the setting and activities can be made as appropriate. For some children, it will be important to encourage them to wear their glasses and so finding books and other positive images of children who wear glasses might be helpful. We may also need to look at ways of supporting other areas of development such as speech and movement that have been affected by the child's visual impairment. It is important that children are encouraged to become self-reliant and learn as many everyday skills as possible. This will help their self-esteem.

Advice as to how best to help children with visual impairments will come from parents and other professionals but you may also find the following guidelines useful:

- Take advice as to how to illuminate the setting to avoid glare and shadows.
- Make sure that steps, ramps or other changes to floor levels are clearly marked, e.g. with fluorescent strips or textured flooring.
- Teach other children to pick up any objects that fall onto these strips.
- Keep the floor areas around the child free of obstacles.
- Make sufficient sound when approaching a child to avoid him or her becoming startled.
- Keep closely to routines so that the child can understand what is happening around him or her.
- Seat children close to adults during activities such as story time and use large books.
- Look for ways of adapting activities to encourage children to participate, e.g. trays so that objects do not fall off tables and out of sight, balls that have bells in them.

Key questions

- Who will act as the child's key worker?
- What support and adaptations does the child need?
- Is everyone in the setting aware of the child's needs?
- How will the child be encouraged to develop physical skills?

Some day-to-day questions

- Has the child brought his or her glasses into the setting?
- Is the lighting sufficient in the setting?
- Are staff aware that the child has a visual impairment?
- Are other children 'mothering' the child?
- In what ways is the child being helped to become independent?
- Is the setting tidy and clear of obstacles?

Contact

Look
National Federation of Families with Visually Impaired Children
c/o Queen Alexandra College
49 Court Oak Road
Birmingham
B17 9TG
www.look-uk.org

Index